The
PYROMANIAC'S
Cookbook

Books by John J. Poister

MEALS FOR MALES

COOKING WITH WINE

THE WINE LOVER'S DRINK BOOK

THE NEW AMERICAN BARTENDER'S GUIDE

THE PYROMANIAC'S COOKBOOK

WRITTEN BY

John J. Poister

ILLUSTRATED BY

Frank Perry

MAIN
STREET
BOOKS

Doubleday
New York London Toronto
Sydney Auckland

THE BEST IN FLAMING FOOD AND DRINK

The PYROMANIAC'S Cookbook

A MAIN STREET BOOK

PUBLISHED BY DOUBLEDAY

a division of Bantam Doubleday Dell Publishing Group, Inc.

1540 Broadway, New York, New York 10036

MAIN STREET BOOKS, DOUBLEDAY, and the portrayal of a building with a tree are trademarks
of Doubleday, a division of Bantam Doubleday Dell Publishing Group, Inc.

Book design by Jennifer Ann Daddio

Library of Congress Cataloging-in-Publication Data
Poister, John J.
The pyromaniac's cookbook : the best in flaming food and drink / John J. Poister.
p.   cm.
"A Main Street book."
1. Cookery (Liquors)   I. Title.
TX726.P6   1996

641.6´25—dc20   95-10157
                                                                                   CIP

ISBN 0-385-47958-1

First Main Street Books Edition: January 1996
1   3   5   7   9   10   8   6   4   2

This book is dedicated

to creative cooks everywhere

who know the difference

between eating and dining.

Acknowledgments

Uncovering exemplary, new recipes is never easy, and I have learned you can't do it alone. So, herewith, I offer my sincere thanks to those who carried the torch in the search for outstanding, and in some instances, even pioneering, flambé food recipes. Karon N. Cullen, The Ritz-Carlton Hotel Company, Atlanta; Henny Santo, The Sign of the Dove, New York; Denise Lemoine Cué, Hotel Ritz, Paris; JoAnn K. Bongiorno, The Drake Hotel, Chicago; Pip, Jimmy, and Ted Brennan, Brennan's Restaurant, New Orleans; Veronique Brown, Hotel de Crillon, Paris; Deanne French, the Ritz-Carlton, Marina del Rey, California; Beverly Barbour (The New York Restaurant Group, Inc.), Post House and Smith

& Wollensky, New York; Tanja Wood, The Dorchester, London; Martine Mercier, Hôtel Plaza Athénée, Paris; George L. Hern, Jr., French Government Tourist Office, New York; Odila Gáler-Noël and Amy Albert, Foods and Wines From France, New York; Elizabeth DeMotte, The Ritz-Carlton, Mauna Lani, Hawaii; Judy Meyenhofer, DHM Group, Inc.; Yvonne Landavazo and Roxanne Marciniak, The Ritz-Carlton, Kapalua, Island of Maui, Hawaii; Patti Hendrix, The Ritz-Carlton, Amelia Island, Florida. Special thanks to Rozanne Gold, Culinary Director of the Joseph Baum & Michael Whiteman Company, a creator of The Rainbow Room menu, who convinced me the time was right for this book, also Andrew Freeman and Robyn E. Massey, The Rainbow Room. And, finally, my grateful thanks to my wife, Carol, who helped me put this book together in more ways than I can count.

Contents

Foreword

This is frankly a book for those who like to play with fire.

Fire has a fascination for everyone. It appeals to the inner being. It is part of our primitive heritage. It separates the civilized from the truly wild. Historically it has been our servant, to give us light, to warm us, to cook our food, and it has made the hearth the timeless symbol of the home. In this context we are all a little afflicted with pyromania: that primordial, universal lure of the open flame.

This, then, is a book about flaming food and drink, written to gratify simply, inexpensively, and beneficially our lifelong love affair with fire. This collection of recipes—many of which appear for the first time—is intended to bring fire out of the kitchen and onto the dining table, to amuse, amaze, and provide some bright, memorable experiences in good eating, gracious entertaining, and pleasant living. The recipes are for the most part simple to prepare and are ideally suited to the needs of the casual cook and the weekend chef.

But most important, it is the intention of this book to go a step beyond the needs of the sometime meal planner, for the majority of those who cook do not always do so by choice. If some of the flambé dishes can bring a little excitement and gladness to the routine but essential job of food preparation, then the prime purpose of this book will have been achieved.

Now a word about what this book is NOT.

This book is not for those who are dedicated to slavishly following recipes that rigidly reflect the traditions of the past. There are many scholarly works on cooking; they represent an important part of the great store of human experience upon which all progress is based. But what is progress if it is not taking the best of the past and adding to it the knowledge gained from our own experience? For this reason many of the recipes included in the following pages are the result of experimentation and innovation. And the reader, by the same token, is encouraged to be bold and inventive, to experiment and innovate. True, some of our experiments fail and we are better off staying with the old. But as long as cooking is considered an art as well as a science, the innovative process must continue, for this is the basis of all creative expression and, incidentally, the source of some of the very best recipes.

Finally, eating should always be an enjoyable experience, and for this reason, if no other, an ingenious cook should have more fun than anybody.

JOHN J. POISTER

How to Flambé
Simply and Safely

1. *Follow the recipe's instructions and do not use more spirits than are called for. Doing so is not just safer; using too much alcohol will detract from the flavor.*

2. *Never pour spirits directly from a bottle into a pan that is on the stove or near an open flame. Do not keep open bottles of spirits anywhere near the cooking area.*

3. *When adding spirits to a pan, use a cup, spoon, or measuring cup that contains only the specified amount for the recipe you are preparing.*

4. *When igniting spirits in a pan, do so at arm's length. You*

wouldn't stand too close to a pan while you were sautéing with butter or cooking oil over high heat; it makes no sense to do so while flambéing.

5. *When flambéing a dish in the dining room, be sure diners are well away from the flames. Do as the professionals do: Use a serving cart or a small table. It gives you more space and enables you to work away from the area where people are seated.*

6. *When flambéing in the dining room, keep clear of draperies or anything flammable, such as a tablecloth or paper party decorations.*

Remember, flambé cooking is no more dangerous than cooking over an open fire at a backyard barbecue. Grease can spatter, sparks can fly, and yes, you can burn your finger even under the best circumstances. If you follow instructions, use common sense, and obey the rules of safety, you can flambé to your heart's content with peace of mind and a free spirit.

The
Pyromaniac's
Cookbook

ONE

Cooking with Flare

$\mathring{A}$ successful restaurateur once said, "We are serving more flaming dishes. They give the customers a nice warm feeling, and the fire doesn't seem to hurt the food very much." If this somewhat cynical statement summarized the only benefits to be derived from flaming food and drink, then the increasing popularity of this branch of the culinary art would hardly be justified.

There are three good reasons for flames at the table. The first two are fairly obvious. One, the food is well heated at the time of serving—an important consideration for large restaurants and hotels but of little import for the amateur chef who is not faced with the logistical problems of mass feeding. And second, the pyrotechnical display connected with flaming dishes does and should have a positive psychological effect on both the server and the servee. At the very least it should be a treat, if not a feast for the eye. The third benefit—and the most subtle—is that a dish properly planned and prepared and set ablaze will be imbued with flavors that will not be duplicated by any other means. The marvelous transformation that results from these baptisms of fire makes it worth all the effort. But we must approach the task of cooking with flare in the proper spirit, with an understanding of the ultimate effect we are striving for, and with attention to the basic principles involved if we are to achieve predictable successes.

So let us be clear on one point: We are not here concerned with simply "breaking even" with our recipes and building a fire for effect that will, it is hoped, not harm the food. But rather, we are *adding flavor with flame*. Therefore, at the risk of overstating the case, let our motto in the kitchen be: IF YOU CAN'T FIND A BETTER WAY, THEN GO TO BLAZES!

Anything, but anything, can be flamed. And as some too-casual chefs have learned, this can include fingers, eyelashes, hair, tablecloths, rugs, and draperies. So we add a note of caution at the outset. Flame with care, for we will be dealing with highly volatile liquids capable of great mischief if misused. As our distant ancestors discovered through trial and terror, fire must be always the servant, never the master. In short, children should never play with fire. This also includes compulsive martini drinkers who have reached a high state of euphoria and anyone else who thinks it might be clever to see how much flammable spirit they can get into their chafing dish. We encourage innovation and experimentation. But please, be prudent and don't waste your booze in overly large tabletop conflagrations. You may spoil both the dinner *and* the dining room.

The principles of flambé cooking are quite simple. Any liquor with sufficient alcoholic content will ignite. First it must be warmed enough to release its flammable vapors. And it usually burns best when used in conjunction with sugar. For this reason, liqueurs that contain relatively large amounts of sugar flame well unless the proof is very low. Some cordials made in Europe may contain less than 30 percent alcohol by volume (under 60 proof) and do not burn well except when fortified with a spirit that is at least 80 proof, such as brandy or a high-proof rum, whisky, or vodka. Desserts are ideal for flaming because of the large amounts of sugar they contain. But remember, always warm the spirits to be used in advance. Failure to do this is the most common cause of burnout or "a flash in the pan," which is the most humiliating failure that can mar an evening of haute cuisine. It is tantamount to a ship that sinks at the moment of launching.

Hot Tips—No. 1

A small copper saucepan tinned on the inside is ideal for heating spirits before blazing. The 6-ounce size is just about right and is large enough for other purposes, such as melting butter. For more elegant service, a long-handled Turkish coffeemaker, complete with its own little burner, is most convenient and easy to use, and saves running back and forth to the kitchen. The latter is to be avoided assiduously since it interferes with the continuity of your presentation and makes your guests feel that you may be going to more trouble than is really necessary . . . which is another way of saying that you need more practice.

The wide range of liquors and spirits available for flamboyant experimentation presents a vast horizon of flavor possibilities to both aficionados and dabbler cooks. The mathematical combinations are such that it is doubtful if anyone has tried them all. Herein lies the challenge. It is hoped that some of the recipes presented will send you reeling down little-trodden paths toward new exotic, offbeat innovations of your own. A listing of many liqueurs with a brief evaluation of their flaming qualities (as well as their myriad other attributes) is given for reference purposes in Chapter 9. But constant experimentation and experience are the only sure ways to master the art of fiery fare. When in doubt, be bold. But learn ye the basics well, lest you spend an inordinate amount of time reinventing the lightbulb—which is a diplomatic way of saying "Nice try. But the dish you invented has been done before—and done better."

Your kitchen equipment need not be elaborate, but it should be the best. You will need a good chafing dish, and you should have no difficulty in obtaining one at a reasonable price. The dish consists of two pans: one to hold hot water, directly over the flame, and a flaming pan or blazer. The two pans nest together and function as a double boiler, or the flaming pan can be used alone. Chafing dishes usually are made of steel, copper, or aluminum. Copper is traditional because of its good heat-conducting qualities, but a nuisance to clean. Aluminum is an excellent cookware material because of the even way it distributes heat, and of course it is light, which makes it easy to handle. Stainless steel is a most durable metal, is very easy to maintain, but tends to develop hot spots close to the heat source. A metal laminate consisting of a stainless steel sheet encased in an outer layer of aluminum combines the marvelous heat conductance of aluminum with the cleaning ease of stainless steel. It is highly recommended for flambé cookery.

There are, of course, other good cookware materials. Silver chafing dishes are elegant by candlelight, and silver is a good heat conductor but not really practical for hard use. Keep a "Sunday" chafing dish in reserve for special occasions, but choose one of the more utilitarian metals for everyday use. When selecting a chafing dish, special care should be given to the type of burner. Some burners consist simply of a container into which canned heat is placed. Other burners utilize alcohol. Whichever type you choose, be sure that it is adjustable so that the size of the flame can be controlled easily. The old-fashioned alcohol burner, employing a wick, went out with the streetcar. It is adequate when used with a warming pan, but it is generally unsatisfactory for cooking purposes. An ideal burner has a series of air vents surrounding the fire hole, ensuring a hot cooking flame. The flame's intensity is controlled by a sliding cover, which partially opens or closes the air vents. The size of your chafing dish is important. A small pan is just right for a cozy supper for two but inadequate for anything else. Pick a good-size pan, 1½ pints capacity, or larger, which will serve equally well for the *dîner intime* and small buffets for six or eight people. The pan should have curved sides to expedite the serving of sauces and liquids with a ladle. All pans, of course, should come with a snug-fitting lid.

Rather than invest at first in several different-size chafing dishes, it is far better to purchase other types of equipment. A good sturdy, adjustable burner with a wide grid for use with flaming pans is invaluable.

Flaming pans can be had in round and oval shapes, and a wide range of sizes. A medium-size oval pan, about 11 by 7 inches, is a good all-purpose utensil. In addition, a shallow crêpe pan will have many uses. Select a round one about 12 inches in diameter. You also will need a ladle with a long handle, with a bowl that is not too deep so that you can serve flaming liquids without having to pour from the pan.

With this basic equipment, you are now ready to meet any challenge. Acquisition of specialized equipment such as *café brûlot* pans and fondue pots should be deferred until you have decided whether you will have a continuing need—and desire—to prepare dishes requiring special purpose utensils.

Hot Tips—No. 2

A small cart or folding table is invaluable for cooking in the dining room. Chafing dish, condiments, and utensils should not clutter up the dining table and interfere with the main task at hand—which is, for your guests, eating, not cooking.

In order to establish the pattern of the major purpose of this book, which is to generate a creative response from you so that you will be not only encouraged but able to strike out on your own, let us explore some variations on a relatively simple dish. Cherries Jubilee is an old standby, the refuge of many a tired maître d'hôtel, but basically a grand alliance of fruit, ice cream, and spirits. It is an ideal subject for innovation because, like all flambé desserts, it is a series of delectable contradictions: hot and cold, bitter and sweet, married in flames to produce a veritable flavor explosion.

Cherries Jubilee was concocted by a chef of the royal household in honor of Queen Victoria's golden jubilee. This was not unusual, as it was the custom in royal circles to commemorate some special occasion, such as the winning of a battle, the observance of a birthday or anniversary, by commissioning some work of art fitting to the circumstances. The fruits of these literally monumental efforts have not been without benefit to posterity. The building of the great gate at Kiev, in Russia, celebrated by Mussorgsky in his *Pictures at an Exhibition*, probably inspired some nameless chef to create Chicken Kiev. The battle of Marengo during which Napoleon trounced the Austrians gave its name to Chicken Marengo, which was reputed to have been concocted on the battlefield immediately after the fray by Napoleon's own personal chef. As is so often the case, the harvest from these notable events is better remembered than the events themselves.

There is little doubt that more people in the world are familiar with Cherries Jubilee today than with the historic occasion that gave it life and a name. The original recipe, created in 1887, did not contain ice cream. This was added later, perhaps as a result of the influence of the great chef Escoffier, who concocted a marvelous dessert of ice cream and peaches in honor of the renowned Madame Melba. It was called, quite naturally, in the manner of the times, *Pêche Melba*. Cherries Jubilee is quite delicious in its original form without ice cream, but it is more appropriate to modern tastes if the flaming mixture is poured over ice cream rather than eaten alone. Here is the recipe in its pristine glory.

CHERRIES JUBILEE

2 TABLESPOONS RED CURRANT
JAM

1¹/₂ CUPS CANNED PITTED
BLACK CHERRIES, DRAINED

¹/₃ CUP COGNAC

1 PINT VANILLA ICE CREAM

Melt red currant jam in flaming pan of chafing dish over direct heat. Add black cherries and a very small amount of juice. When thoroughly heated, pour in cognac and blaze. Serve over vanilla ice cream. Serves 2.

When adding spirits such as cognac to a sauce being heated in a chafing dish, it is not necessary to heat the brandy in advance. However, after adding cold spirits of any kind to a mixture in the chafing dish, be sure to wait several minutes before attempting to flame so that the alcohol is warmed and the fumes are released. When serving a blazing sauce such as Cherries Jubilee at table, the dramatic effect will be heightened if at the moment of blastoff you take up some of the sauce in your serving ladle and ignite it, pouring a cascade of flames into the pan, which then in turn catches fire. To prolong the effect and make certain that most of the alcohol is burned off, while serving shake the flaming pan back and forth and stir the mixture with your ladle. Alcohol, unburned, is not desirable in most foods because it often leaves an aftertaste that will sabotage subtle flavors as effectively as a good dash of cleaning fluid. The purpose of flambé cookery is to combine and enhance flavors—not to prolong the cocktail hour, as desirable upon occasion as that might be.

Some recipes call for the use of arrowroot in place of red currant jam. The substitution is quite acceptable since arrowroot smooths and thickens the sauce and is a good binder, but currant or some other fruit preserve is preferable because the high sugar content aids the flaming, and the flavor combines well with the cherries. Here are some variations that provide generous servings for two.

CHERRIES JUBILEE À L'ORANGE

2 HEAPING TABLESPOONS
ORANGE MARMALADE

$1/4$ CUP FRESH ORANGE JUICE

$1^1/2$ CUPS CANNED PITTED
BLACK CHERRIES, DRAINED

GROUND CINNAMON

$1/3$ CUP GRAND MARNIER

1 PINT VANILLA ICE CREAM

Melt orange marmalade in flaming pan of chafing dish over direct heat. Mix in orange juice and add drained cherries. Sprinkle with cinnamon. When thoroughly heated, pour in Grand Marnier (or equal parts of cognac and Grand Marnier if less sweetness is desired). Blaze and serve over vanilla ice cream.

SWEET AND SOUR CHERRIES JUBILEE
(Cerises Aigres-Douces Flambées)

2 TABLESPOONS CHERRY JAM OR
   PRESERVES

ORANGE BITTERS

GROUND CINNAMON OR
   GRATED NUTMEG

1 CUP CANNED PITTED BLACK
   CHERRIES, DRAINED

$^1/_2$ CUP CANNED PITTED SOUR
   RED CHERRIES, DRAINED

1 TEASPOON HONEY

$^1/_3$ CUP KIRSCHWASSER

1 PINT VANILLA OR BLACK
   CHERRY ICE CREAM

Melt cherry jam or preserves in flaming pan of chafing dish over direct heat with dash of orange bitters and pinch of cinnamon or nutmeg. Add all cherries and stir in honey. When thoroughly heated, pour in kirschwasser and blaze. Serve over vanilla or black cherry ice cream.

You may wish to vary the above—or any other recipe in this book—according to your own personal tastes. Experience and experimentation are the building blocks of good cuisine. When trying out your own innovations for Cherries Jubilee, you may want to use various sweetening agents, such as grenadine or orgeat syrup. More sophisticated tastes may spark to Falernum, an intriguing syrup from the West Indies island of Barbados. You should explore the shelves of your favorite food specialty store or gourmet shop for exotic syrups made from currants (red and black), raspberries, passion fruit, and tamarind. These are interesting basic sweeteners for many of the flaming desserts that will be encountered later. Or you can make your own syrup by adding various flavor extracts and fruit juices to plain sugar syrup. In its unflavored form, Simple Syrup is a must for the well-equipped bar, since sugar in crystalline or powdered form does not dissolve well in alcohol. This simple fact explains why so many tall drinks of the summer variety seem to get sweeter as we near the bottom of the glass. That's where all the sugar is that was supposed to be dissolved—but wasn't.

To make Simple Syrup, add 6 cups white sugar to 1 quart water that has been brought to the boiling point. Boil until all sugar is dissolved and solution thickens. Be sure to strain the syrup before bottling to remove any foreign matter that may cause crystals to form in the bottle. Simple Syrup keeps well and will help ensure well-blended mixed drinks that require sugar.

The spirits used to flame and flavor Cherries Jubilee are traditionally cognac or kirschwasser, but there are others that you may find more interesting and exciting. Demerara rum of the 151-proof type provides an unusual flavor and a truly spectacular blaze. It should be used judiciously and handled with care. Here is a recipe for Cherries Jubilee with a Caribbean accent.

CHERRIES JUBILEE PORT ROYAL

2 GENEROUS TABLESPOONS
    GUAVA JELLY

BROWN SUGAR

1 TEASPOON LEMON JUICE

PINCH OF GROUND CINNAMON

DASH OF ANGOSTURA BITTERS

$1^1/_2$ CUPS CANNED PITTED
    BLACK CHERRIES; DRAIN AND
    RESERVE JUICE

2 TABLESPOONS PUERTO RICAN
    OR BARBADOS RUM

2 TABLESPOONS
    151-PROOF DEMERARA RUM

1 PINT BUTTER PECAN OR
    VANILLA ICE CREAM

Melt guava jelly in flaming pan of chafing dish over direct heat and sprinkle well with brown sugar. Add lemon juice, cinnamon, Angostura bitters, cherries, and a little of their juice. When thoroughly heated, pour in both rums and blaze. Serve over butter pecan or vanilla ice cream.

This British colonial version can be varied in a number of interesting ways. The addition of a thickly sliced ripe banana and the substitution of dark Jamaica rum in place of the high-proof Demerara make a good flavor combination. In this case, omit the guava jelly and add 2 tablespoons brown sugar and 1 tablespoon butter. Cook banana slices gently before adding the black cherries. The banana should not be allowed to get mushy.

Since, for purposes of illustration, this chapter has been devoted almost entirely to the cult of a dessert created in honor of an illustrious queen, it seems only fair to pay homage to her son, Edward VII, with a variation of Cherries Jubilee that was probably popular during his reign. This recipe differs from the others in that you begin with uncooked cherries and prepare them with spices and claret in a time-honored Anglo-French tradition that dates back to Edward I—and beyond.

CHERRIES JUBILEE EDWARD VII

1 POUND FRESH BLACK CHERRIES

1 BOTTLE CLARET OR DRY RED WINE

1 DOZEN WHOLE CLOVES

1 TEASPOON GROUND ALLSPICE

PINCH OF GROUND GINGER

CINNAMON STICKS

SUGAR OR SIMPLE SYRUP (SEE INDEX)

2 TABLESPOONS RED CURRANT JAM

$^1/_3$ CUP COGNAC

1 PINT VANILLA ICE CREAM

Select well-ripened cherries, remove pits and stems, cover with a good claret or dry red wine in saucepan to which have been added cloves, allspice, ground ginger, and several cinnamon sticks. Sweeten mixture to taste with sugar or Simple Syrup. Bring to a boil, then simmer gently for about 15 minutes. Remove cherries and continue simmering until liquid is reduced by at least half. Pour liquid into flaming pan of chafing dish, and mix in currant jam. Add cherries, and when thoroughly heated, pour in cognac and blaze. Serve over vanilla ice cream.

Hot Tips—No. 3

Some well-meaning home economist (in the most literal sense) planted the idea that wines and spirits used in cooking need not be of good quality, and the fiction has grown to mammoth proportions. Poor wines and cheap liqueurs taste just as bad hot as they do at room temperature—perhaps worse. What's more, they contaminate the other ingredients. Buy the best. The small amounts called for in most recipes do not justify the theoretical savings involved.

A more modern creation—also in a royal vein—is this recipe that makes use of Queen Anne cherries, thus providing a pleasant deviation from the traditional black cherries called for in most versions of this dessert. For lack of a better name, we have called it quite naturally:

CHERRIES JUBILEE QUEEN ANNE

8-OUNCE CAN PITTED QUEEN
ANNE CHERRIES, DRAINED
GROUND CINNAMON
2 TABLESPOONS LIGHT CORN
SYRUP

1/3 CUP SHREDDED COCONUT
1 DOZEN ALMONDS, SLIVERED
1 PINT VANILLA ICE CREAM
FRESHLY GRATED NUTMEG
1/2 CUP SOUTHERN COMFORT

Sprinkle cherries with ground cinnamon, and mix with corn syrup in flaming pan of chafing dish over direct heat. Toast coconut with almonds briefly under broiler of hot oven (450° F.). Serve ice cream in individual dishes, cover with almonds and coconut, and sprinkle with nutmeg. Pour Southern Comfort into chafing dish, warm, ignite, and ladle blazing cherries and sauce over ice cream. Serves 2 or 3.

For the hurried and the harried who must prepare in advance for weekend soirées or who want to be able to meet any situation that may arise suddenly, all of the sauces we have considered thus far can be premixed, jarred, and refrigerated. They will keep a reasonable time under ordinary conditions and almost indefinitely when frozen. For that glorious moment when the boss arrives for a quick bite after the cocktail party, you will only have to dechill or defrost your Cherries Jubilee sauce, heat with appropriate spirits in a chafing dish, ignite, and ladle blazing over ice cream. The effect will be impressive (and sobering), and the flavor . . . well, it won't be quite the same, but after a cocktail party even a confirmed culinary pyromaniac won't be able to taste (or tell) the difference.

⚘

No collection of Cherries Jubilee recipes would be complete without a typically American version. This variation employs bourbon whisky to achieve a delightful and unusual flavor. We recommend 100-proof bourbon whisky. Actually any good straight bourbon will do, and the chances are that your favorite sippin' whisky will work as well for eatin' purposes as far as your own personal tastes are concerned.

CHERRIES JUBILEE BLUEGRASS

2 GENEROUS TABLESPOONS
    MINT JELLY
1 1/2 CUPS CANNED PITTED
    BLACK CHERRIES, DRAINED
1 SCANT TEASPOON LEMON
    JUICE

1 TABLESPOON HONEY OR
    SIMPLE SYRUP (SEE INDEX)
PINCH OF GROUND CINNAMON
DASH OF ANGOSTURA BITTERS
1/3 CUP 100-PROOF BOURBON
1 PINT VANILLA ICE CREAM

Melt mint jelly in flaming pan of chafing dish over direct heat. Add drained cherries, lemon juice, honey or Simple Syrup, cinnamon, and Angostura bitters. When well heated, add bourbon and blaze. Serve over vanilla ice cream.

If you wish to experiment with hard liquor as a flambé fuel, by all means do so. Rye drinkers and lovers of blended whiskies, rum, and cognac will rise to the challenge, but we do not recommend that devotees of Highland whisky attempt to satisfy their lust for Scotch in this man-

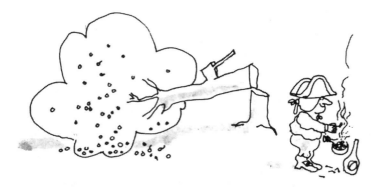

ner. Unfortunately, the smokiness of peat does not live well with other ingredients. Scotch is unique and in a class by itself. A friendly but opinionated publican in Aberdeen, Scotland, summed it up well when a drinking companion ordered his Scotch with a lemon twist. He said sardonically, "If a wee bit o' lemon was meant to be in there, aye, they'd a' put it in at the distillery." Martini lovers are enjoined also from straying too far from their own little path of Juniper. It *could* be done, of course (anything is possible after the second martini), but the vermouth would be hopelessly lost in the conflagration, and who can really abide olives or onions served flaming on their ice cream?

Hot Tips—No. 4

Spirits needed in large quantities for flaming can be warmed effectively by placing the loosely corked *bottle of spirits upright in a saucepan of water. Heat water to boiling point, but do not boil. Turn off heat,* then *place bottle in pan. This method is ideal when spirits are to be used in their free state for flaming and not mixed with other ingredients in advance.* Never *heat spirits in a microwave oven, as this can create dangerous vapor build-up.*

For those who feel that the whole subject of Cherries Jubilee is on the verge of being exhausted—even for the purposes of illustrating the *raison d'être* of this dissertation—we modestly present a final recipe not to be construed in any way as an "end-all," but rather as an inspiration of sorts to motivate you to forge on to more flamboyant heights and brighter tonights. Since this may well be one of the most compatible formulas for Cherries Jubilee in existence, it seemed appropriate to name it in honor of the place where it was born.

SUTTON HOUSE CHERRIES JUBILEE

2 TABLESPOONS RED CURRANT JAM

1 1/2 CUPS CANNED PITTED BLACK CHERRIES; DRAIN AND RESERVE JUICE

DASH OF LEMON JUICE

PINCH OF GROUND CINNAMON

1/2 CUP CHOPPED BLACK WALNUTS

2 TABLESPOONS Cherry Heering

1/4 CUP DRY GIN

1 PINT VANILLA ICE CREAM

Melt red currant jam in flaming pan of chafing dish over direct heat. Add cherries with a scant amount of juice, lemon juice, cinnamon, and walnuts. When well heated, pour in Cherry Heering and gin and blaze. Serve over vanilla ice cream.

The possibilities for innovation in flambé cookery are limitless for the brash experimenter, the intrepid chef who hopes to titillate a jaded palate, and those of us who are goaded by a persistent intuitive feeling that there is always a better way. But beware of running roughshod over the well-trodden paths of human experience in your headlong pursuit of those toothsome moments of culinary glory. The road to success at the dinner table is paved with many blunders in the kitchen. In short, it is wise to learn the rules before deciding to break them. Failures usually must be eaten, and this is punishment enough. In the byways and backwaters of *cuisine flambée* efforts that fizzle out take on a graver aspect, for a really poor showing is tantamount to committing arson. And arson is purely and simply a felony, whether perpetrated in the street or in the chafing dish.

TWO

Casual Conflagrations

The true satisfaction of good flambé cooking comes not only in the eating but in the preparation and the serving as well. For this reason, the cook theoretically should have more fun than those who simply partake of the results, however sumptuous they may be. The secret lies in the approach. It should be casual rather than intense, relaxed instead of frenetic, and above all positive. Experience and practice eventually will bring you a sense of disciplined freedom that is the mark of good cooks and great chefs. The best recipes are simple; but paradoxically, simple dishes are often the most difficult to prepare. The recipes in this chapter are basically uncomplicated. The fact that they are all flambéed may awe your friends, but you must accept these conflagrations with a philosophical detachment. In short, don't let the fire get in the way of the food.

Breakfast is a likely place to begin thinking about the day's menus, and in addition it offers some truly eye-opening possibilities for those members of the family who habitually get off to a slow start. Surely nothing could be more calculated to put things in motion at Sunday breakfast than a plump omelet ablaze in rum or a chafing dish of sausages surrounded by an electric-blue aura of flaming cognac. The old family circle really starts revolving when you serve something in flames. And when someone says, "Let's have something different for a change," you've got the pyrophile's perfect rejoinder: "Okay, we'll burn something."

Here are a couple of omelet dishes you can "burn" some morning or fire off at your next bruncheon. Omelets are especially delicious when properly flambéed, but of course they have to be made properly to begin with. A few basic points on omelet making may be in order before putting one to the match. The best results seem to come from small omelets—the two- or three-egg variety—and they are easier to handle in the pan. Don't beat the daylights out of your eggs; just give them about a half minute's worth of good licks with a fork in a mixing bowl. A tiny bit of water added for each egg gives them body. Be sure your pan is well lubricated with a light coating of cooking oil, then add butter. Be careful not to overheat the pan. When cooking, keep the eggs well distributed in the pan so they cook evenly. When eggs start to firm up, be sure that the omelet is "mobile" and slides easily in the pan. When cooked, tilt the pan and fold over the omelet, using a spatula if necessary, then turn the omelet out onto serving platter, which should be held at an angle adjacent to pan. With practice, your omelets will fold neatly and you will have no difficulty in gently flipping them out of the pan. A well-cooked omelet should be firm on the outside and tender and moist on the inside.

L'OMELETTE FLAMBÉE

$^1/_2$ TABLESPOON WATER

4 LARGE EGGS

$^1/_8$ TEASPOON SALT

BLACK PEPPER

1 TABLESPOON BUTTER

$^1/_4$ CUP AQUAVIT OR VODKA

Add water to eggs and beat vigorously for 30 seconds. Season with salt and freshly ground pepper. Heat omelet pan after coating with a few drops of oil. Immediately add butter and let it become frothy but not brown. Add eggs and stir with fork until well distributed in pan. Shuffle pan over burner while eggs cook and lift up edges of omelet to make sure all liquid is in contact with bottom of pan. While omelet is still soft, tilt pan, fold over omelet, add aquavit or vodka, warm a second or two, blaze, and turn out on preheated platter. Serves 2.

Hot Tips—No. 5

Reserve a special pan for omelets. Aluminum or cast iron is highly recommended, although some prefer an enameled pan because of its smooth finish. Whatever type you select, make sure it has gently sloping or curved sides and is not more than 10 inches in overall diameter. Keep it lightly oiled, and never wash it in the conventional way; rather clean it with paper towels and salt.

After you have had an opportunity to practice with simple omelet recipes, you will want to experiment with various fillings, such as chopped ham, salami, or cheese, and combinations of herbs and seasonings. The possibilities are limitless. Here is one of them that makes a very satisfying entrée for lunch.

MAYFAIR OMELET

2 GREEN ONIONS, SLICED

1 1/2 GENEROUS TABLESPOONS
   BUTTER

8 LARGE EGGS

2 TABLESPOONS CREAM OR
   HOMOGENIZED MILK

2 TABLESPOONS WATER

PINCH OF SALT

BLACK PEPPER

6 GREEN OLIVES, SLICED

2 TABLESPOONS CHOPPED
   FRESH PARSLEY

3 TABLESPOONS CRUMBLED
   ROQUEFORT CHEESE

1/4 CUP DRY GIN, WARMED

Sauté green onions lightly in butter but do not brown; remove from pan and put aside. Add additional butter to pan if needed and pour in beaten mixture of eggs, cream, or milk, water, salt, and a little freshly ground pepper. When eggs begin to set, spoon on onions, olives, and parsley; sprinkle with Roquefort cheese. While top of omelet is still creamy, fold over, add warmed gin, and serve blazing on platter. Makes approximately 4 servings.

A popular breakfast dish that can be flamed easily and deliciously is sausage. Small pork sausage links are preferable and can be prepared at table in your chafing dish. Here is an old colonial recipe we have modified and named for the day of the week when this dish presumably can be enjoyed at leisure.

SUNDAY SAUSAGE

1 POUND LITTLE PORK LINK
  SAUSAGES

1 TABLESPOON BUTTER

1/2 CUP FIRMLY PACKED BROWN
  SUGAR

1/2 TEASPOON LEMON JUICE

PINCH OF GROUND CINNAMON

1/3 CUP PUERTO RICAN OR
  BARBADOS RUM

Place sausages in enough water to barely cover flaming pan of chafing dish. Cook sausages, covered, over direct heat. When sausages have been rendered of excess fat, remove lid and brown lightly on all sides. Pour off all fat and add butter, brown sugar, lemon juice, and cinnamon. When sugar is melted, add rum, ignite, and serve blazing on individual plates. Makes 2 to 3 servings.

Another sausage dish that can be served on Sunday or any other day is this variation made with D.O.M. Benedictine liqueur and cognac. You can mix your own proportions of Benedictine and brandy, but it is much easier simply to buy a bottle of B and B liqueur, which already has been carefully blended to save you the trouble.

SAUSAGE BENEDICTINE

1 POUND LITTLE PORK	¹/₂ TEASPOON LEMON JUICE
SAUSAGES	¹/₃ CUP B AND B LIQUEUR
1 TABLESPOON BUTTER	

Prepare sausages in flaming pan of chafing dish as described in preceding recipe. After pouring off all fat, add butter and lemon juice and complete browning of sausages. Add B and B liqueur, ignite, and serve blazing. Makes 2 to 3 servings.

Breakfast dishes provide many unexpected opportunities for flambé fare for the simple reason that most people mistakenly associate flaming dishes with posh surroundings and formalized dining situations. Actually, flaming cuisine is appropriate any time and any place unless you happen to be taking your breakfast break in a munitions factory. Try this quick and easy recipe next time you serve bacon and eggs.

BACON AND BOURBON

| ¹/₂ POUND LEAN SUGAR-CURED | ¹/₄ CUP 100-PROOF STRAIGHT |
| BACON | BOURBON |

Cook bacon slowly in flaming pan of chafing dish over direct heat to desired degree of doneness. Pour off all excess fat and add bourbon. Allow whisky to warm in pan for a few seconds, then ignite and serve blazing on hot plates. Serves 2.

If your tastes run to viands in the English tradition and you fancy kippers, kidneys, and the proper accoutrements in gleaming Georgian silver serving dishes on a groaning oaken sideboard, here are two spirited recipes that will add a little tang to your next hunt breakfast.

FLAMING KIPPERS

12-ounce can Scottish kippers (or 6 freshly smoked herring)

3 tablespoons butter

1 tablespoon lemon juice

Black pepper

$^1/_3$ cup Scotch or bourbon

Sauté kippers in flaming pan of chafing dish over direct heat with butter and lemon juice until thoroughly heated. Season with several generous grinds of pepper. Add extra butter if necessary. Warm Scotch or bourbon in small saucepan, ignite, and pour over kippers. Serve blazing on hot plates. Enough for 6.

VEAL KIDNEYS FLAMBÉ

6 veal kidneys

3 tablespoons butter

Salt

Black pepper

$^1/_3$ cup cognac

Trim most of excess fat from kidneys but do not wash. Melt butter in flaming pan of chafing dish over direct heat. When butter begins to bubble, place kidneys in chafing dish, season with salt and freshly ground pepper, and sauté for 10 minutes. Remove kidneys to cutting board and slice crosswise into pieces about $1/8$-inch thick. Place sliced kidneys in chafing dish, add additional butter if necessary, and quickly reheat. Pour in cognac, blaze, and serve on toast points with juices from pan. Serves 6 unless they are kidney lovers. A full-bodied Nuits-Saint-Georges (or a good West Coast pinot noir) is the traditional accompaniment.

If you would like to add even more variety to your English buffet, chicken livers flambé alongside flaming kippers and blazing veal kidneys surely would seem to comprise a formidable Anglo-Saxon triumvirate.

CHICKEN LIVERS FLAMBÉ

2 GENEROUS CUPS CHICKEN LIVERS	BLACK PEPPER
	3 TABLESPOONS BUTTER
SALT	$1/4$ CUP DRY GIN

Sauté chicken livers with salt, freshly ground pepper, and butter in flaming pan of chafing dish over direct heat. Cook until livers are brown. Add gin and blaze. Excellent with broiled bacon. Makes 4 servings.

Another favorite way of serving chicken livers is *en brochette*, but like so many other recipes that are good but time-worn, the old reliable skewered chicken liver blossoms forth in aureate splendor with the addition of a good peg of dry gin. And if the juniper essence seems to clash with the strong flavor of liver, this presents a fine opportunity for you to begin a little pyromaniacal innovating on your own. You might substitute vodka. But vodka is neutral in flavor and is a safe retreat, though not a sound solution. It is best utilized in its 100-proof form in conjunction with other, less highly endowed (alcoholically speaking) spirits to provide that much-needed flash in the pan . . . but with a purpose. If our prime interest in *cuisine flambée* is only flash, as some people mistakenly suppose, and not flavor, then we might as well use straight grain alcohol. But this is not the best way to buy fire insurance. It is far better to experiment with the many-splendored spiritual opportunities that exist in the pantheon of volatile victuals. Chicken livers are a challenge because liver flavor is hard to deal with. Livers obliterate other flavors around them and thus are served best in their own juice. But flaming can contribute materially to their flavor and add subtle overtones that are achieved only by the most skillful *saucier* using conventional means of cooking. Chicken livers can be sautéed easily in the chafing dish with a little butter and successfully flambéed with rum, bourbon or rye, aquavit, Jenever gin (not to be confused with London dry gin), kümmel, Calvados or applejack, arak, and even tequila. Only experimentation and a *soupçon* of audacity will yield up the best recipe for your palate.

You can begin your explorations with this recipe for impaled chicken livers, which are easily broiled in the oven or grilled over charcoal out of doors.

CHICKEN LIVERS
EN BROCHETTE FLAMBÉ

16 CHICKEN LIVERS

6 SLICES BACON

SALT

BLACK PEPPER

OLIVE OIL

16 MUSHROOMS

3 TABLESPOONS BUTTER

1 TEASPOON LEMON JUICE

PINCH OF CHOPPED FRESH
    PARSLEY

PINCH OF DRIED TARRAGON

$1/3$ CUP ARMAGNAC

Rinse chicken livers in cold water, dry thoroughly, and slice in half. Broil bacon slices for less than a minute on each side, or until about half cooked; remove from heat and slice into thirds. Season livers with salt and freshly ground pepper and brush with olive oil. Fill four long skewers with alternating pieces of bacon, liver, and mushrooms and broil until livers are brown. In small saucepan, melt butter and add lemon juice, generous pinches of chopped parsley, and tarragon. Remove skewers to heated metal platter. Add Armagnac to butter mixture, ignite, and pour blazing over livers. Serves 4.

Armagnac is recommended instead of cognac for this dish as it has a strong, characteristic flavor that will stand up better when flambéed with livers. You may wish to try a flaming agent of your own choosing. If so, make some small extra portions of the recipe and blaze some new trails on your own.

If The Sign of the Dove is not one of the most stunning restaurants in New York, it is certainly the most romantic. Who can resist flower-filled, comfortable rooms, charmingly decorated, such as a gardenlike conservatory with a roof that opens to the sun and the stars in summer? Best of all, the service is caring, and attention to detail brings everything together in a genteel place to dine. The cuisine is inspired; an example is this sumptuous salad recipe created by Executive Chef Andrew D'Amico.

CHICKEN SALAD FLAMBÉ WITH ORANGE AND WALNUT VINAIGRETTE

2 TABLESPOONS PEANUT OIL

1 CUP SLICED SHIITAKE
   MUSHROOMS

$1/4$ CUP DICED LEEKS

1 GARLIC CLOVE, SLICED THIN

$1/4$ CUP DICED, SEEDED, PEELED
   TOMATO

$1/4$ CUP GRAND MARNIER

1 CUP GOOD CHICKEN STOCK
   OR BROTH

2 CUPS DICED COOKED
   CHICKEN MEAT

$1/2$ CUP SHERRY WINE VINEGAR

$1/2$ CUP WALNUT OIL

SALT

BLACK PEPPER

4 DINNER PLATES COVERED
   WITH ASSORTED GREENS
   (ENDIVE, ESCAROLE,
   ARUGULA, SPINACH,
   RADICCHIO, ETC.)

3 TABLESPOONS TOASTED
   SLIVERED ALMONDS

4 TEASPOONS CHOPPED FRESH
   CHIVES

1 LARGE ORANGE, CUT INTO
   SEGMENTS

In 14-inch sauté pan, heat peanut oil over high heat. Add mushrooms and cook until crisp. Add leeks and garlic, cook for 1 minute, add tomato with juice, and cook until tomato juice has evaporated. Add Grand Marnier with measuring cup; ignite and flambé until flames are exhausted and reduce until almost dry. Add chicken stock or broth and reduce by half. Add chicken meat and vinegar; return to boil. Whisk in walnut oil and season with salt and freshly ground pepper. Serve over torn salad greens that have been arranged attractively on large individual plates. Garnish with almonds, chives, and orange segments. Makes 4 servings.

Hot Tips—No. 6

Pure grain alcohol in its strongest, commonly available form is known and sold as grain neutral spirits and is 190 proof. It's powerful stuff. If imbibed straight, it's guaranteed to take the hide right off the roof of your mouth. It should never be used alone in flambé cookery even though you can use it to build a banquet-size fire. Occasionally it is valuable in adding alcoholic content to a weak, underproof cordial so it can be flamed, but it contributes nothing to the flavor of food.

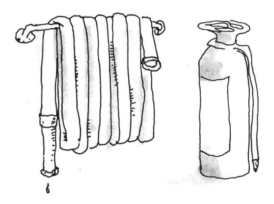

Vegetables also lend themselves to flambéing, but only the more robust types are recommended. Mushrooms respond extremely well to the flaming process, which endows them with new and exciting flavors.

CHAMPIGNONS AU RHUM

$^1/_2$ POUND (2 CUPS) WHITE
    MUSHROOMS

SALT

3 TABLESPOONS BUTTER

$^1/_3$ CUP LIGHT PUERTO RICAN
    RUM

$^1/_2$ CUP CREAM OR
    HOMOGENIZED MILK, HEATED

Wash mushrooms thoroughly in cold water, cut away bottoms of stems and season to taste with salt. Melt butter in flaming pan of chafing dish over direct heat and sauté mushrooms until brown. Pour in rum and blaze. When flames are extinguished, stir in heated cream or milk. Serve on toast points or rice pilaf. Makes 4 servings.

Here is a more traditional version of the last recipe using sherry and cognac in place of rum, which makes it a good choice as a luncheon entrée or the *pièce de résistance* for a light after-theater supper.

CHAMPIGNONS FLAMBÉS

1/2 POUND (2 CUPS) MUSHROOMS	1 CUP MEDIUM-DRY SHERRY
SALT	1/3 CUP COGNAC
6 TABLESPOONS BUTTER	1/2 CUP CREAM OR HOMOGENIZED MILK, HEATED

Wash mushrooms and trim stems. Season with salt and sauté mushrooms with butter in flaming pan of chafing dish over direct heat until brown. Add sherry and cook over low flame until wine has almost entirely evaporated. Pour in cognac and blaze. When flames are extinguished, stir in heated cream or milk and serve on toast points. Serves 4.

Cooked carrots, whose flavor is not always the world's most interesting, can be enlivened considerably by flambéing them in cognac, after which they become quite a presentable side dish.

CAROTTES FLAMBÉES

1 1/2 POUNDS CARROTS	1/3 CUP COGNAC
1/2 TEASPOON SALT	2 TABLESPOONS CHOPPED FRESH CHERVIL OR PARSLEY
4 TABLESPOONS BUTTER	
1 TABLESPOON SUGAR	

Wash carrots, trim off tops, and peel with vegetable peeler. Quarter carrots lengthwise, cut into 2-inch pieces, and boil in salted water for about 30 minutes or until tender. Remove, drain, and sauté carrots in butter and sugar. Pour in cognac, blaze, and sprinkle with chervil or parsley before serving. Makes enough for 6.

Rum is famous as a great flavor catalyst for fruits (in addition to its therapeutic values for people), but its energizing effects on vegetables are relatively unknown. Dark Jamaica rum is especially good for flambé cookery because the alcohol content is relatively high (90 to 100 proof) and it has a distinctive "rummy" molasses flavor which persists after the flaming process. The following recipes are good examples of its potential in the cooking of vegetables.

KINGSTOWN YAMS

4 YAMS OR SWEET POTATOES

$1/4$ CUP BUTTER

$3/4$ CUP FIRMLY PACKED BROWN
    SUGAR

PINCH OF SALT

DASH OF LEMON JUICE

$1/3$ CUP DARK JAMAICA RUM

Cook yams in boiling water for about 30 minutes or until tender. Remove, drain, and when cool, peel and slice yams crosswise into pieces about $1/2$-inch thick. Sauté yam slices with butter, brown sugar, salt, and lemon juice in flaming pan of chafing dish over direct heat. When thoroughly heated, pour in rum and blaze. Serves 4.

SUGAR WHARF SQUASH

ACORN SQUASH (¹/₂ PER PERSON)

BUTTER

BROWN SUGAR

SALT

GROUND GINGER

BLACK PEPPER

DARK JAMAICA RUM

Wash each squash, split, and remove seeds. Cover inside with thick coating of butter, thin layer of brown sugar, and light sprinklings of salt, ginger, and freshly ground pepper. Bake in 350° F. oven for about 1 hour or until tender. Add additional butter while baking if necessary. Remove squash from oven and place on heated flameproof platter. Warm enough rum in a saucepan to allow 1 tablespoon for each half squash. Ignite rum and ladle small amount while blazing into each portion.

Rum even can be used to give as prosaic a dish as baked beans a tinge of glamour that they somehow never seem to have when they are just sitting there looking up at you from the plate. If you find the rum flavor too pronounced, try substituting bourbon, which works just as well. One thing is certain, once you've set fire to baked beans, you may find it difficult to go back to the less flamboyant kind.

BAKED BEANS AU GLOW-GLOW

4 CUPS CANNED BAKED BEANS

1/2 CUP CHOPPED ONION

1/4 CUP BROWN SUGAR, PLUS
    EXTRA

2 TABLESPOONS MOLASSES

1 TABLESPOON PREPARED
    MUSTARD

1/2 CUP KETCHUP

1 TABLESPOON A-1 SAUCE

1/4 TEASPOON SALT

BLACK PEPPER

8 SLICES BACON

1/2 CUP DARK JAMAICA RUM OR
    BOURBON

Empty 4 cups (that's two 1-pound cans) of your favorite brand of baked beans into heated flameproof casserole and stir in onion, brown sugar, molasses, mustard, ketchup, A-1 Sauce, salt, and several grinds of pepper. Cut bacon slices in half and place on top of beans. Sprinkle with additional brown sugar, and bake in medium oven (325 to 350° F.) for at least 2 hours. Warm rum in saucepan. Remove casserole to table and ladle flaming rum over beans. Serves 4 men, or 8 women, or 2 famished teenagers.

If flaming beans with rum give you a lift, perhaps you are ready for something really way out. How about something in flaming beer? Yes, it can be done, but we have to "needle it" Prohibition-style to bring up the alcohol content so it will ignite. If you've ever eaten freshly caught jumbo Gulf shrimp steamed in beer and have luxuriated in the experience, you may want to give this recipe, with an ingenious, igneous twist, a try.

YAZOO SHRIMP

2 POUNDS RAW JUMBO SHRIMP

BEER

1 TABLESPOON LEMON JUICE

4 OR 5 FRESH DILL SPRIGS, OR

 1 TABLESPOON CRUMBLED

 DRIED DILL, PLUS EXTRA FOR

 GARNISH

1 TABLESPOON SALT

1/2 CUP 100-PROOF VODKA

Place raw shrimp in large saucepan and pour in enough beer to cover. Add lemon juice, fresh dill sprigs or tablespoon dried dill, and salt. Simmer very slowly for about 15 minutes. When cool enough to handle, take out shrimp, remove shells and vein running along back, and place on heated flameproof platter. Warm 1/2 cup beer in saucepan and add enough vodka to ensure ignition (a generous 1/2 cup). Ladle blazing mixture over shrimp. Garnish with additional dill and serve on rice pilaf. Serves 4 shrimp lovers. Should be accompanied with tall steins of cold beer or a light dry Riesling.

Swedish meatballs (*köttbullar*) is one of the basic indispensable dishes that make up a classic smorgasbord. The added touch of flaming these meatballs with aquavit is just liable to make someone stand up and shout, "Great Balls of Fire!"

GREAT BALLS OF FIRE!

1 TABLESPOON BUTTER

3 TABLESPOONS CHOPPED
ONION

1/4 CUP BREAD CRUMBS

2 TO 3 TABLESPOONS CREAM OR
HOMOGENIZED MILK

2/3 POUND GROUND BEEF

1/3 POUND GROUND LEAN PORK

1 EGG

1 TEASPOON ARROWROOT

SALT

BLACK PEPPER

2 OUNCES AQUAVIT

Melt butter in skillet and sauté onion until golden brown. In a bowl mix
bread crumbs with cream or milk and blend in meats, egg, arrowroot
moistened with a little water, salt to taste, and several grinds of pepper.
Add sautéed onions and mix well. Shape into small balls, return to skil-

let in small batches, adding a little butter if necessary, and sauté until evenly browned. Just before serving, add aquavit, allow it to warm for several minutes, and ignite, shaking skillet back and forth until all the alcohol is burned off. To flame at table, use blazer pan of chafing dish over direct heat with a touch of butter if necessary to prevent sticking. Add meatballs and aquavit, making certain that diners are well away from the flames. Serves 4.

It is not really necessary to go far afield in search of bizarre methods of flambéing food. Actually the most commonplace dishes are the ones that lend themselves most naturally to culinary pyrotechnics. Many of your old favorites, which have perhaps lost their luster over the years, can be brightened up considerably when paired with some blithe spirits. This is what the incorrigible firebrand means when he exclaims, "We're always on the lookout for the perfect match."

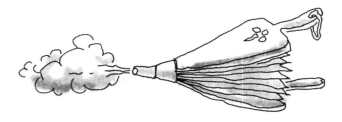

Hot Tips—No. 7

Although wines and spirits and good food are traditional running mates, don't overlook the frequent opportunities to use beer and ale in recipes. Beer is basic to a hearty Welsh rabbit or a good cheese sauce, and a marvelous replacement for water in pot roast and beef stew. And if you enjoy it as a beverage, be sure to keep a special set of mugs or glasses set aside especially for beer drinking. These containers should never be washed with soap or detergent—only rinsed in hot water after use. Try it and see how it improves the flavor and the "head."

Chicken and cognac make a delectable combination, as this variation of a classic French recipe adapted for the chafing dish will prove.

CHICKEN BREASTS FLAMBÉ

4 TABLESPOONS BUTTER

4 CHICKEN BREASTS, BONED

1 TEASPOON LEMON JUICE

SALT

BLACK PEPPER

$^1/_3$ CUP COGNAC

$^1/_2$ CUP BEEF BOUILLON

$^1/_2$ CUP MADEIRA WINE

1 CUP CREAM OR HOMOGENIZED
    MILK

CHOPPED FRESH PARSLEY

Melt butter in flaming pan of chafing dish over direct heat. Place chicken breasts in pan, add lemon juice, season with salt and freshly ground pepper, and sear on both sides. Reduce flame, cover, and cook for about 15 minutes or until tender. Pour in cognac and blaze. Remove breasts to heated platter. Pour in bouillon and Madeira and bring to boil over high flame. Pour in cream or milk and stir constantly over medium heat until sauce has thickened. Season to taste with salt and pepper, ladle sauce over chicken, and sprinkle with parsley. Serves 4. A dry Graves or, if you prefer a red wine with chicken, a light California cabernet will heighten your enjoyment of this dish.

Duck is one of the great traditional flaming entrées of all time. Here is a delightful method of preparing waterfowl with an Irish brogue.

DUBLIN DUCK

4¹/₂-POUND DUCK

SALT

BLACK PEPPER

1 ONION

1 TABLESPOON COOKING OIL

2 CUPS CANNED BEEF BOUILLON

PINCH OF DRIED THYME

1 TABLESPOON CHOPPED FRESH
    PARSLEY

¹/₂ BAY LEAF

1 CUP BITTER ORANGE
    MARMALADE OR COCKTAIL
    ORANGES IN SUGAR SYRUP

¹/₂ CUP IRISH WHISKEY OR
    IRISH MIST LIQUEUR OR
    EQUAL PARTS OF BOTH

Rinse duck, remove all excess fat from cavity, dry, season with salt and freshly ground pepper, and place on rack in roasting pan in preheated moderate oven (350° F.) for about 1¹/₂ hours. While duck is roasting, prepare stock as follows: Dice liver, heart, neck meat, and gizzard and cook in saucepan with sliced onion and oil until brown. Remove fat from saucepan and add bouillon, thyme, parsley, and bay leaf. Simmer for at least 1¹/₂ hours, adding water if necessary. By the time duck is ready to serve, stock should be reduced to less than 1 cup. Immediately before serving, remove and discard bay leaf; add marmalade or oranges to stock and heat through. Remove duck to hot platter and pour on blazing whiskey or liqueur. Ladle stock over duck. Serves 4. A fine Chambertin will make everything taste even better.

If the foregoing Hibernian recipe for waterfowl seems like too much fuss (actually duck is the easiest of all birds to prepare because of its abundance of fat), we offer this considerably more casual recipe, which can be tossed off in a trice—providing a trice can last at least long enough to roast a nice plump duck. Prepare duck as directed in the last recipe but omit the stock. In its stead, make the following sauce while the duck is roasting.

WILLIAM OF ORANGE SAUCE

1 CUP FRESH ORANGE JUICE

PEEL OF 1 ORANGE

3 TABLESPOONS RED CURRANT
    JAM

$^1/_4$ CUP TRIPLE SEC

$^1/_4$ CUP COGNAC

Pour orange juice into saucepan and add orange peel, which has been scraped clean of pulp and cut into strips about $^1/_8$-inch wide. Stir in jam, cover, and simmer over very low heat for about 20 minutes. Remove lid and cook until liquid is reduced by half. Pour in triple sec and cognac, ignite, and ladle over duck, which has been placed on heated flameproof platter.

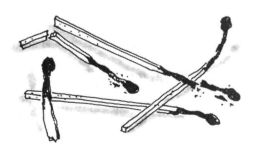

Orange liqueurs are called for in many flambé dishes. Their selection depends on the degree of sweetness desired and alcoholic strength. Generally speaking, cordials with more sugar are selected for desserts, and those with less are more suitable for entrées. High-proof spirits are best when combined with other ingredients because they are more easily flamed. Grand Marnier, triple sec, and Cointreau (a brand of triple sec) all run about 80 proof. Curaçao and Mandarine Napoléon, a cordial made from tangerines, are usually only 60 proof. Taste is a matter of judgment, but flammability is a matter of proof. Remember, the lower-proof spirits should be beefed up with cognac, vodka, gin, or, in some instances, 190-proof neutral spirits.

Veal, which is considerably more popular in Europe than in the United States, is the epicenter of many traditional dishes and the basis of some truly flavorful flammables. The French prize young, milk-fed veal, which produces a fine-grained meat with a very light pink color. And this is what you should look for when you buy veal in the market. If you are not a confirmed veal lover, you might try this easy recipe for veal chops by way of introduction.

VEAL VESUVIO

3 TABLESPOONS CHOPPED
SHALLOTS

4 TABLESPOONS BUTTER

$^1/_2$ TEASPOON CHOPPED
TARRAGON

$^1/_2$ TEASPOON CHOPPED FRESH
CHERVIL OR PARSLEY

6 LARGE VEAL CHOPS

SALT

BLACK PEPPER

$^1/_3$ CUP CALVADOS OR
APPLEJACK

In skillet or flaming pan of chafing dish over direct heat, sauté shallots lightly in 1 tablespoon butter with tarragon and chervil or parsley. Remove and put aside. Add remaining butter to pan and cook veal chops 4 or 5 minutes on each side, depending on heat. Season with salt and freshly ground pepper. Remove chops to heated flameproof platter and stand each group of three chops together like a teepee or tripod. Add butter-and-herb mixture to pan, reheat, pour in Calvados or applejack, ignite, and ladle blazing over chops. Serves 6. A chilled Chablis or California sauvignon blanc will make a good dinner companion.

This dish is the centerpiece for a cozy dinner for two. The flaming Calvados adds more than festivity to the table. It permeates the veal with a subtle apple flavor.

VEAL MIGNONETTES FLAMED WITH CALVADOS

8 MEDIUM-THICK BONELESS
    SLICES OF VEAL (AS FOR
    VEAL SCALLOPINE)
SALT
BLACK PEPPER

FLOUR
SWEET BUTTER
8 LARGE MUSHROOMS, SLICED
3 TABLESPOONS CALVADOS
$1/4$ TO $1/2$ CUP HEAVY CREAM

Season each slice of veal with salt to taste and several grinds of pepper. Dredge veal slices in flour and sauté in butter lightly on both sides over medium heat for about 6 minutes. Add mushrooms and brown lightly. Pour in Calvados and ignite, stirring briskly so that all alcohol is burned off. Remove veal and mushrooms from skillet and pour in heavy cream (amount depending on richness desired). Simmer over low heat until sauce is reduced slightly. Ladle hot sauce over veal and mushrooms. Makes 2 servings.

Another excellent veal dish is scallops flambé, which can be turned out effortlessly for a light luncheon or an "after-something" supper. Have your butcher slice a boneless tender cut of veal in thin slices so when pounded out with the side of a meat cleaver they end up about $1/2$-inch thick. They should be light pink in color and devoid of gristle and fat.

VEAL SCALLOPS FLAMBÉ

12 VEAL SCALLOPS

4 TABLESPOONS BUTTER

SALT

BLACK PEPPER

$^1/_3$ CUP COGNAC

CHOPPED FRESH PARSLEY

Sauté scallops in large skillet with butter until lightly browned on both sides. Season with salt and freshly ground pepper. Pour cognac in skillet and blaze. Remove to hot platter and sprinkle with chopped parsley. Serves 6. A Montrachet is a good choice of wine for this dish.

If your tastes run to Italian cooking, here is a variation of veal scallops that is a real scorcher.

VEAL SCALLOPINE FUOCO

3 TABLESPOONS OLIVE OIL

12 VEAL SCALLOPS

FLOUR

1 GARLIC CLOVE, MINCED

1 TABLESPOON CHOPPED

    CAPERS

6 ANCHOVY FILLETS, SLICED

1 TEASPOON CHOPPED FRESH

    PARSLEY

$^1/_2$ TEASPOON DRIED OREGANO

DASH OF LEMON JUICE

SALT

BLACK PEPPER

$^1/_3$ CUP COGNAC, WARMED

Heat olive oil in skillet, give veal a light coating of flour, and sauté on both sides until brown. When scallops are almost done, add garlic, capers, anchovies, herbs, and lemon juice. Season with salt and freshly ground pepper. Remove to heated flameproof platter, pour on warmed cognac and blaze. Serves 6. A good Valpolicella or Bardolino will complement this zesty dish.

Many kinds of crabs are readily available fresh or frozen. Two particularly good ones for flambé cookery are king crab and Dungeness (blue) crab. Either will work beautifully in this recipe.

As a general rule of thumb, fresh herbs are not available, use half the amount of dried herbs.

CRAB IMPERATUR

3/4 CUP BUTTER

2 TABLESPOONS CHOPPED
    FRESH CHIVES

1/4 CUP CHOPPED GREEN
    ONIONS

1 TABLESPOON CHOPPED FRESH
    PARSLEY

2 TEASPOONS CHOPPED FRESH
    TARRAGON

SALT

BLACK PEPPER

2 POUNDS KING CRABMEAT

1/3 CUP DRY WHITE WINE

DASH OF LEMON JUICE

1/3 CUP COGNAC

Melt butter in flaming pan of chafing dish over direct heat. Add chives, green onions, parsley, and tarragon, and season with salt and several grinds of pepper. Add crabmeat, wine, and lemon juice. Add additional butter if necessary. Heat crabmeat through but do not brown. Reduce liquid by half, pour in cognac, and blaze. Serve on rice pilaf or toast points. Serves 4. A well-chilled Chablis or dry Graves will spark this dish.

When blue crabs, which are as well known on the East Coast as Dungeness crabs are in the Pacific Northwest, are molting, soft-shell crabs are in season. Actually, soft-shell crabs are simply blue (and other) crabs with a new exterior that hasn't had a chance to change from skin to shell. When these succulent little soft-shell crabs are readily available, try this recipe. It is a crab lovers' delight.

CRAB BEATRICE

12 SMALL SOFT-SHELL CRABS

MILK

FLOUR

$^3/_4$ CUP BUTTER

1 TABLESPOON CHOPPED FRESH
   PARSLEY

$^1/_2$ TABLESPOON CHOPPED
   FRESH DILL

$^1/_2$ TABLESPOON CHOPPED
   FRESH TARRAGON

DASH OF LEMON JUICE

SALT

BLACK PEPPER

$^1/_3$ CUP DRY GIN

Bathe cleaned crabs for 1 hour in enough fresh milk to cover. Remove and dredge in flour. Melt butter in flaming pan of chafing dish over direct heat. When butter froths, add crabs, herbs, and lemon juice, and sauté until brown on each side. Season with salt and several grinds of pepper. Remove crabs to heated flameproof platter. Pour gin into chafing dish, ignite, and ladle over crabs. Serves 4. A chilled dry Rhine wine or California chardonnay will go well with this dish.

Good pans, whether made of iron, aluminum, stainless steel, or copper, should be given proper care if you want predictable cooking results. A new pan should be "broken in" by being gradually heated the first few times it is used. Never leave an empty pan over heat for an extended period of time. Food seems to have a tendency to stick to a pan that has been severely overheated or in which food has been burned. The metallurgy of modern cookware is complex, and it is important that a good pan should not lose its temper. Don't douse very hot pans in cold water. Let them cool gradually before washing.

FROGS' LEGS MIRABELLE

16 MEDIUM PAIRS FROGS' LEGS

MILK

SALT

BLACK PEPPER

FLOUR

3 TABLESPOONS BUTTER

1 GARLIC CLOVE, MINCED

2 TABLESPOONS CHOPPED
FRESH PARSLEY, PLUS EXTRA
FOR GARNISH

JUICE OF 1 LEMON

1/4 CUP 100-PROOF VODKA

2 TABLESPOONS MIRABELLE OR
SLIVOVITZ

LEMON WEDGES (FOR GARNISH)

Soak frogs' legs in milk for at least 1 hour. Remove, drain, and season with salt and several good grinds of pepper. Cross legs, dust lightly with flour, and sauté with butter in flaming pan of chafing dish over direct heat. As frogs' legs are browning, add garlic, parsley, and half of lemon juice. When legs are lightly browned, pour in vodka and mirabelle or slivovitz and blaze. Serve with remainder of lemon juice, garnish with lemon wedges, and sprinkle on additional parsley. Serves 4. A chilled Pouilly-Fuissé or California pinot blanc is a good wine selection.

Located in a beautiful, quiet, and very elegant section of Paris, the Hôtel Plaza Athénée has always been a retreat for merchant princes (and real princes), world travelers, and knowledgeable Parisians who come here to enjoy the ambience, the fine food, and service. In warm weather, the centerpiece for social activity is the lovely open-air Garden Court where the cuisine has a celebratory aura that quickens the most jaded appetite.

MONKFISH AND SQUID EN CASSEROLE

1 GENEROUS POUND MONKFISH

SALT

BLACK PEPPER

OLIVE OIL

$1/4$ CUP PERNOD

FINELY CHOPPED FRESH THYME

FINELY CHOPPED FRESH
    ROSEMARY

GENEROUS $3/4$ POUND NEW
    POTATOES, SCRUBBED AND
    SCRAPED

SEVERAL PINCHES OF SAFFRON

2 CUPS FISH STOCK (SEE
    INDEX) OR CHICKEN BROTH
    (SEE NOTE)

$3/4$ POUND SMALL SQUID

$3/4$ POUND FRESH BROCCOLI
    WITH LEAVES

2 SMALL TOMATOES, SEEDED
    AND CHOPPED

When you buy whole monkfish and squid ask your fish market to pre-pare them so they are ready for cooking. Season monkfish with salt and pepper and place in a casserole with olive oil; sear over heat on both sides for 5 to 8 minutes. Pour in Pernod, and when it is warmed, ignite and flambé until flames are extinguished. Season with thyme and rosemary; add potatoes and sprinkle with a little saffron. Cook monkfish for 18 minutes over medium heat, remove, and set aside and keep warm. Add fish stock or chicken broth and squid. While squid is cooking, lightly steam broccoli. After a few minutes, when squid is nearly done (do not overcook), blend chopped tomato into stock, return monkfish to casse-role, and arrange broccoli around it. Serve in casserole or on individual plates. This fine dish deserves a chilled Montrachet. Makes 2 servings.

NOTE: You can substitute a mixture of equal parts chicken broth and clam juice for the fish stock or chicken broth.

Lobster tails can be deliciously flambéed and are more convenient to use in their frozen form than fresh live lobsters. The lobster tail available in most of our markets is known in France as *langouste* and is not really a lobster at all, but rather a seagoing crawfish, except that it has no claws. It is sometimes referred to as a spiny or rock lobster. Lobster tails can be broiled or boiled. Many cooks prefer to boil lobster because it can be cooked longer without drying out. This is the time-honored method of cooking seafood in New England, where shellfish are abundant. Before preparing lobster tails, allow them to thaw out if they are frozen, since this permits more even cooking.

LOBSTER TAILS FLAMBÉ

4 LARGE LOBSTER TAILS

SALT

1 CUP MELTED BUTTER

1 TEASPOON LEMON JUICE

2 TABLESPOONS CHOPPED
    FRESH PARSLEY, PLUS EXTRA
    FOR GARNISH

1 TABLESPOON CHOPPED FRESH
    TARRAGON

$^1/_3$ CUP DRY GIN

LEMON WEDGES (FOR GARNISH)

Boil lobster tails in lightly salted water for 30 to 40 minutes, depending on size. Remove to cutting board, slit undershell lengthwise along each side, remove meat in one piece, and place on heated flameproof platter. While lobster is cooking, boil butter in small saucepan until it begins to brown, then add lemon juice, parsley, and tarragon. Serve in individual cups. Warm gin in saucepan used to prepare butter mixture, then ignite and pour blazing over tails. Garnish with fresh parsley and lemon wedges. Serves 4. Wash down with cold beer or a chilled Meursault.

The Ritz-Carlton, Kapalua, on the island of Maui fronts the ocean and overlooks the nearby island of Molokai. Its setting amid a 23,000-acre pineapple plantation with the majestic West Maui mountain range as a backdrop makes this a prime Hawaiian playground. Here you can enjoy nature's culinary treasures, such as tiger prawns, pineapple, and macadamia nuts, at the source. This recipe was created by Executive Chef Patrick Callarec.

TIGER PRAWNS FLAMBÉ

UNSALTED BUTTER

6 RAW TIGER PRAWNS, SHELLED
AND DEVEINED

$^1/_2$ SHALLOT, FINELY CHOPPED

1 TABLESPOON DICED FRESH
PINEAPPLE

$^1/_4$ TABLESPOON DICED
MACADAMIA NUTS

HANA RUM (OR ANY DARK RUM)

$^1/_2$ CUP HEAVY CREAM

SALT

BLACK PEPPER

In butter, sauté prawns on both sides in skillet or saucepan. Add shallot, pineapple, and macadamia nuts. Pour in rum. When warmed, ignite and flambé, shaking pan vigorously, until flames die out. Stir in cream and reduce by about one-third. Add 1 teaspoon butter and salt and pepper to taste. Serve on sticky rice, if you wish. Makes 1 serving.

NOTE: Any large prawns or shrimps may be substituted for tiger prawns, which usually are only available frozen in mainland United States.

American beef is the standard of excellence by which beef throughout the world is compared. It is the leading favorite for broiling, roasting, barbecuing and just about every other means of cooking imaginable, including, of course, flambéing. And whether it is served up on a sterling silver platter, amid elegant surroundings, as Tournedos Henri IV, or as a hot dog broiled on the end of a stick over a driftwood fire at the beach, it is universally enjoyed for its great nutritional value and marvelous flavor. Cooking techniques have a great deal to do with amplifying the natural flavor of beef. For this reason, the application of direct flame plays a particularly important role in beef cookery, and flambéing is a means of adding that perfect final touch to a great steak.

Steaks, generally speaking, should be broiled under a high heat in the oven or grilled over a hot fire out-of-doors. Whether you prefer your steaks charred on the outside and rare on the inside—a condition pyromaniacs refer to as "black and blue"—or bordering on incineration, it is essential that you always are in complete control of the cooking process.

Hot Tips—No. 10

Various chefs have favorite ways of testing the degree to which beef has been cooked. This includes looking at the color of the juices that bubble out of the meat and pressing on the meat to determine its resiliency or "springiness"—or lack of it. Professionals, thoroughly familiar with the cuts of meat they regularly prepare and with their kitchen equipment, can time a steak down to seconds. For the amateur, the best method is simply to make a small cut into the meat on the "done" side (near the bone if there is one) and look at the color. If it's bright red, it's rare, and if it's pink, it's medium, and if it's gray, you looked too late. Remember, meat continues to cook for a few minutes after it is removed from its heat source. Try not to cook your meat too long, no matter what someone tells you about cooking times. A dry, drab piece of meat is overcooked *by any standard.*

Curiously enough, the more expensive cuts of beef need the greater amount of attention in the kitchen, for the cheaper cuts usually have a greater abundance of natural beef flavor that is so highly prized. The two recipes given here involve expensive cuts of beef; consequently, flambéing will add measurably to their flavor and your enjoyment.

STEAK AU POIVRE FLAMBÉ

1 LARGE PRIME
    PORTERHOUSE STEAK
    (2 INCHES THICK)
2 TABLESPOONS PEPPERCORNS
SALT
3 TABLESPOONS BUTTER

1 TABLESPOON CHOPPED
    SHALLOTS OR GREEN ONIONS
1 TABLESPOON CHOPPED FRESH
    PARSLEY
1/2 CUP COGNAC OR AQUAVIT

Dry steak thoroughly with paper towels. Crack peppercorns with mortar and pestle or rolling pin and press into steak with palm of hand. Salt to taste. Broil steak in preheated oven. While steak is broiling, melt butter in saucepan. Add shallots or green onions and parsley and sauté lightly. Remove steak to heated flameproof platter and pour on butter mixture. Add cognac or aquavit to saucepan used for butter. Warm and pour blazing over steak. Serves 4. A full-bodied Médoc or Burgundy will counter the pronounced flavor of the peppered beef beautifully.

Filet mignon is lean and very tender but not long on flavor. This simple recipe will help give this aristocratic cut of beef a needed fillip.

FILET MIGNON FLAMBÉ

4 PRIME FILETS MIGNONS
  (2 INCHES THICK)
SALT
BLACK PEPPER
2 TABLESPOONS BUTTER

1 TABLESPOON CHOPPED FRESH
  PARSLEY
1 TABLESPOON CHOPPED
  SHALLOTS
1/3 CUP COGNAC

Season filets mignons with salt and freshly ground pepper, brush with a little butter, and broil in preheated oven. While steaks are cooking, melt remaining butter in saucepan with parsley and shallots and sauté lightly. Remove filets to heated flameproof platter. Add cognac to butter mixture, heat, and pour blazing over steaks. Serves 4. Try a Châteauneuf-du-Pape or California cabernet sauvignon with this dish.

One restaurant critic called New York's Post House "a chauvinist monument to meat and Martinis." Meaning that this is where the guys get together to have hearty food and drink and lots of it. Every time I've visited this busy, crowded, cheerful establishment, I've seen plenty of women dining with gusto on a variety of entrées as well as some of the biggest and best beefsteaks in town. So chauvinist or not, people are standing in line for exceptional, old-fashioned steakhouse fare, like this creation by Post House Executive Chef Bob Mignola.

TENNESSEE PEPPER STEAK

FOUR ¹/₂-POUND FILETS
   MIGNONS
1 TABLESPOON WHOLE WHITE
   PEPPERCORNS
1 TABLESPOON WHOLE
   CORIANDER SEEDS
2 TABLESPOONS MUSTARD
   SEEDS
1 TEASPOON CELERY SEEDS
SALT

BLACK PEPPER
4 TABLESPOONS VEGETABLE OIL
³/₄ CUP JACK DANIEL'S
   TENNESSEE SOUR MASH
   WHISKEY
1 CUP CAMPBELL'S BEEF BROTH
   (DOUBLE CONSOMMÉ)
1 CUP HEAVY CREAM
¹/₂ CUP UNSALTED BUTTER

Flatten the steaks with the flat side of a cleaver. Using a spice grinder, coarsely grind peppercorns, coriander, and mustard, and celery seeds, and spread out on a cutting board. Press both sides of steak firmly into spice mixture, and season with salt and pepper. Add vegetable oil to sauté pan just large enough for all the steaks, and heat until oil is almost smoking. Carefully lay steaks in pan and sauté for about 3 or 4 minutes per side (for medium rare), being careful not to burn spice coating. Remove steaks to warm platter. Drain oil from pan, return to heat, pour in Jack Daniel's; when warm, ignite and flame for 10 or 15 seconds. Before flames subside, add beef broth and heavy cream, and reduce mixture over high heat, stirring constantly with a wire whip. When mixture reaches sauce consistency (coats a spoon), whisk in butter; check seasoning and correct if necessary. Remove steaks to warm dinner plates, spoon sauce over meat, and serve immediately. Serves 4.

Undoubtedly the most famous flambé beef dish of recent times was the "flaming sword" dinner devised by the late Ernie Byfield for his splendiforous Pump Room at the Ambassador East Hotel in Chicago. In its halcyon days, it was an elegant place to dine, and the fascination of watching a never-ending parade of turbaned torchbearers proudly carrying their flaring family-sized *brochettes* aloft never seemed to wane. The flame was provided by impaled cotton balls soaked in alcohol and ignited.

Perhaps its main benefit, as far as the food was concerned, was to keep it warm. But the psychological effects on the clientele were substantial indeed, for the flaming sword ultimately was equated with haute cuisine for the haut monde. If you happen to have any rapiers around, you can approximate this spectacle in the confines of your very own dining room.

FLAMING BEEF EN BROCHETTE

2 POUNDS PRIME SIRLOIN OR
    BEEF TENDERLOIN
SALT
BLACK PEPPER
1¹/₂ TABLESPOONS BUTTER
1¹/₂ TABLESPOONS PEANUT OIL

DASH OF LEMON JUICE
CHERRY TOMATOES
LARGE MUSHROOM CAPS
GREEN PEPPERS, QUARTERED
COGNAC, WARMED
RICE PILAF (PREPARED)

Trim all fat and gristle from beef and dice into 1¹/₂-inch cubes. Season with salt and freshly ground pepper. Melt butter in saucepan with oil and lemon juice. Brush meat with butter-and-oil mixture and place on four long skewers, alternating meat, tomatoes, mushroom caps, and green peppers. Broil in oven, turning frequently and brushing with additional butter and oil as needed. Remove from oven. With string, tie cotton balls on top and bottom of skewers. Saturate with warmed cognac, ignite, and bring to table blazing. Place on rice pilaf. Serves 4. Enjoy with a bright Beaujolais Moulin-à-Vent.

Cuisine flambée is by nature flamboyant and exuberant; it can be performed discreetly, but hardly inconspicuously. It is a bright, glittering showcase for good cooking, but never a substitute for ordinary fare.

For these reasons, perhaps, there is some truth in the old adage: "The pan is mightier than the sword!"

THREE

Flaming Feasts
in the Great Tradition

Combustible comestibles once comprised a very substantial part of the gastronomy of France as well as all of Europe. It was but one aspect of the lusty approach to life that made the taking of food such a thoroughly pleasurable event for our ancestors. The remnants of more dynamic eras of eating are still well within the recollection of some of our fathers and our grandfathers who may have participated in the extended tabletop bouts that were commonplace in the Gay Nineties and the Edwardian Age that followed. The French had a much better name for it. They called it *La Belle Époque.*

And that it was! When it came to an end, it signaled the passing of an era of graciousness and culinary opulence that is not likely to be surpassed. True, there were excesses, and there was gluttony, but let it be firmly stated that the availability of a vast array of food, however elegantly prepared, and the practice of stuffing oneself far beyond reasonable limits of human capacity do not necessarily go hand in hand. It is not quantity or even variety that matters, it is the attitude and the orientation to good food and good living that separate the gourmet from the gourmand. True epicureanism is not even really a matter of money, for while money alone can buy the best that a great chef is able to produce, it by no means ensures that the enjoyment of his or her handiwork will be in direct proportion to the prices on the menu.

This philosophical approach to pot and pan is intended only to provide an explanation for the selection of recipes that follow. Some are classic, in the true tradition of haute cuisine; others are modern interpretations, and some are new. All were selected, however, because they provide the nucleus of good—and in a few instances, perhaps even great—dinners. They all have connotations of elegance, imagination, and vitality that are rooted deeply in our past. And finally, these dishes have a good flammability quotient, and although this will be subject to varying shades of opinion, I believe all of these particular recipes taste better *en flambeau* than without a touch of fire. For one of the first principles of pyromania and a good rule to follow in the kitchen is: "Out of the frying pan and into the fire."

This is more than a saying—it is a gastronomic way of life.

Of all the ways of preparing lobster, one of the most delicious and deservedly famous is *Lobster à l'Américaine* or, as it is often called, *Lobster à l'Armoricaine*. From the very beginning, this classical dish has been a maverick. There is even disagreement as to its proper name. The method of cooking is partially traditional—one that is used in the ancient region of Armorique, in Brittany. But the use of tomatoes is indigenous to Mediterranean cooking, particularly in Provence. Whether it was named in honor of an American or after an old section of France is not of great consequence. Inasmuch as our recipe was developed by the talented and capable chefs of Air France, and they have classified this dish as a *spécialité* from Brittany, it would seem the name to use should be the one that they themselves have selected.

HOMARD À L'ARMORICAINE

2 LIVE LOBSTERS ($1^{1}/_{2}$ TO 2 POUNDS EACH)

$^{3}/_{4}$ CUP PEANUT OR OLIVE OIL

$^{1}/_{2}$ POUND BUTTER

SALT

CAYENNE PEPPER

$^{1}/_{2}$ TABLESPOON CHOPPED ONION

2 TABLESPOONS CHOPPED SHALLOTS

1 GARLIC CLOVE, CHOPPED

$^{3}/_{4}$ CUP COGNAC

6 CUPS DRY WHITE WINE

3 CUPS FISH STOCK (SEE NEXT RECIPE)

4 TOMATOES

2 TABLESPOONS TOMATO PASTE

2 PARSLEY SPRIGS, PLUS CHOPPED FRESH PARSLEY (FOR GARNISH)

CHOPPED FRESH TARRAGON

2 TABLESPOONS FLOUR

TABASCO SAUCE

Split lobsters lengthwise with sharp knife, remove legs and claws. Remove sand sack in head, which contains gravel, and intestinal vein, and discard. Remove coral and green tomalley and set aside. Pour peanut or olive oil into large skillet or casserole and heat with 2 tablespoons butter. Cut tail sections into four pieces and crack claws with knife handle, but do not remove meat. Add lobster pieces. Season with salt and cayenne pepper, and stir with wooden spoon over high heat. When shells turn red and meat is firm and opaque, pour off oil-and-butter mixture. Sprinkle onion, shallots, and garlic on lobster. Mix rapidly. Add three-quarters of the cognac (saving the rest for later use), ignite, and blaze. Add wine and enough Fish Stock to cover lobster. Add tomatoes, which have been skinned, seeded, pressed to squeeze out juice, and chopped. Add tomato paste, parsley, and tarragon. Cover and cook for 20 minutes over low heat. Remove meat from shells, place in vegetable dish, and keep warm. Reduce liquid in skillet by half and with whisk beat in coral and tomalley. Add 5 tablespoons butter and the flour. Cook for a short time. Push through fine strainer and add remaining cognac and butter. Correct seasoning with salt, pepper, and a few drops of Tabasco sauce. Place lobster meat on heated serving platter and pour sauce over lobster. Sprinkle with chopped parsley and tarragon. Shells can be used for decoration by placing lobster tails *en accolade*—balancing tails vertically against each other in center of platter. Serve on rice pilaf, if you wish. Serves 4. A fine Graves or Montrachet makes the perfect accompaniment.

Fish stock (*fumet de poisson*) is an important ingredient in the preceding and certain other recipes. It may seem like an extra complication, but making it is worth the effort. It will keep for a considerable period of time if frozen.

FUMET DE POISSON
(Fish Stock)

2 POUNDS FRESH FISH, FISH HEADS, BONES, AND TRIMMINGS OF SOLE OR FLOUNDER

1/2 TABLESPOON BUTTER

1 ONION, SLICED

2 PARSLEY SPRIGS

1 BAY LEAF

6 PEPPERCORNS

PINCH OF SALT

2 CUPS DRY WHITE WINE

2 CUPS COLD WATER

JUICE OF 1 LEMON

Cut fish into small pieces and carefully wash heads, bones, and trimmings. Heat butter in large skillet or casserole. Add fish, fish heads, bones, trimmings, onion, parsley, bay leaf, peppercorns, and salt. Cook over medium heat for about 10 minutes; if necessary, add a little water. Then add wine, cold water, and lemon juice. Bring to boil, lower heat, and simmer for 20 minutes. Stir from time to time. Strain into container with tight-fitting lid. Can be refrigerated for several days or placed in freezer until needed.

Marina del Rey boasts the largest man-made small-craft harbor in the world, and believe it or not, it's only 10 minutes from Los Angeles International Airport. The Ritz-Carlton, situated on the water's edge of the marina with a beautiful view of the Pacific Ocean, offers many conveniences and diversions, among them a fine kitchen, expertly managed by Executive Chef Bruno Lopez, who created this succulent lobster dish.

AMERICAN LOBSTER LOPEZ

2 LIVE MAINE LOBSTERS
　(1¹/₂ POUNDS EACH)

SALT

¹/₃ CUP OLIVE OIL

1 ONION, DICED

1 CARROT, DICED

1 STALK CELERY, DICED

3 SHALLOTS, CHOPPED

3 TABLESPOONS COGNAC

1 CUP WHITE WINE

1 CUP FISH STOCK (SEE INDEX)
　OR WATER

1 TABLESPOON TOMATO PASTE

3 TOMATOES, DICED

BLACK PEPPER

CAYENNE PEPPER

2 BAY LEAVES

1 THYME SPRIG

1 PARSLEY SPRIG

¹/₂ CUP HEAVY CREAM

1 TABLESPOON FRESH
　TARRAGON

2 TABLESPOONS BUTTER

1 TABLESPOON CHOPPED FRESH
　CHERVIL (FOR GARNISH)

Plunge live lobsters into rapidly boiling water that has been lightly salted and cook for 6 to 8 minutes. Remove, drain, and with large knife, cut off head and claws and chop head into large pieces. Cut lobsters in half, lengthwise, and drain. Remove meat from claws; reserve and keep warm. Heat olive oil in large skillet; add lobster pieces, onion, carrots, celery, and shallots and cook until lightly browned. Add cognac, ignite, and flambé until flame dies. Add white wine, Fish Stock, tomato paste, and diced tomatoes. Season lightly with salt, peppers, bay leaves, and sprigs of thyme and parsley. Bring to boil, lower heat, and simmer for 15 to 20 minutes. Strain out lobster pieces and reduce to one-third. Stir in heavy cream, add chopped tarragon, and reduce to one-third. Strain sauce, check seasonings, and add butter. Place lobsters on platter. Chop claw meat and place on lobsters. Serve hot sauce on top of lobsters and sprinkle with chopped chervil. Serves 4.

The tremendous increase in the demand for lobsters, coupled with the fact that they can be flown anywhere and arrive alive and fresh, has resulted in not only higher prices but a shortage of this delicious commodity. Consequently, fish markets are forced to sell more and more smaller lobsters of the "chicken" size in the one-pound range. This has led to the propagation of the myth that these small lobsters are especially desirable because they are young and tender. The truth is that the larger sizes of lobsters can be just as tender as the small ones. Tenderness is not exclusively a matter of size, but is influenced by other factors, such as the method of cooking that is used; according to some authorities, it is dependent on sex—with the female being regarded as the tender gender. When you buy lobsters, you will find the 2-pound size far easier to work with than the "chickens." Be sure the lobsters you select are alive and kicking—the more energetic they are, the better.

Cognac's fame as the reigning monarch of brandies has completely overshadowed its royal cousin Armagnac. Armagnac is very popular in France, is frequently used in cooking, and has a very pleasant nutty flavor that is somewhat drier, harder, and a little more full-bodied than that of cognac. As this next recipe demonstrates, Armagnac and lobster make a fine, flavorful pair.

HOMARD ARMAGNAC

2 LIVE LOBSTERS ($1^1/2$ TO 2
   POUNDS EACH)
$^3/_4$ CUP BUTTER
1 ONION, CHOPPED
2 SHALLOTS, CHOPPED
BOUQUET GARNI OF SWEET
   HERBS:
   1 TABLESPOON EACH
   CHOPPED FRESH PARSLEY,
   THYME, AND TARRAGON
$^1/_2$ CUP ARMAGNAC

1 TABLESPOON FLOUR
$^1/_2$ CUP FISH STOCK
   (SEE INDEX)
BLACK PEPPER
1 OR 2 PINCHES CAYENNE
   PEPPER
SALT
1 CUP CREAM OR HOMOGENIZED
   MILK
1 OUNCE SWISS OR GRUYÈRE
   CHEESE, GRATED

Slice lobsters in half, lengthwise, remove sand sack from head and intestinal vein, then take meat from tail and claws and cut up into small pieces. Reserve coral, tomalley, and juice. Melt $^1/_2$ cup of the butter in skillet and sauté lobster meat until it turns opaque. Remove and set aside. Add onion, shallots, and bouquet garni and sauté lightly for a few minutes. Then place lobster pieces back in skillet. Warm Armagnac, pour into skillet, ignite, and blaze. When flame is extinguished, sprinkle lobster pieces lightly with flour, add Fish Stock, remainder of butter, several good grinds of pepper, cayenne pepper, and salt to taste. Simmer slowly, uncovered, for 15 to 20 minutes. Lower heat, add cream or milk and cheese, and cook, stirring constantly, until sauce thickens. Correct seasonings. Makes 4 servings. Serve with a good Montrachet, Sancerre, or California sauvignon blanc.

Another popular method of cooking lobster in France is to prepare it with herbs and absinthe. Since absinthe is no longer available legally, you will have to use Pernod, Herbsaint, or some other absinthe substitute.

HOMARD À L'ABSINTHE FLAMBÉ

2 LIVE LOBSTERS (1¹/₂ TO 2 POUNDS EACH)

1 BOTTLE DRY WHITE WINE

1 DOZEN SPRIGS TARRAGON

4 TABLESPOONS BUTTER

FLOUR

2 TABLESPOONS CHOPPED FRESH CHERVIL

1 TEASPOON CHOPPED FRESH DILL

PINCH OF SALT

BLACK PEPPER

¹/₂ CUP PERNOD

Place lobsters in large skillet or saucepan. Cover them with wine. Add 8 or 9 sprigs tarragon, bring to boil, and simmer for 20 to 25 minutes. Turn off heat and allow to cool. Reserve cooking liquid. Split lobsters lengthwise, remove sand sack in head and intestinal vein running along the back. Remove coral and green tomalley and set aside. Take out lobster meat from tail and claws, cut into bite-size pieces, and place in large heatproof casserole with 1 or 2 tablespoons of the butter. Put casserole in warm oven (about 200° F.) and heat lobster pieces slowly. While lobster is warming, prepare sauce as follows: Place remaining butter in small saucepan with coral and tomalley, and mix in enough flour to make a smooth paste. Heat gently and stir in a little of the wine in which the lobsters were boiled until mixture is light and creamy. Chop remainder of fresh tarragon sprigs finely (about 2 to 2¹/₂ tablespoons) and add to sauce with chervil, dill, salt, and several grinds of pepper. Blend well. Remove casserole from oven. Pour Pernod over lobster pieces, ignite, and blaze.

Flaming Feasts in the Great Tradition
69

When flames are extinguished, cover lobster pieces with sauce and heat in oven for another 10 to 15 minutes. Correct seasoning and add additional dill or tarragon if you wish. Serves 4. A good Meursault or Montrachet is recommended with this dish.

Sometimes it is more convenient to use lobster tails than to begin with live lobster. While frozen lobster tails do not have the flavor of a freshly prepared lobster, they nevertheless are good and convenient to use, and they retain their flavor satisfactorily through the freezing process. Here is a good dish employing lobster tails flambéed with gin.

LOBSTER CHATELAINE

4 LARGE ROCK LOBSTER TAILS

BAY LEAF

JUICE OF 1 LEMON

SALT

2 TABLESPOONS BUTTER

2 TABLESPOONS FLOUR

1 SMALL CAN BUTTON
    MUSHROOMS

1 CUP CREAM OR HOMOGENIZED
    MILK

1 TEASPOON SAUCE DIABLE

1/2 TEASPOON CHILI SAUCE

2 TABLESPOONS KETCHUP

1 1/2 TEASPOONS SOY SAUCE

LEMON JUICE

ONION POWDER

DRIED CHERVIL

DRIED TARRAGON

DRIED BASIL

DRIED OREGANO

CELERY SALT

2 EGG YOLKS

1/4 CUP DRY SHERRY

1/2 CUP DRY GIN, WARMED

1/2 CUP EQUAL PORTIONS OF
    GRATED PARMESAN AND
    ROMANO CHEESE

Place lobster tails in saucepan with water to which has been added bay leaf, lemon juice, and 1 teaspoon salt. Boil gently for about 10 minutes. To make sauce: Melt butter in small saucepan. Stir in flour, juice from mushrooms, cream or milk and a little water. Blend well, add Sauce Diable, chili sauce, ketchup, soy sauce, a dash of lemon juice, and pinch each of onion powder, chervil, tarragon, basil, oregano, and celery salt. Add salt to taste. After bringing to a boil, stirring constantly, simmer for a few minutes over a very low heat. Beat egg yolks in bowl, remove saucepan from heat, and pour sauce, stirring, into eggs. Return to saucepan, stirring continually. Bring just to boiling point. Pour in sherry and mix well. Remove lobster tails from water and drain. Remove meat and cut into bite-size pieces. Place meat in saucepan with a little tarragon. Pour in warmed gin, ignite, and blaze. When fire is extinguished, place lobster meat with mushrooms in sauce and continue cooking over medium heat until lobster is warmed through. Pour lobster meat and sauce into heatproof casserole. Sprinkle generously with Parmesan and Romano cheese mixture and broil a few inches from heat for several minutes until cheese is golden brown. Can be served on sautéed bread slices, artichoke bottoms, or rice pilaf. Serves 4 generously. Accompany with a chilled Chablis, or perhaps something a little bolder, a Gewürztraminer.

Other shellfish also can be fired up with considerable success. These include shrimp and crab, which can be prepared in any number of conventional ways, but you will find that few of them are as rewarding as the next three recipes, prepared by a French master chef, a New York advertising man, and a London hostess. While all of the approaches are different, the ritual of fire in each case is used effectively to properly accent the essential flavor of each entrée.

This superb recipe for king crab was originated by Camille Marcadier, a former *chef de cuisine* for Air France at Orly Airport. When you partake of this creation, you will see why the cuisine on Air France flights is so highly regarded.

KING CRAB AU WHISKY

2½ POUNDS KING CRAB LEGS

½ POUND BUTTER

5 TABLESPOONS FINELY
  CHOPPED SHALLOTS

1 CUP SCOTCH

1¾ CUPS DRY WHITE WINE
  (CHABLIS IS RECOMMENDED)

½ CUP FISH STOCK (SEE
  INDEX)

2 TABLESPOONS TOMATO PASTE

SALT

BLACK PEPPER

1½ POUNDS LARGE
  MUSHROOMS

JUICE OF 1 LEMON

2 CUPS HEAVY CREAM

CROUTONS

CHOPPED FRESH PARSLEY

1 TRUFFLE (OPTIONAL)

Remove crab from shells. Melt ¼ pound butter in large skillet or flat pan. Add shallots and sauté gently until shallots turn transparent, but do not brown. Place crab legs in pan, cover, and cook slowly over low heat for 10 minutes. Add ⅔ cup of the Scotch, ignite, and blaze. When flames are extinguished, pour in wine and Fish Stock. Add tomato paste, salt, and freshly ground pepper and simmer for 25 minutes. While crab is cooking, wash mushrooms well. Choose 10 of the smallest ones and keep whole. Cut remainder into julienne strips and place in pan together with lemon juice, 2 tablespoons of the butter, pinch of salt, and several grinds pepper. When mushrooms begin to brown, pour in cream and cook until it thickens, then add julienned mushroom mixture to simmering crab. Remove crab legs from pan and arrange on heated platter. Place whole mushrooms on top. Cover with aluminum foil and keep warm. Add remainder of Scotch to sauce with remaining butter and stir gently with wire whisk. Correct seasoning, remove foil from platter, and pour sauce over crab legs. Place any extra sauce in gravy boat and serve hot. Croutons can be cut into heart shapes. Dip points in parsley and use to decorate platter. A truffle can be cut into circles and also used as decoration. Serves 6. Try a young Vouvray, a Sancerre, or a fine Champagne with this one.

Advertising people are a resourceful lot, by and large, because it is basic to their business. This also extends into the kitchen, proving once again that creative expression takes many forms. This recipe came from Mike Reise, advertising copywriter and inventor of good things to eat.

SHRIMP NORMAND

2 MEDIUM ONIONS, CHOPPED

4 TABLESPOONS BUTTER

2 TABLESPOONS OLIVE OIL

SALT

BLACK PEPPER

1 GARLIC CLOVE, MINCED

1 POUND RAW SHRIMP, PEELED
   AND DEVEINED

$^2/_3$ CUP DRY WHITE WINE

2 EGG YOLKS

$^1/_3$ CUP CREAM OR
   HOMOGENIZED MILK

$^1/_3$ CUP COGNAC, WARMED

In skillet, cook onions in butter and olive oil until mushy. Discard onion. Add salt, several grinds of pepper, garlic, and shrimp. Cook for about 15 minutes, until shrimp are done. Remove shrimp to heated flameproof platter and keep warm. Pour wine into sauce and reduce by about one-third. Beat egg yolks and cream or milk together and add to sauce. Stir until it begins to thicken. Do not boil. Pour warm cognac over shrimp, ignite and blaze, then pour on sauce. Serves 2. Try a chilled muscadet or chardonnay with this dish.

Eileen Best is a charming and vivacious London hostess and a marvelous cook. Eileen, who can serve up almost anything, from old traditional English recipes to the very best of French cuisine, concocted this delicious recipe for prawns flambé with cream and brandy sauce. Her recipe for preparing rice, which she recommends with this dish, is also included.

Shrimp or scampi can be substituted if prawns are not available. Contrary to popular misconception, prawns and scampi are *not* different names for the same thing. While both are crustaceans, they are different branches of the family, with markedly different cooking and flavor characteristics.

PRAWNS FLAMBÉ

$3/4$ CUP BUTTER

1 POUND COOKED, SHELLED
    PRAWNS

2 TABLESPOONS LEMON JUICE

SEVERAL PINCHES OF GRATED
    NUTMEG

PINCH OF SALT

BLACK PEPPER

$1/2$ CUP COGNAC, WARMED

1 CUP CREAM OR HOMOGENIZED
    MILK

1 TABLESPOON CHOPPED FRESH
    PARSLEY

Melt butter in large skillet and sauté prawns with lemon juice, nutmeg, salt, and several grinds of pepper. After about 7 minutes of cooking, add warmed cognac, ignite, and blaze. Turn heat down very low. After a few minutes increase heat, add cream or milk, and let it bubble until it starts to thicken, stirring constantly. Mix in parsley, correct seasoning, and serve on rice pilaf (see below). Serves 3 or 4. A chilled muscadet,

Pouilly-Fuissé, or California sauvignon blanc makes a good drinking companion.

EILEEN'S RICE

2 TO 3 QUARTS WATER

1 TABLESPOON SALT

1 CUP UNCOOKED ITALIAN OR
   PATNA RICE (ITALIAN
   PREFERRED)

2 TABLESPOONS OLIVE OIL

Pour water in large saucepan, add salt, and bring to boil. When water boils, add rice a little at a time and keep water boiling uncovered. Add olive oil to prevent water from boiling over. Test after 12 minutes. When cooked, drain. Place on heatproof platter, fluff up with fork, and keep warm in oven. Makes about 3 cups of rice.

Hot Tips—No. 12

It goes without saying that good cooks invariably follow the example of great chefs and continually taste and test throughout the cooking process. In fact, an old adage admonishes us to "beware the lean chef." Tasting is a must if the seasoning is to be adjusted properly before serving. It is also wise to "taste" with the nose as well as with the mouth. A highly sensitive and experienced nose frequently can be as valuable as an educated palate in telling how things are going with the culinary business at hand.

The Drake, Chicago's Gold Coast hostelry on the lakefront where Lake Shore Drive meets Michigan Avenue's "Magnificent Mile," has been dispensing hospitality of the highest order along with fabulous food (the Cape Cod Room) and drink (the Coq d'Or) since its opening in 1933. A genuine landmark—listed in *The National Register of Historic Places*—and in recent years expertly refurbished without losing its classic but warm elegance, it is blessed with one of the best hotel kitchen staffs anywhere. From Executive Chef Leo Waldmeier comes this fine seafood recipe.

EL PESCADOR

4 FRESH OR FROZEN CRAWFISH TAILS

12 RAW MEDIUM PRAWNS IN SHELL

1 CUP LONG-GRAIN RICE

$1/4$ TO $1/2$ TEASPOON SAFFRON THREADS

$1^3/4$ CUPS WATER

$1/3$ CUP BLANCHED OR FROZEN PEAS, DEFROSTED

1 WHOLE LARGE CANNED PIMIENTO, FINELY DICED

2 TABLESPOONS SWEET BUTTER

2 OUNCES SALT PORK, CUT INTO $1/2$-INCH DICE

2 OUNCES COOKED HAM, CUT INTO $1/2$-INCH DICE

2 TEASPOONS FINELY CHOPPED GARLIC

1 MEDIUM GREEN PEPPER, CUT INTO $1/4$-INCH DICE

$1/3$ CUP THINLY SLICED SMALL MUSHROOMS

1 MEDIUM TOMATO, PEELED, SEEDED, AND CUT INTO $1/2$-INCH DICE

$1/2$ TEASPOON DRIED CORIANDER

3 TABLESPOONS SPANISH BRANDY

1 CUP CHICKEN STOCK OR BROTH

SALT AND PEPPER TO TASTE

Fill a skillet with enough water to cover crawfish tails. Bring to boil, add crawfish, and simmer for 3 minutes. Add prawns and simmer for another minute. Drain shellfish and cool until you can remove shells. Devein prawns, and cut crawfish into $1/2$-inch slices and set aside. In small saucepan, combine rice and saffron with the water and, while stirring, bring to boil. Turn down heat to the absolute minimum, cover, and cook for 20 minutes. Remove from heat and let stand, covered, for about 15 minutes. Stir in peas and pimiento. In a very wide skillet or crêpe pan, heat butter, add salt pork, and sauté over moderately high heat for a minute or until pork is lightly browned. Add ham to skillet and toss. Add garlic and toss for 30 seconds. Add green pepper, mushrooms, tomato, and coriander and toss for 2 minutes. Pour in brandy, and when warm, ignite and shake pan vigorously until flames subside. Add stock or broth and boil for 1 minute. Add seafood, return to a boil, tossing. Add rice and vegetable mixture, and toss for about 2 minutes to heat through. Add salt and pepper to taste. Makes 4 servings.

Here is a fine recipe for American shrimp flambéed with Pernod.

SHRIMP PERNOD

APPROXIMATELY 3 DOZEN RAW
    SELECT JUMBO SHRIMP
SALT
$^1/_2$ CUP BUTTER
2 TABLESPOONS CHOPPED
    GREEN ONIONS
BLACK PEPPER
2 TABLESPOONS CHOPPED
    FRESH TARRAGON

$^1/_2$ CUP PERNOD, WARMED
CHOPPED FRESH DILL
CHOPPED FRESH CHERVIL OR
    PARSLEY
LEMON SLICES (FOR GARNISH)
BÉARNAISE SAUCE (SEE INDEX)
    (OPTIONAL)

Boil shrimp in salted water. Drain, shell, and devein. Slice in half lengthwise, so they will lie flat in skillet. Melt butter in flaming pan of chafing dish over direct, heat and sauté shrimp and green onions over high heat for 3 or 4 minutes. Add salt, several grinds of pepper, and tarragon. Pour in Pernod, ignite, and blaze. Sprinkle with dill and chervil or parsley. Garnish with lemon slices and serve with a dollop of béarnaise sauce if you wish. Makes enough for 4. Accompany with a chilled sauvignon blanc or dry Graves.

While this crab dish can be whipped up in a hurry, it nevertheless has all the requisites for crab. Prepared in the finest tradition of *cuisine classique*.

CRAB RELAIS

$1/2$ CUP BUTTER

8 THIN SLICES BREAD

4 GREEN ONIONS, THINLY
   SLICED

2 POUNDS FROZEN KING CRAB
   OR DUNGENESS CRAB

$1/2$ CUP DRY WHITE WINE

PINCH OF SALT

BLACK PEPPER

2 TEASPOONS CHOPPED FRESH
   TARRAGON

$1/2$ CUP COGNAC

CHOPPED FRESH PARSLEY

Melt butter in flaming pan of chafing dish over direct heat. Over high heat, sauté bread slices rapidly and remove to hot platter. Sauté green onions lightly, using additional butter if needed. Add crabmeat (well drained), wine, salt, several grinds of pepper, and tarragon. Stir occasionally until crabmeat is heated through. Warm cognac in ladle, ignite, and pour blazing into chafing dish. Give final stirring. Serve crabmeat with a little sauce on sautéed toast slices, sprinkled with parsley. Serves 4. Eat with a chilled Sancerre or Pouilly-Fumé.

Hiram Walker & Sons, Inc., which produces and imports a number of premium brands of wine and spirits, decided to try combining two of our favorites—Harvey's Bristol Cream and Irish Mist liqueur—into a food recipe. The experiment was successful but we had difficulty with the name (Irish Mist Steamed Halibut with Harveys Bristol Cream–Irish Mist Liqueur Sauce) as it was overly long. So we shortened it.

HOT MISTED HALIBUT WITH IRISH BRISTOL CREAM SAUCE

4 FISH STEAKS (HALIBUT, SEA BASS, SALMON, OR OTHER FIRM-FLESHED FISH, BONED, BUT WITH SKIN LEFT ON

1 1/2 CUPS IRISH MIST LIQUEUR

1 1/2 CUPS VEGETABLE STOCK OR WATER

1 BAY LEAF

SALT TO TASTE

IRISH BRISTOL CREAM SAUCE (SEE NEXT RECIPE)

Place fish steaks on a rack in a steamer or large kettle. Pour liquid into bottom of pan. Add bay leaf, salt fish lightly, and steam with lid on until meat is opaque but still firm, adding additional liquid if necessary. Turn off heat and keep fish warm in steamer, but do not continue to cook. Remove skin just before serving and ladle Irish Bristol Cream sauce over fish steaks.

IRISH BRISTOL CREAM SAUCE

1 GARLIC CLOVE, QUARTERED

$^1/_4$ CUP PEANUT OIL

$^1/_3$ CUP HONEY

$^1/_4$ CUP SOY SAUCE

$^1/_4$ CUP MUSHROOM SOY SAUCE
(SEE NOTE)

$^1/_3$ CUP IRISH MIST LIQUEUR

2 TABLESPOONS HARVEYS
BRISTOL CREAM

2 TABLESPOONS RICE WINE
VINEGAR

BLACK PEPPER

2 TABLESPOONS SESAME OIL

2 TABLESPOONS SWEET BUTTER
(OPTIONAL)

$^1/_4$ CUP JULIENNED GREEN
ONIONS

$^1/_4$ CUP ALMONDS, TOASTED
AND SLIVERED

In a skillet, over low heat, sauté garlic in peanut oil. Remove and discard garlic before it is browned. Add honey and soy sauces and stir until blended. Increase heat, add Irish Mist and Harveys Bristol Cream, ignite, and flambé for a few moments. Pour in vinegar and simmer over medium heat until mixture is reduced by one-third. Season with pepper to taste and slowly stir sesame oil into sauce. If you wish, you may swirl in some butter for flavor. After saucing individual fish portions, sprinkle with green onions and almonds. Serves 4.

NOTE: If mushroom soy sauce is not available, add a little more regular soy sauce to taste.

One of the great champions of eating and drinking in the grand manner was Henri IV of France. This is attested to by the fact that many dishes, both traditional and modern, are named in his honor. Henri loved to eat well, and he believed that others should too. It was Henri who popularized the idea that at least every Sunday "there should be a chicken in every pot." The French citizenry apparently agreed with their king, for chicken in the pot, or *coq au vin,* is to this day one of the most popular of all French dietary staples.

We are indebted to the French Embassy in Washington for allowing us to reprint this authentic sixteenth-century recipe for *coq au vin,* which has been translated from the old French. It is perfectly acceptable by even today's gastronomic standards. Why not try it next Sunday?

COQ AU VIN ANCIEN

*When thou wilst cook a coq au vin, take first a goodly young
limaigne capon and having slain it, quarter it in six.
Then in an earthen vessel, or crock, lightly brown conjoined*

some 3 ounces of lean, firm lard, well diced, half that much fresh butter and divers little onions.

At the moment that this fair mixture shall become brown, throw in the crock thy chicken, cut up and stuffed with garlic cloves chopped fine. To this add parsley-bunch and other odorous herbs, as thyme and bay, forgetting not morels or mushrooms. Keep thou pot well-lidded on a bright fire, and thus let all take on a golden, roasted hue, alike on every side.

Lift then the lid and banish with care the over-abundant fat.

Now mark thee well, if thou hast a finger of fine old brandy, sprinkle the fowl with all.

Then put fowl and spirit to the torch, and upon all spread speedily a pint of old good wine (let it be Bailly of Champturgue) and then once fowl be well done, serve the whole piping hot, baptized with melted butter to which shall be added fine wheat flour.

Here is a more modern version of *coq au vin* that you may want to prepare as an alternative to the last recipe. Essentially it has not changed in four hundred years.

COQ AU VIN

3 BREASTS AND 6 LEGS FROM
   FRYING CHICKENS
SALT
BLACK PEPPER
2 DOZEN SMALL MUSHROOMS
2 DOZEN SMALL WHITE ONIONS
$1/4$ POUND BACON, THINLY
   SLICED
6 TABLESPOONS BUTTER
2 GARLIC CLOVES, MINCED

$1/4$ CUP COGNAC
2 CUPS CHICKEN BROTH OR
   BEEF BOUILLON
3 CUPS RED BURGUNDY WINE
$1/2$ TEASPOON DRIED THYME
1 BAY LEAF
2 TABLESPOONS CHOPPED
   FRESH PARSLEY, PLUS EXTRA
   FOR GARNISH
2 TABLESPOONS FLOUR

Cut chicken breasts in half and separate second joint from chicken leg. Dry chicken pieces thoroughly to ensure browning. Sprinkle with salt and several grinds of pepper. Wash mushrooms and remove stems. Peel onions and slice bacon into small pieces. Cook bacon in 4 tablespoons of the butter in casserole. Remove bacon, drain, and set aside. Brown chicken pieces in bacon fat–butter mixture. When evenly browned, remove and set aside. Brown onions, mushrooms, and garlic in casserole. Add chicken and pour in cognac; ignite, and blaze. Pour in chicken broth or beef bouillon, wine, thyme, bay leaf, and parsley. Cover and simmer for about 30 minutes until chicken is well cooked and tender. Remove chicken, bacon pieces, mushrooms, and onions and discard bay leaf. Raise heat and boil rapidly, reducing liquid to about 3 cups. Skim off fat from surface of liquid and correct seasoning. Remove from heat. Blend flour in remaining butter to make a smooth paste. Stir this *beurre manié* into stock and cook until sauce thickens. Place chicken pieces on hot platter with onions and mushrooms and baste with sauce. Garnish with parsley. Serves 4. A fine Burgundy such as a Chambertin or a good Bordeaux such as a St. Émilion will add to your enjoyment of *coq au vin*.

A tender roast duckling with a succulent, blazing orange sauce is one of the greatest gifts that French cookery has bestowed upon us. There are as many ways of preparing it as there are French restaurants. Here is one of the better recipes.

CANETON AU GRAND MARNIER

$5^1/_2$- TO 6-POUND READY-TO-COOK DUCKLING	BLACK PEPPER
LEMON JUICE	2 PEELED ORANGES, QUARTERED
SALT	$^1/_4$ CUP MELTED BUTTER
1 GARLIC CLOVE, CHOPPED, OR 1 SMALL ONION, SLICED	GRAND MARNIER SAUCE (SEE NEXT RECIPE)
PINCH OF DRIED SAGE	

Preheat oven to 425° F. Prepare duck as follows: Pull out all loose fat from inside of cavity and be sure fat gland at base of tail has been removed. Trim wing tips and cut off neck. Wash thoroughly with cold water inside and out, and dry very carefully with paper towels. Rub cavity with lemon juice and 1 teaspoon salt. Stuff cavity with garlic or onion, sage, $^1/_2$ teaspoon freshly ground pepper, and orange quarters. Bring skin of neck over back and fasten with skewer, close body cavity with poultry pins or lace with twine. Bend wing tips under body and tie ends of legs together. Place duckling, breast side up, in shallow baking pan and brush with 2 tablespoons of the butter. Roast duck uncovered for 15 to 20 minutes, until it browns. Reduce oven to 375° F. Turn duck on side and brush with a little butter. After 15 minutes, turn duck on other side and again brush with butter. Remove accumulated fat with baster from time to time. After another 15 to 20 minutes, turn duck breast up and roast until done. Duck should be cooked within 1½ hours, more or less, if medium-rare meat is desired. A few minutes before removing from oven, add more salt and a little pepper. Place on heated flameproof serving platter. Remove skewers and strings and keep warm while making sauce.

GRAND MARNIER SAUCE

BUTTER

PEEL OF ½ ORANGE,
  JULIENNED

3 TABLESPOONS SUGAR

1 TABLESPOON WINE VINEGAR

⅔ CUP ORANGE JUICE

GRATED OUTER RIND (ZEST) OF
  1 ORANGE

½ CUP GRAND MARNIER

JUICE FROM ROASTED DUCK

¼ CUP COGNAC

In small saucepan, sauté lightly, in a little butter, julienned strips of orange peel. When cooked, remove from heat and set aside. In same saucepan cook mixture of sugar and vinegar over medium heat until sugar melts and caramelizes. Add orange juice, grated orange rind, and sautéed orange peel. Pour in Grand Marnier and simmer for 10 minutes, stirring from time to time. Skim off excess fat from juices in roasting pan and add drippings to orange mixture. Adjust seasonings and pour into heated gravy boat. Heat cognac in ladle, ignite, and pour blazing over duck. Then pour on orange sauce. Serves 4. A fine Bonnes Mares, Aloxe-Corton, or Grands-Échézeaux would make a fitting complement.

Hot Tips—No. 13

Flambéing can play a very important part in the preparation of meat sauces. The use of blazing spirits is one of the best ways to dissolve coagulated juices that form in a pan as a result of roasting or sautéing. This procedure is known as deglazing. The usual practice is to remove meat from pan and degrease remaining juices by skimming off excess fat. Loosen crust and other congealed drippings with spoon, pour in spirits, stirring well, then ignite and burn off alcohol. You are now ready to add other necessary ingredients to complete the sauce.

Duckling with cherries is almost as popular as that served with orange. *Caneton aux cerises* utilizes the basic method of preparing duckling as described in the foregoing recipe.

CANETON AUX CERISES

Use basic seasonings and method of preparation for Caneton au Grand Marnier above. While duck is roasting, you can make the duck stock, which you will need for sauce.

DUCK NECK, HEART, GIZZARD,
AND TRIMMINGS
1 MEDIUM ONION, SLICED
SALT
BLACK PEPPER
1 TABLESPOON COOKING OIL
2 CUPS BEEF BOUILLON OR
CHICKEN BROTH

2 TEASPOONS DRIED PARSLEY
DRIED THYME
DRIED SAGE OR $^{1}/_{2}$ BAY LEAF
JUICE FROM ROASTED DUCK
$^{2}/_{3}$ CUP KIRSCH
$1^{1}/_{2}$ CUPS CANNED PITTED
MONTMORENCY SOUR
CHERRIES, DRAINED

Slice duck giblets and trimmings into small pieces and brown in sauce-pan with onion, dash of salt, dash of pepper, and oil. Pour out oil. Add beef bouillon or chicken broth, herbs, and a little water so that duck pieces are covered. Simmer while duck is roasting, about 90 minutes. Remove excess fat from surface of liquid with baster and strain. When duck is roasted, remove to heated flameproof platter. Skim off excess fat in roasting pan and deglaze with about half the kirsch. Add kirsch and roasting pan juices to small saucepan with 1 cup duck stock. Bring to boil and reduce slightly. Add cherries and simmer until warmed through. Correct seasonings. Place remainder of kirsch in ladle, warm, ignite, and pour blazing over duck. Pour hot sauce and cherries over duck. Serves 4. Try a full-bodied Médoc or good California cabernet sauvignon with this one.

Wild fowl, whether duck, pheasant, or some other form of upland game, should always be treated with the utmost respect. If game is carefully prepared (and here we are speaking of conventional game, not smoked Kodiak bear or potted penguin meat), the chances are that it will be eaten with appreciation, if not gusto.

The somewhat primitive cooking procedures of Henri IV's era are hopelessly antiquated by today's standards, but the time-tested way of cooking fowl on a spit over an open fire has not been materially improved upon. If you are fortunate enough to have the facilities for spit-roasting in your fireplace or on a grill out-of-doors, you will find that this method of roasting wild duck is unexcelled.

CANARD ST. HUBERT

2 LARGE WILD DUCKS

SALT

LEMON JUICE

1 LARGE APPLE, OR 2 CRAB
    APPLES

2 MEDIUM ONIONS

2 SHALLOTS

PARSLEY SPRIGS

BLACK PEPPER

1 CUP MELTED BUTTER

1 BOTTLE DRY RED WINE
    (PREFERABLY BURGUNDY)

$^{1}/_{2}$ CUP COGNAC, WARMED

Wipe ducks inside and out with damp towel and rub with a little salt and lemon juice. Pare, core, and quarter apples and place inside cavity with whole onions, shallots, and parsley sprigs. Sprinkle with freshly ground pepper. Sew up cavity opening and brush duck with some melted butter. Place on rotary spit and roast over hot fire for 15 to 30 minutes, depending on size of ducks. Baste alternately with melted butter and Burgundy. While ducks are still rare, remove from spit to heated flameproof platter, pour on warmed cognac, ignite, and blaze. If you can collect drippings from the roasting ducks, prepare a sauce using degreased pan juices and a little Burgundy, which can be thickened with a *beurre manié* made of $^{1}/_{2}$ tablespoon butter blended with $^{1}/_{2}$ tablespoon flour, depending on thickness desired. Serves 4. The classic accompaniment is a fine Pommard or full-bodied Saint-Estèphe.

For those who do not possess roasting facilities employing a spit, here is another extremely popular French recipe for wild duck.

CANARD SAUVAGE AU COGNAC

2 LARGE WILD DUCKS

1/2 CUP FLOUR

6 TO 8 THICK, LEAN SLICES
    BACON

2/3 CUP BUTTER

1/2 TEASPOON DRIED THYME

1 TABLESPOON CHOPPED FRESH
    PARSLEY OR CHERVIL

SALT

BLACK PEPPER

1 GARLIC CLOVE, MINCED
    (OPTIONAL)

1 BAY LEAF

1 BOTTLE DRY RED WINE
    (PREFERABLY BURGUNDY)

18 TO 20 LITTLE ONIONS

18 TO 20 MUSHROOMS

1/2 CUP COGNAC

Remove breasts and legs from ducks and cover lightly with flour. Cut bacon into 1-inch pieces and sauté with 2 tablespoons of the butter in saucepan. After bacon has cooked for several minutes, add duck and sauté until evenly browned. Remove duck, cover with remainder of flour, season with herbs, salt, and several grinds of pepper, and place in skillet with minced garlic (optional), bay leaf, and wine. Simmer for approximately 45 minutes to 1 hour. Remove onion skins by immersing onions in boiling water for about 5 seconds. Outer skin should slip off without difficulty. Place remaining butter in saucepan, sauté onions, and add to skillet after duck has cooked for approximately 30 minutes. Trim stems from mushrooms and add to skillet with duck a few minutes before serving. Remove bay leaf, correct seasoning, and place duck with sauce on heated flameproof platter. Warm cognac, ignite, and ladle blazing on duck. Serves 4. A Musigny or Aloxe-Corton makes a good drinking companion with this dish.

Amelia Island, Florida, is home base for Matthew Medure, chef of the Grill at The Ritz-Carlton, and the only chef in the state to be honored with a AAA Five-Diamond award. This is indeed a resort for gourmets. In addition to outstanding cuisine, the hotel has a well-stocked gourmet shop and offers courses at its in-house cooking school. Here is a sampling of Chef Medure's cuisine: a recipe for squab breasts that is creative in its combination of ingredients.

SQUAB BREASTS AND ARTICHOKES WITH FLAMING YAMS

2 YAMS	4 LARGE ARTICHOKES, LEAVES
4 SQUAB BREASTS	AND CHOKES REMOVED
SALT	12 CHANTERELLES, PEELED
BLACK PEPPER	1 TABLESPOON BUTTER
OLIVE OIL	1 TABLESPOON HONEY
2 SHALLOTS, CHOPPED	2 TABLESPOONS DRAMBUIE
1 GARLIC CLOVE, CHOPPED	
3 CUPS CHICKEN STOCK OR	
BROTH	

For candied pecan garnish:

1/4 CUP DRAMBUIE	1/4 CUP PECAN HALVES

Bake yams in a 375° F. oven for approximately 45 minutes until done. Debone squabs (or your butcher can do this for you), season with salt, freshly ground pepper, and olive oil, and set aside. Chop remaining bones and sear in saucepan over high heat. Add shallots and garlic and cook for 2 minutes. Add chicken stock, artichokes, and chanterelles and simmer for 10 minutes. Remove artichokes and chanterelles and continue simmering sauce for 10 more minutes. Strain sauce and set aside. Lay squab breast in each artichoke, place on sheet pan, and bake at 350° F. for 10 minutes. Remove skin from yams and discard. Place yams in skillet over low heat. Add butter, honey, and salt and pepper to taste. Pour in Drambuie and flambé. Mound yams on warm serving platter and top with baked artichoke and squab. Heat sauce and drizzle around platter. Garnish with chanterelles and candied pecan halves. Makes 4 servings.

To make candied pecan garnish, pour Drambuie into a small nonstick saucepan and reduce by half over low heat. Add pecans, stir, and transfer to a buttered baking sheet. They will harden as they cool.

New York City's '21' Club easily ranks as one of the world's great restaurants. The decor *is* clublike, the food is majestic, and the service is superb. If there's any secret to '21's success—and it has been phenomenal—it is that this is probably one of the best-managed restaurants you will ever encounter. It is *the* place to take very important visitors. One of the things that '21' does best is to cook game. This recipe for pheasant was given to us by Peter Kriendler, one of '21's genial proprietors.

PHEASANT '21'

BREASTS FROM TWO 2$^{1}/_{2}$- TO 3-POUND PHEASANTS

2 TABLESPOONS BUTTER

SALT

BLACK PEPPER

2 TABLESPOONS CURRANT JELLY

$^{1}/_{2}$ CUP SHERRY

20 CANNED PITTED BLACK CHERRIES, DRAINED

SUPRÊME (MEAT WITHOUT SEEDS AND PULP) OF 2 ORANGES

$^{1}/_{4}$ CUP COGNAC

Place pheasant breasts in skillet with butter, add salt and several grinds of pepper, and sauté for 20 to 25 minutes. Remove pheasant breasts to flaming pan of chafing dish over very low heat; cover and keep warm. In skillet in which pheasant was sautéed, add currant jelly and stir until dissolved. Then add sherry and simmer slowly until thick. Place cherries and oranges into skillet and heat thoroughly. Pour sauce over pheasant breasts in chafing dish. Replace cover and heat for a few seconds. Remove cover. Sprinkle cognac on pheasant, ignite, and blaze. Serves 2. Wild rice is recommended as an accompaniment, along with a very fine Vosne-Romanée, Pomerol, or Châteauneuf-du-Pape.

Sautéing is one of the great classical methods of cooking. It is traditionally accomplished in France in a heavy frying pan or skillet called a sauteuse *or* sautoir. *Since a brisk heat usually is called for and the favorite fat for sautéing is butter, when preparing a delicately flavored dish it is often wise to use what is known as clarified butter. When butter is melted, a sediment settles to the bottom of the pan which burns easily, imparting a bitter taste to food. Clarified butter eliminates this and can be made very simply by melting butter in a small pan until it begins to froth. Simply remove froth with spoon and then pour off the clear portion of the butter, leaving the sediment in the bottom of the pan.*

I have found that if a chef prepares game with real flair, you can be certain that the meat, fish, and fowl of domestic origin that he or she cooks will be excellent also. On this basis, the Rex Restaurant in its heyday was one of the best in New York City, for its preparation of game was outstanding. The restaurant is gone, but it has left us a legacy of extraordinary game recipes. This is one of the best.

WILD DUCK REX

2 WILD DUCKS	CHOPPED FRESH ROSEMARY
SALT	6 THICK SLICES BACON
BLACK PEPPER	1/2 CUP COGNAC

Preheat oven to 280° F. Season inside of ducks with salt, freshly ground pepper, and rosemary. Put ducks in roasting pan, breast side down, and place in oven. After 30 minutes, turn ducks breast side up. Cook approximately 45 minutes longer. Remove from oven and place 3 slices of bacon over each bird. Return to oven and cook for another 10 minutes. When duck is done (average cooking time is about $1\frac{1}{2}$ hours), remove from oven and place birds on hot platter. Discard bacon. Carve all meat off duck and place in flaming pan of chafing dish over low heat. Warm cognac in ladle, ignite, and pour blazing over duck pieces. Serve with White Crumb Sauce, Brown Crumb Sauce, and Currant Sauce (recipes follow), in addition to wild rice. Serves 4. Enjoy with a full-bodied dry red wine of your choice such as a Margaux, a Beaujolais Brouilly, or a Pommard.

While your ducks are roasting, you will want to prepare these sauces which are *de rigueur* for duck as well as for all upland game.

BROWN CRUMB SAUCE

8 SLICES WHITE SANDWICH	$^3/_4$ CUP MELTED BUTTER
BREAD	SALT

Remove crust from bread and discard. Crumble bread into very fine pieces. Sauté with melted butter and pinch of salt in skillet for approximately 15 minutes, stirring constantly so crumbs are browned evenly. They should be served crisp and while still warm.

WHITE CRUMB SAUCE

8 SLICES WHITE SANDWICH BREAD

3/4 CUP MELTED BUTTER

SALT

2 TABLESPOONS SHERRY

1/2 CUP HEAVY CREAM

Remove crust from bread and discard. Crumble bread into very fine pieces. Sauté lightly with melted butter in skillet. Add pinch of salt, sherry, and heavy cream, and cook slowly for about 15 minutes, stirring frequently.

CURRANT SAUCE

1 SHALLOT, CHOPPED

3/4 CUP BUTTER

3 TABLESPOONS CURRANT JELLY

1/4 CUP SHERRY

1/2 CUP CONSOMMÉ

2 TABLESPOONS COGNAC

1 TABLESPOON GRAND MARNIER

Sauté shallot in butter in saucepan and add currant jelly, sherry, and consommé. Cook over medium heat until jelly melts and mixture is heated through. Strain mixture, pour in cognac and Grand Marnier, and mix well.

James Beard was one of America's great cooks and certainly one of the most influential of those who wrote about food. His approach to food preparation was eclectic and dynamic; he knew the rules of the *cuisine*

classique, but he was not afraid to try old things in new ways, especially if he believed that the result would taste better. And who could, or would, ever question James Beard's taste? In the kitchen it has proven to be impeccable. Here is Mr. Beard's favorite chicken recipe. He called it:

CHICKEN PANNE

4 WHOLE CHICKEN BREASTS,
    BONED AND HALVED

4 TABLESPOONS FLOUR

SALT

BLACK PEPPER

2 EGGS, PLUS 4 EGG YOLKS

$1/4$ CUP CREAM OR
    HOMOGENIZED MILK

1 CUP FRESHLY MADE BREAD
    CRUMBS

4 TABLESPOONS BUTTER

3 TABLESPOONS VEGETABLE OIL

$1/3$ CUP COGNAC

$1^1/2$ CUPS CREAM OR
    HOMOGENIZED MILK

Flatten chicken breasts by pounding with heavy cleaver and trim if necessary. Season flour with a little salt and freshly ground pepper, and dredge chicken breasts in mixture. Beat whole eggs with $1/4$ cup cream or milk. Dip chicken breasts in this batter and roll in bread crumbs. In skillet, melt butter mixed with vegetable oil and brown chicken breasts on both sides, then cook for approximately 4 minutes on each side. Add salt and pepper to taste. Remove skillet from heat. Pour in cognac, ignite, and blaze. Place chicken on hot platter. Mix $1^1/2$ cups cream or milk and egg yolks and stir into skillet that was used for sautéing. Heat slowly, stirring constantly, until sauce is slightly thickened. Correct seasoning and pour sauce over chicken on platter. Serves 8. Serve with a Côte Rôtie, or California chardonnay.

In Normandy, the home of Calvados, they have a wonderful way of cooking chicken using this marvelous apple brandy. There are many good recipes. This one is named after a lovely old town on the beautiful Normandy coast.

CHICKEN LE TOUQUET

3 POUNDS CUT-UP FRYING CHICKEN

1 TABLESPOON COOKING OIL

2 TABLESPOONS BUTTER

SALT

BLACK PEPPER

2 TEASPOONS CHOPPED FRESH TARRAGON

$1/2$ CUP CALVADOS

2 TABLESPOONS CHOPPED SHALLOTS OR GREEN ONIONS

2 CRAB APPLES, PEELED, CORED, AND DICED

$1/2$ CUP DRY WHITE WINE

$1/2$ CUP BEEF BOUILLON OR CHICKEN BROTH

1 CUP CREAM OR HOMOGENIZED MILK

2 EGG YOLKS

CAYENNE PEPPER

2 TABLESPOONS CHOPPED FRESH PARSLEY OR CHERVIL (FOR GARNISH)

Dry chicken pieces thoroughly and place in skillet with oil and butter over fairly high heat. Brown each piece well on both sides. Keep fat hot but do not allow it to burn. Season chicken with salt, freshly ground black pepper, and tarragon. Add additional butter if necessary. When chicken is completely browned, pour in Calvados, ignite, and blaze. Remove all but 2 tablespoons fat from skillet. Add shallots or green onions and crab apples to skillet, and sauté lightly for several minutes. Add wine and beef bouillon or chicken broth. Cover and simmer slowly, basting occasionally, for 25 to 30 minutes or until chicken is done. When cooked, remove chicken pieces from skillet and place on hot platter. Raise heat and reduce sauce in skillet to about $^1/_3$ to $^1/_2$ cup. Reduce heat, combine cream or milk and egg yolks and add to skillet, stirring constantly until sauce has thickened. Add cayenne pepper and additional tarragon, if you wish. Correct seasonings. Pour sauce over chicken pieces on platter and sprinkle with parsley or chervil. Serves 4. Enjoy with a dry Graves or light Beaujolais.

The succeeding flambé meat recipes provide a happy and reciprocal relationship between Bacchus and Vulcan, achieving a glorious comingling of spirit and flame with proportionately gratifying results.

TOURNEDOS SAUTÉS AU BOURBON

12 TO 16 SLICES PRIME FILET
   OF BEEF ($^1/_4$-INCH THICK)
SALT
BLACK PEPPER
CLARIFIED BUTTER (SEE
   INDEX)
3 TABLESPOONS CHOPPED
   SHALLOTS OR GREEN ONIONS

$^1/_2$ CUP DRY RED WINE
DASH OF WORCESTERSHIRE
   SAUCE
$^1/_3$ TO $^1/_2$ CUP BOURBON,
   WARMED
PARSLEY SPRIGS (FOR GARNISH)

Season beef slices with salt and freshly ground pepper. In flaming pan of chafing dish over direct heat, add enough clarified butter to cover bottom of pan. Place layer of beef in bottom of chafing dish and sauté over high heat 2 to 3 minutes on each side, depending on degree of doneness desired. As tournedos are cooked, place in heated flameproof platter and keep warm. When all meat is cooked, add shallots to chafing dish, season with salt and pepper, and sauté lightly for a minute or two. Add additional butter if necessary, pour in wine, add Worcestershire sauce, and cook until sauce is reduced by half. Pour warm bourbon over tournedos, ignite, and blaze. Ladle sauce over meat and garnish with parsley sprigs. Serves 4. A choice St.-Julien or a West Coast pinot noir will make you glad you're hungry.

Here is a more patrician version of the foregoing recipe. The secret to cooking this steak is plenty of heat and plenty of speed.

STEAK DIANE

4 PRIME SIRLOIN STEAKS (12
    OUNCES EACH)
SALT
BLACK PEPPER
CLARIFIED BUTTER (SEE
    INDEX)
1/2 CUP COGNAC, WARMED

2 TABLESPOONS CHOPPED
    SHALLOTS
1 TABLESPOON CHOPPED FRESH
    PARSLEY
1/4 CUP SHERRY (OPTIONAL)

Steaks must be selected with care, and completely free of fat and gristle. Pound each steak with mallet until it is as thin as a dessert crêpe. Season with salt and freshly ground pepper. In flaming pan of chafing dish over high heat, add enough clarified butter to cover bottom of pan. When butter reaches cooking temperature, very quickly brown steaks on both sides. Pour in warmed cognac, ignite, and blaze. Remove steaks to heated platter. Add additional butter, shallots, and parsley, and sauté lightly. Add sherry if you wish. Mix well, then pour hot sauce over steaks. Serves 4. A Côtes-du-Rhône or California cabernet sauvignon is a good wine selection.

STEAK AU POIVRE FLAMBÉ ARMAGNAC

1 POUND PRIME SIRLOIN STEAK

2 TABLESPOONS WHOLE BLACK
   PEPPERCORNS

SALT

2 TABLESPOONS COOKING OIL

2 TABLESPOONS BUTTER

3 TABLESPOONS ARMAGNAC

1 TABLESPOON DIJON MUSTARD

$^1/_2$ CUP BORDELAISE SAUCE
   (SEE NEXT RECIPE)

Dry steak thoroughly. Crush peppercorns with bottle or rolling pin, and pound into steak with heel of hand. Sprinkle with salt. Place oil and butter in skillet over high heat. When mixture begins to brown, add steak. Sear on both sides, then cook to desired state of doneness. Pour out fat from skillet and discard. Pour in half of the Armagnac, ignite, and blaze. Remove steak from pan and keep warm. Add mustard and Bordelaise Sauce to pan and mix well with deglazed juices. Add additional butter if you wish and remainder of the Armagnac. Replace steak in pan, heat, and serve with sauce. Serves 1. A full-bodied St.-Émilion or a red Hermitage is a good choice of wine for this dish.

BORDELAISE SAUCE

2 SHALLOTS, CHOPPED

1/2 CUP DRY RED WINE

1 CUP BROWN SAUCE (SEE
INDEX) OR CANNED GRAVY

1 TEASPOON DIJON MUSTARD

1/2 TEASPOON DRIED PARSLEY

In a saucepan, cook shallots in wine until reduced to at least one-quarter the original quantity. Add Brown Sauce or canned gravy and mustard, and boil gently for 10 minutes. Just before serving, add parsley to sauce.

Hot Tips—No. 15

One of the secrets of sautéing meat successfully is to make certain that all pieces are completely dry before they are placed in the pan. This also applies to fowl, fish, and vegetables. If there is any appreciable amount of water or moisture on the outside, steam is produced between the food and the pan surface, which effectively retards browning. Since meats usually are sautéed with a little fat over high heat in order to sear the surface and seal in the juices, the presence of moisture inhibits this all-important searing process. Use paper towels to dry whatever is to be sautéed before it is placed in pan.

Here is a different treatment of beef, which is a variation of a Scottish recipe.

INVERCAULD STEAK

24 MEDIUM MUSHROOMS	1 CUP BROWN SAUCE (SEE
BUTTER	NEXT RECIPE)
SALT	$^1/_2$ CUP CREAM OR
BLACK PEPPER	HOMEGENIZED MILK
4 PRIME STRIP SIRLOIN OR	ROQUEFORT CHEESE,
SHELL STEAKS	CRUMBLED
$^1/_2$ CUP SCOTCH, WARMED	PARSLEY SPRIGS (FOR GARNISH)

Cut stems from mushrooms. Chop into very small pieces and sauté lightly with a little butter in skillet. Season with salt and freshly ground pepper. When mushrooms are lightly browned, remove and set aside. Sprinkle steaks with salt and freshly ground pepper, add additional butter to skillet, and sauté them quickly over high heat, until they are well seared on both sides. Pour in Scotch, ignite, and blaze. When flames are extinguished, remove steaks to hot plate and cover with foil to retain heat. Pour Brown Sauce in skillet and reduce mixture until about $^1/_2$ to $^2/_3$ cup remains. Stir in cream or milk and bring sauce to boiling point. Remove from heat and add 1 tablespoon butter. Stir well. Spread chopped mushrooms on top of steaks and cover with layer of sauce, sprinkle with crumbled Roquefort cheese and place in broiler of hot oven (475° F.) for a few minutes until browned. Remove to hot platter and garnish with parsley. Serves 4. Serve with a St.-Émilion or California pinot noir.

BROWN SAUCE FOR INVERCAULD STEAK

1 TABLESPOON FINELY
CHOPPED CARROT

1 TABLESPOON FINELY
CHOPPED ONION

1 TABLESPOON FINELY
CHOPPED CELERY

1 SLICE LEAN BACON, DICED

2 TABLESPOONS BUTTER

1 TABLESPOON FLOUR

2 CUPS BEEF BOUILLON

BOUQUET GARNI: 1 TEASPOON
DRIED PARSLEY, 1 SMALL BAY
LEAF, $^1/_2$ TEASPOON DRIED
THYME

SALT

BLACK PEPPER

Cook vegetables and bacon in saucepan with butter over low heat for about 10 minutes. Blend in flour, stir continually, and cook until it turns golden brown. Do not overcook or flour will be burned and will not thicken properly. Gradually add bouillon and bouquet garni. Bring to boil and let cook for a few minutes, then reduce heat and simmer sauce for about an hour. Skim off fat from time to time. Correct seasonings, adding additional salt and pepper if necessary. Remove bouquet garni. Be sure all fat has been skimmed off surface of sauce and strain. Should yield about 1 cup Brown Sauce.

Here is a fine flambé recipe for lovers of roast pork.

RÔTI DE PORC FLAMBÉ

6-POUND CENTER-CUT LOIN OF PORK

1 GARLIC CLOVE, MINCED (OPTIONAL)

CRUSHED DRIED ROSEMARY

SALT

BLACK PEPPER

1 CUP DRY WHITE WINE

$^1/_2$ CUP DRY GIN OR CALVADOS, WARMED

Preheat oven to 325° F. Rub pork roast with garlic, rosemary, generous amount of salt, and freshly ground pepper. Place in roasting pan for about 3 hours or until tender. Baste frequently with white wine. After roast has heated through, meat thermometer should register 180° F. When done, remove roast to heated flameproof platter. Pour warmed gin or Calvados on roast, ignite, and blaze. Can be accompanied with potatoes, onions, turnips, or sauerkraut, which can be cooked along with the roast. Serves 4 to 6. A good Sancerre or Riesling will make it taste even better.

And for those who like saltimbocca, here is a recipe that will satisfy the most devoted Italian fire lover.

BLAZING SALTIMBOCCA

4 THINLY SLICED VEAL
   CUTLETS
SALT
BLACK PEPPER
PINCH OF DRIED SAGE
4 THIN SLICES PROSCIUTTO
   HAM
BUTTER

$1/2$ CUP COGNAC, WARMED
FLOUR
$1/3$ CUP CREAM OR
   HOMOGENIZED MILK
$1/4$ CUP MARSALA
2 TABLESPOONS CHOPPED
   FRESH CHERVIL

Sprinkle veal cutlets with salt, a little freshly ground pepper, and sage. Place slice of Prosciutto over each cutlet and fasten in place with wooden toothpicks. Melt enough butter to cover bottom of flaming pan of chafing dish. Sauté meat over high heat for several minutes on each side. Pour in warmed cognac, ignite, and blaze. When flames are extinguished, remove meat to hot serving platter with Prosciutto face up. Reduce heat in chafing dish. Add a little flour to thicken sauce. Stir in cream or milk and Marsala. Cook until thickened. Pour sauce over saltimbocca and sprinkle with chervil. Serves 4. A light California sauvignon blanc or a zinfandel will do nicely with this dish.

To those of you who run the gauntlet of fire with these recipes in order to set a festive (if not a smoldering) board, remember that whether your approach to food is in the great tradition of Henri IV or that of Brillat-Savrin or Escoffier, it's always the spirit that matters most. This knowledge will enable you to brave the taunts of envious friends and shrug off the jibes of jealous neighbors who bruit it about that your food is cooked in a veritable "hell's kitchen" and that you use a flamethrower instead of a stove. You will, of course, eventually become inured to these well-intentioned barbs and continue undaunted with chafing dish, matches, and Sterno poised and ready, remembering that it takes both talent and fortitude to set off a miniature five-alarm fire in the dining room every night at eight-thirty.

After all, it is one thing to be a good cook, but only a real keeper of the flame can prepare food—whether snack or feast—in a true blaze of glory.

FOUR

Incandescent Cocktails and Matchless Coolers

The best rule to follow while waiting around for lunch or dinner is: Never be caught empty-handed. But it is not whether you drink, but what and how much that counts. A really civilized society can be judged by its use of alcohol, among other things. Nowhere is this reflected with more clarity than in that hallowed American institution—the cocktail hour. It is basic that cocktail party hosts extend themselves to please their guests. It is not the effort that is important, but rather the degree of imagination and ingenuity that they bring into play in planning and preparing refreshments for the multitude.

They will surely have no difficulty in finding many ways to slake the thirst of friends, for there are literally thousands of solutions at hand. Cataloged in a plethora of mixing manuals is the sum total of human experience in formulating and concocting all manner and types of cocktails, cobblers, cups, coolers, collinses, crustas, daisies, flips, fixes, frappés, juleps, toddies, grogs, bucks, mojitos, possets, punches, rickies, swizzles, sours, shrubs, smashes, scaffas, sangarees, syllabubs, and slings, to name some of the more common kinds of popular potations.

In a work dedicated to the cause of innovation, it would be unseemly to write of apéritifs and other assorted refreshments that can be found in lush profusion in any bibbers' Baedeker of standard drink recipes. It is the purpose of this brief dissertation on drinkery to consider only a few of the more familiar mixed drinks, and concentrate on a number of esoteric formulations, some of which are bizarre, a few of which are original, and all of which you will perchance find tempting and satisfying. Even if only a few of these draughts strike a responsive chord, perhaps you will be moved to join that small but loyal company of those who carry the torch in the interests of bringing more artistry, originality, and variety to those pleasant hours whiled away with ice cube and mixing glass.

First, the flaming drinks. This is a challenging category, for the extant recipes are rare and hard to come by. They have one outstanding attribute, however, for apéritifs aflame seem to fulfill their therapeutic functions with greater rapidity than their counterparts served on-the-rocks. Consequently, when these lovelies are put to the match, it can be said literally and figuratively that *you are going to get a glow on.*

England hasn't been called merry all these years for nothing. Whether it's the climate, the people, or the indomitable British spirits, one cannot say, but Great Britain has contributed substantially to the lore of stout-hearted drinking, as some of these formulas will attest.

ENGLISH CHRISTMAS PUNCH

2 FIFTHS RED BORDEAUX WINE

3 CUPS STRONG TEA

JUICE OF 1 LEMON

JUICE OF 1 ORANGE

2 POUNDS GRANULATED SUGAR

1 FIFTH JAMAICA OR PUERTO
   RICAN RUM

Mix together well wine, tea, and juices. Warm thoroughly and pour into a heatproof punch bowl. Soak sugar in rum in a covered container. With a long-handled ladle, dip out a portion of sugar-rum mixture and warm by holding over chafing-dish burner. Ignite and blaze. When fire is extinguished, pour remainder of rum and sugar mixture into punch bowl and stir well. Makes a little over 3 quarts.

PICCADILLY PUNCH

2 LEMONS

1 DOZEN WHOLE CLOVES

2 CINNAMON STICKS

1/4 TEASPOON GRATED NUTMEG

1 3/4 CUPS GRANULATED SUGAR

2 CUPS HOT WATER

1 FIFTH COGNAC

Cut peel from both lemons, stud peel with cloves, and place in flaming pan of chafing dish over direct heat with cinnamon sticks, nutmeg, sugar, and hot water. Add juice of both lemons and let simmer slowly until all sugar is dissolved. Pour some cognac in ladle, warm in simmering mixture, ignite, and pour blazing into chafing dish. Stir in remainder of cognac and serve piping hot. Makes nearly 1$^1/_2$ quarts.

ENGLISH BISHOP NO. 1

6 LARGE ORANGES

WHOLE CLOVES

$^1/_2$ CUP FIRMLY PACKED BROWN
    SUGAR

3 CINNAMON STICKS

1 QUART BARBADOS RUM,
    WARMED

2 QUARTS HOT APPLE CIDER

FRESHLY GRATED NUTMEG

Stud each orange with 12 whole cloves. Coat with brown sugar, place under broiler in medium oven (350° F.), and brown well, until sugar caramelizes and juice begins to seep out of oranges. Quarter oranges and place in heatproof punch bowl. Add cinnamon sticks and additional brown sugar. Pour in warmed rum, ignite, blaze for a few moments, and then extinguish by pouring in hot cider. Stir and sprinkle with nutmeg. Makes a little over 3 quarts.

ENGLISH BISHOP NO. 2

6 LARGE ORANGES

WHOLE CLOVES

$^1/_2$ CUP FIRMLY PACKED BROWN
    SUGAR

2 CINNAMON STICKS

2 FIFTHS RED PORT WINE

4 OUNCES COGNAC

Prepare oranges as in last recipe. Place in punch bowl with cinnamon sticks and wine. Cover and simmer slowly for 15 minutes. Uncover and pour in cognac gently so it floats on surface. Remove 1 orange with ladle from bowl, douse with cognac, ignite, and lower blazing into punch. After punch has flamed for a few moments, extinguish and serve. Makes about $1^1/_2$ quarts.

ABERDEEN ANGUS

Juice of 1 lime

1 tablespoon honey

2 ounces Scotch

Boiling water

1 ounce Drambuie

Mix all ingredients except Drambuie in flameproof mug. Add boiling water. Warm Drambuie, ignite, and pour blazing into mug. Makes 1 drink.

EAST OF SUEZ

1 quart hot tea

1 lemon, sliced

2 ounces lime juice

1 cup granulated sugar

$^1/_2$ pint Batavia arak

$^1/_2$ pint triple sec or

    Curaçao

1 pint Jamaica rum

1 pint cognac

Put tea, sliced lemon, lime juice, and sugar in flaming pan of chafing dish over direct heat. Simmer for a few minutes until sugar is completely dissolved. Add arak, triple sec or Curaçao, and rum. Heat but do not boil. Warm some cognac in a long-handled ladle by holding partially immersed in hot liquid, then ignite and pour blazing into chafing dish. Extinguish after a minute, using cover if necessary. Pour in remainder of cognac. Makes a little less than 3 quarts.

CORONATION CUP

1 LARGE ORANGE

1 CUBE SUGAR

1 WHOLE CLOVE

1 SMALL PIECE CINNAMON
   STICK

2 OUNCES COGNAC, OR
$1^{1}/_{2}$ OUNCES COGNAC AND 1
   OUNCE TRIPLE SEC, WARMED

Cut rind around middle of orange and place in boiling water for about 5 minutes or until rind becomes loose. Remove orange. As soon as it is cool enough to touch, carefully pull up half of rind to form cup and other half to form base. Place sugar, clove, cinnamon stick, and warmed cognac or cognac/triple sec combination in cup, ignite, and serve blazing. Makes 1 drink.

Hot Tips—No. 16

The fine art of blazing hot drinks requires a modicum of restraint. Beware the mazes of the dancing flames, for they can have the same hypnotic effect when issuing forth from a chafing dish that they have in a fireplace on a cold winter's night. After but a few moments of blazing, extinguish the flame by covering the chafing

dish lest your firewater end up plain water when the fire goes out.
In other words, do not allow the life of the party to go up in smoke.
In drink-making, spirits are never boiled.

OLD OXFORD UNIVERSITY PUNCH

1 CUP FIRMLY PACKED BROWN
   SUGAR
2 QUARTS BOILING WATER
1 PINT LEMON JUICE
1 FIFTH COGNAC

1 FIFTH 151-PROOF DEMERARA
   RUM
WHOLE CLOVES OR CINNAMON
   STICKS (OPTIONAL)

Dissolve sugar in boiling water in flaming pan of chafing dish over direct heat. Add lemon juice. When sugar is completely dissolved, reduce heat and add cognac. Warm a little Demerara rum in long-handled ladle by partially immersing in punch; ignite, and pour blazing into chafing dish. When flames are extinguished, add remainder of rum. Whole cloves or cinnamon sticks can be added if desired. Makes about 4 quarts.

GUARDSMEN'S PUNCH

1 QUART GREEN TEA
1 CUP FIRMLY PACKED BROWN
   SUGAR
PEEL OF 1 LEMON

2 OUNCES PORT WINE
1 FIFTH SCOTCH
$1/2$ PINT COGNAC

Simmer tea, sugar, and lemon peel in flaming pan of chafing dish over direct heat until all sugar is dissolved. Add wine and Scotch. When heated, pour a little cognac in long-handled ladle and warm by partially immersing in hot punch. Ignite and pour blazing into chafing dish. Add remainder of cognac. Makes about 2 quarts.

This drink was much venerated by the old British establishment in the Caribbean, particularly on the island of Jamaica. It can be served either hot or cold. The hot recipe is given here.

THE BLACK STRIPE

2 TEASPOONS HONEY OR	1 CINNAMON STICK
MOLASSES	2 OUNCES DARK JAMAICA RUM,
BOILING WATER	WARMED
1 PIECE LEMON PEEL	FRESHLY GRATED NUTMEG

Dissolve honey or molasses in heatproof mug with a little boiling water. Add lemon peel, cinnamon stick, rum, and additional boiling water, if desired. Float a little warmed rum on top, ignite, and blaze. Sprinkle with nutmeg. Makes 1 drink.

And now, here are a succession of hot drinks from around the world. Some can be flambéed, but in most cases it is not necessary. If, however, the night is very raw, do not underestimate the stimulating effect of a hot, hearty mug presented *en flamant* to cold and weary travelers as they enter the family circle to partake of the warmth of your friendship and your fireside. Some of these drinks are hoary with tradition, but a few are contemporary.

DOWN EAST HOT BUTTERED RUM

2 TEASPOONS FIRMLY PACKED BROWN SUGAR

1 CUP BOILING HOT APPLE CIDER

1/2 CINNAMON STICK

3 WHOLE CLOVES

1 PIECE LEMON PEEL

2 OUNCES LIGHT JAMAICA OR GOLD LABEL PUERTO RICAN RUM

1 TABLESPOON BUTTER

FRESHLY GRATED NUTMEG

In a large heatproof mug dissolve sugar in a little boiling hot cider. Add cinnamon, cloves, lemon peel, and rum. Fill remainder of cup with hot cider. Top with butter and sprinkle with grated nutmeg. Makes 1 drink.

KRAMBAMBULI PUNCH

2 FIFTHS DRY RED WINE

2 ORANGES

2 LEMONS

1 CUP GRANULATED SUGAR

1 PINT JAMAICA RUM

1 PINT BATAVIA ARAK

Heat wine but do not boil. Pour into flameproof punch bowl with juice from oranges and lemons and some rind from each. Place sugar in long-handled ladle. Saturate with a little rum and arak. Ignite and flame. Add additional rum and arak if necessary until all sugar is melted, and use ladle to stir. Pour remainder of spirits into punch. Stir again and serve in mugs. Makes about 3 quarts.

Occasionally recipes for drinks will call for powdered sugar, which also is known as confectioners' sugar. Using it is not too satisfactory because it cakes and takes considerably longer to dissolve than granulated sugar. Many professional bartenders prefer a superfine granulated sugar, which dissolves rapidly or Simple Syrup, which can be easily made. (See Index.) Good drink-mixing technique requires that all sugar be dissolved before the drink is served.

THE AMBER JACK

1 TEASPOON FIRMLY PACKED
    BROWN SUGAR
HOT WATER
1 GENEROUS TABLESPOON
    BAKED APPLE

GROUND CINNAMON
FRESHLY GRATED NUTMEG
2 OUNCES CALVADOS OR
    APPLEJACK

Dissolve sugar in a little hot water in bottom of large mug. Add baked apple and sprinkle with cinnamon and nutmeg. Pour in Calvados or applejack and fill with hot water. Makes 1 drink.

In an age of jet propulsion, you will find that this old reliable "locomotive" still has plenty of steam to take you where you want to go.

THE LOCOMOTIVE

6 OUNCES RED BURGUNDY OR
  BORDEAUX WINE

$^1/_2$ OUNCE ORANGE CURAÇAO

2 TABLESPOONS HONEY

$1^1/_2$ TEASPOONS GRANULATED
  SUGAR

1 EGG, LIGHTLY BEATEN

1 LEMON SLICE

PINCH OF GROUND CINNAMON

Combine wine, Curaçao, honey, and sugar and mix well until honey and sugar have dissolved. Place in flaming pan of chafing dish over direct heat. Stir in egg (or just the egg yolk, if you wish) and bring to a simmer. Pour into mug, add lemon slice, and cinnamon. Makes 1 drink.

Hot buttered rum originally was intended as a bibulous resuscitant back in the days before central heating. It's meant to be potent. If you're worried about its aftereffects, just drink less. Here is a Caribbean version that profits considerably from the addition of crème de cacao.

ST. VINCENT HOT BUTTERED RUM

BOILING WATER

2 HEAPING TEASPOONS BROWN
  SUGAR

1 SMALL PIECE LEMON PEEL

WHOLE CLOVES

1 CINNAMON STICK

2 OUNCES DARK JAMAICA RUM

1 OUNCE CRÈME DE CACAO

1 TABLESPOON BUTTER

FRESHLY GRATED NUTMEG

Heat a large mug by rinsing in boiling water. Place brown sugar in mug with lemon peel studded with cloves and cinnamon stick. Pour in a little boiling water and stir until sugar is dissolved. Add Jamaica rum, crème de cacao, and additional boiling water. Place butter on top and sprinkle with nutmeg. Makes 1 drink.

BEACHCOMBER'S BRACER

1 TEASPOON CONFECTIONERS'
SUGAR
DASH OF LEMON JUICE
BOILING WATER
1 OUNCE RYE OR BOURBON

1 OUNCE LIGHT JAMAICA RUM
1 OUNCE ORANGE CURAÇAO
DASH OF ANGOSTURA BITTERS
(OPTIONAL)

Place sugar and lemon juice in mug with a little boiling water. Stir until sugar is dissolved. Add whisky, rum, and Curaçao, and bitters if you wish. Fill mug with boiling water. Makes 1 drink.

The Tom and Jerry is a traditional holiday drink, particularly in the United States—which is fitting and proper, since it was invented in New York City. Jerry Thomas, who was the father of the Blue Blazer (see Index), generally is given credit for inventing this traditional Christmas cup—hence the name. What part Tom played in this enterprise is not known, but since the recipe bears his name as well, in all likelihood he was the boss. This would suggest that bartenders, then as now, were pos-

sessed of a good deal of diplomacy. Here is the original recipe, which has not been improved upon substantially through the years.

TOM AND JERRY

1 EGG

1 TABLESPOON GRANULATED
   SUGAR

1 OUNCE DARK JAMAICA RUM

1 OUNCE COGNAC

BOILING WATER

FRESHLY GRATED NUTMEG

Separate egg and beat yolk and white individually. Blend beaten yolk and white together. Add sugar and place in mug. Pour in rum and cognac and fill up with boiling water. Sprinkle with nutmeg. Makes 1 drink.

After a short cruise, you may want to tie on to this.

LONDON DOCK

2 TEASPOONS GRANULATED
    SUGAR

BOILING WATER

1 SMALL PIECE LEMON PEEL

CINNAMON STICK

$1^1/_2$ OUNCES DARK JAMAICA
    RUM

$1^1/_2$ OUNCES RED BURGUNDY
    OR BORDEAUX WINE

FRESHLY GRATED NUTMEG

Dissolve sugar in mug with a little boiling water. Add lemon peel, cinnamon stick, rum, and wine. Fill up with boiling water and top with nutmeg. Makes 1 drink.

Try this if in need of a blustery, nautical nog.

WINDJAMMER

PEEL OF $^1/_2$ ORANGE

BROWN SUGAR

$1^1/_2$ OUNCES LIGHT JAMAICA
    OR BARBADOS RUM

1 OUNCE ROCK & RYE

1 OUNCE ORANGE CURAÇAO

1 SMALL PIECE LEMON PEEL

BOILING WATER

Cut orange peel in spiral, and coat with brown sugar. Place in heatproof mug and flame with $^1/_2$ ounce warmed rum until sugar is caramelized. Add Rock & Rye, Curaçao, remaining rum, and lemon peel. Fill with boiling water and mix well. Makes 1 drink.

HOT MILK PUNCH

GRANULATED SUGAR

1 CUP HOT MILK

1 OUNCE DARK JAMAICA RUM

1 OUNCE COGNAC

1 OUNCE DRY GIN OR VODKA

DASH OF ANGOSTURA BITTERS

FRESHLY GRATED NUTMEG

Dissolve sugar to taste in milk and heat in saucepan. When milk is hot, add rum, cognac, gin, and bitters. Pour into electric blender. Mix at high speed until frothy, and serve in mug that has been scalded with hot water. Top with nutmeg. Makes 1 drink.

REGENT'S PUNCH

DOLLOP OF HONEY

HOT TEA

4 OUNCES SAUTERNE WINE

2 OUNCES MADEIRA WINE

1 OUNCE DARK JAMAICA RUM

Add honey to preheated mug and pour in a little hot tea. When honey is dissolved, add Sauterne, Madeira, and rum. Mix well and fill up with additional hot tea. Makes 1 drink.

THE ZOMBIE'S REVENGE

1 OUNCE LEMON JUICE   1 OUNCE DARK JAMAICA RUM

1 OUNCE ORANGE JUICE   2 OUNCES PUERTO RICAN RUM

GRENADINE   DASH OF PERNOD

BOILING WATER OR TEA   1 OUNCE DEMERARA

1 OUNCE ORANGE CURAÇAO   151-PROOF RUM

Mix lemon juice, orange juice, and grenadine to taste with a little boiling water or tea in large preheated flameproof mug. Pour in Curaçao, Jamaica rum, Puerto Rican rum, and Pernod. Warm 151-proof Demerara rum in ladle, ignite, and pour blazing into mug. Extinguish and serve. Makes 1 drink with a vengeance.

If you have tried every one of these recipes, by now you will have had enough incendiary imbibing to gag the entire complement of Engine Company No. 16. Besides that, while flambé dishes are appropriate at any time of the year, thermal tippling really satisfies best when there is a touch of frost in the air. So it is appropriate that we include some coolers to bring some relief to parched palates and singed chin whiskers. The following formulations have been culled through assiduous personal research at the world's best bars; they are not necessarily new, just great drinks to be drunk in the grand manner.

The secret of making a good mint julep is so disarmingly simple that many people never get the hang of it, including a few bartenders who are so busy learning the tricks of the trade that they never get around to learning the trade. All you need is the right equipment, the right ingredients, and the right recipe. First you must have a quantity of tender, fresh mint leaves. Then you need a bottle of fine, aged straight bourbon whisky, a little superfine granulated sugar, ice, and an electric ice crusher (or a canvas bag and a mallet) with which to frappé it properly.

MINT JULEP

12 FRESH MINT LEAVES, PLUS 1
   SPRIG
1 TO 2 TEASPOONS SUPERFINE
   GRANULATED SUGAR
   (DEPENDING ON SWEETNESS
   DESIRED)

ICE CUBES
3 OR 4 OUNCES 100-PROOF
   STRAIGHT BOURBON
CONFECTIONERS' SUGAR
   (OPTIONAL)

Take largest glass you can find—at least 12 to 14 ounces in capacity—and place mint leaves in bottom. Add sugar and bruise mint leaves with muddler, until sugar is well mashed into them. Chill glass in freezer for at least $1/2$ hour. Be sure outside of glass is dry, or it will not frost properly. Place a quantity of ice cubes in electric ice crusher and frappé until ice is pea size. Remove glass from freezer, pack with frappéed ice, and pour in bourbon. Give mixture a good working over with swizzle stick until frost begins to form on outside of glass. Add additional crushed ice if necessary. Garnish with sprig of mint leaves and top with sprinkling of confectioners' sugar, if you wish. Makes 1 monumental drink.

Hot Tips—No. 18

Throughout the Spanish Main many, many drinks are swizzled with a swizzle stick. It is simply a small, rather longish stick with roots or little branches that have been trimmed so that it can be in-

*serted without difficulty into the mouth of a pitcher or glass,
whereupon it is rotated rapidly, by moving the palms of the hands
back and forth vigorously. Actually, any instrument capable of ag-
itating the solution into which it is inserted and bringing about the
desired aeration will do. In most drinks it is a boon. In those that
call for soda water or are blessed with natural carbonation it is a
bane. And it is painful indeed to see certain misguided people in-
dulge in the unfortunate European practice of swizzling a lovely
glass of fine champagne and removing in minutes the precious ef-
fervescence that man and nature spent so much time to put there in
the first place.*

To many people the word Sazerac is only a name, but in the city of New
Orleans, be assured that it is a tradition. There are many recipes for Saz-
eracs in standard bartenders' guides. This one came right from Royal
Street in the heart of the Vieux Carré.

THE SAZERAC

1 SUGAR CUBE	2 OUNCES RYE OR BOURBON
2 DASHES OF PEYCHAUD'S	1 DASH HERBSAINT OR PERNOD
BITTERS	1 PIECE LEMON PEEL
DASH OF ANGOSTURA BITTERS	

Take two Old-Fashioned glasses. Fill one with shaved ice and set aside
to chill. In other, place sugar cube with a small amount of water. Add
bitters and crush sugar with muddler until dissolved. Add rye or bourbon, 2 or 3 ice cubes, and stir until mixture is well chilled. Now discard

shaved ice from first glass. To it add Herbsaint or Pernod, and carefully rotate glass until sides and bottom are coated with thin layer of liqueur. Pour off excess. Pour mixture of whisky, bitters, and sugar into coated glass. Twist lemon peel over Sazerac but do not place peel in glass. Do not add more ice. Makes 1 fine drink.

Although it is about as bartenderproof as any mixed drink can be, the Bloody Mary is shabbily treated often. Dill adds a refreshing touch.

THE COMPATIBLE BLOODY MARY

$1/2$ TEASPOON CHOPPED FRESH OR DRIED DILL WEED

$1/4$ TEASPOON CELERY SALT OR ACCORDING TO TASTE

PINCH OF WHITE PEPPER

2 DROPS OF TABASCO SAUCE

$1/4$ TEASPOON WORCESTERSHIRE SAUCE

1 TEASPOON LEMON JUICE

2 OUNCES VODKA

6 OUNCES BEST TOMATO JUICE

Mix all ingredients well with ice and serve in tall glass with 1 or 2 ice cubes. Makes 1 drink.

V-8 Juice makes a marvelous Bloody Mary when it is mixed with the right ingredients. This is a great morning-after drink, right before a Sunday brunch. We were so happy with this potion that we called it:

THE HAPPY MARY

GENEROUS PINCH OF CELERY
    SALT
GENEROUS PINCH OF WHITE
    PEPPER
2 DROPS OF TABASCO SAUCE
$1/4$ TEASPOON
    WORCESTERSHIRE SAUCE

PINCH OF DRIED OREGANO (OR
    DILL WEED OR TARRAGON)
$1/2$ TEASPOON HORSERADISH
    (OPTIONAL)
JUICE OF $1/4$ FRESH LIME
2 OUNCES VODKA
6 OUNCES V-8 JUICE

Mix all ingredients well with ice in order listed. Makes 1 happy drink.

If you have traveled in the Caribbean, perhaps you have wondered why it is so easy to get a good Planter's Punch almost anywhere and yet when you get back home, while you have no difficulty in ordering a drink with the name of Planter's Punch, the resemblance seems to end there. Two of the secrets are good rum and fresh fruit. Here is a recipe you might try next time you yearn for a presentable Planter's Punch.

A PRESENTABLE PLANTER'S PUNCH

2 OUNCES JAMAICA,
    DEMERARA, HAITIAN, OR
    MARTINIQUE RUM
1 OUNCE FRESH PINEAPPLE
    JUICE
1 OUNCE FRESH ORANGE JUICE
1 OUNCE FRESH LIME JUICE

$1/4$ TEASPOON ORANGE
    CURAÇAO
CLUB SODA
SLICE OF PINEAPPLE AND
    ORANGE
MARASCHINO CHERRY

Shake together rum, juices, and Curaçao or mix in electric blender. Strain into 14- or 16-ounce glass. Add a little soda water. Mix again or swizzle if you wish. Garnish with slice of pineapple, slice of orange, and maraschino cherry. Makes 1 drink.

Hot Tips—No. 19

There are many substitutes available for fresh fruit juice. Some of them are excellent, and they have a legitimate use when convenience and storage space are a factor (as on shipboard). But if you want absolutely first-class drinks, please use freshly squeezed fruit juices whenever possible. Frozen juices are also quite acceptable, but remember, you can't go wrong if you squeeze your own. And it makes a whale of a difference in the taste of the drinks you make.

These next few recipes were chosen not because they are unusual but simply because in my opinion they have never received their just due. This moonraker's moonshine is a good example.

OLD NAVY PUNCH

JUICE OF 4 FRESHLY SQUEEZED
    LEMONS
MEAT OF 1 FRESH PINEAPPLE
$^1/_2$ BOTTLE DARK JAMAICA RUM

$^1/_2$ BOTTLE COGNAC
$^1/_2$ BOTTLE PEACH BRANDY
SUGAR TO TASTE
4 FIFTHS CHAMPAGNE

Mix all ingredients well, except champagne. Chill and pour over block of ice in punch bowl. Immediately before serving, pour in champagne and stir gently into punch. Makes about $4^1/_2$ quarts.

And speaking of good punches, here is one that has made the rounds in Jamaica.

PEPPER TREE PUNCH

1 OUNCE FRESHLY SQUEEZED
    LIME JUICE
1 TABLESPOON GRANULATED
    SUGAR
2 DASHES OF ANGOSTURA
    BITTERS

PINCH OF CAYENNE PEPPER
PINCH OF GROUND CINNAMON
2 OUNCES LIGHT JAMAICA RUM
1 OUNCE DARK JAMAICA RUM

Mix all ingredients in shaker or electric blender with cracked ice and serve in double Old-Fashioned glass. Makes 1 drink.

Here is a colorful zoological specimen.

THE RED LION COCKTAIL

1 OUNCE DRY GIN	1/2 OUNCE ORANGE JUICE
1 OUNCE GRAND MARNIER	1/2 OUNCE LEMON JUICE

Shake all ingredients vigorously with cracked ice and serve in a stemmed cocktail glass. Makes 1 drink.

Ounce for ounce, there are very few cocktails that can stand up to the ubiquitous and indomitable martini. The Hunter Cocktail is one of them. This little atomic apéritif will really stir things up, and what's more, it's a cracking good drink as well.

THE HUNTER COCKTAIL

3/4 OUNCE CHERRY BRANDY	MARASCHINO CHERRY
1 1/2 OUNCES STRAIGHT RYE	(OPTIONAL)

Stir brandy and rye with ice and strain into stemmed cocktail glass. You can garnish with maraschino cherry if you wish. The original formula calls for straight rye, but blended whisky can be substituted. As far as the cherry brandy is concerned, be sure to use a real cherry brandy and not a liqueur, which is much too sweet. Makes 1 very authoritative drink.

PRINCE GEORGE COCKTAIL

$^3/_4$ OUNCE GRAND MARNIER   LEMON PEEL (OPTIONAL)

$1^1/_2$ OUNCES LIGHT RUM

JUICE OF $^1/_2$ FRESHLY

   SQUEEZED LIME

Mix all ingredients with ice, strain, and serve in stemmed cocktail glass. A lemon peel can be twisted over this drink, if you so desire. Makes 1 drink.

This British colonial favorite, typical of the regional drinks that became famous at the hill stations, clubs, and other retreats during the palmy days of the British Raj in India and Burma, originated at the Pegu Club in Pegu, Burma. To find its way from there to here, it *had* to be good. And it is.

PEGU CLUB COCKTAIL

DASH OF ANGOSTURA BITTERS $^3/_4$ OUNCE ORANGE CURAÇAO

DASH OF ORANGE BITTERS $1^1/_2$ OUNCES DRY GIN

1 TEASPOON FRESHLY

   SQUEEZED LIME JUICE

Shake all ingredients well with ice, strain, and serve in stemmed cocktail glass. Makes 1 drink.

This is the famous old pacifier of the Scots Guards Officer's Mess. It has traveled around the world under many names.

The original recipe calls for equal parts of orange juice, lemon juice, and whisky. But this does not seem quite dry enough for modern tastes.

THE SCOTS GUARDS COCKTAIL

1 TEASPOON GRENADINE

1 1/2 OUNCES CANADIAN
   WHISKY

1/2 OUNCE LEMON JUICE

1 OUNCE ORANGE JUICE

Shake all ingredients well with ice, strain, and pour into stemmed cocktail glass. Makes 1 drink.

THE ROYAL SMILE COCKTAIL

JUICE OF 1/2 FRESH LIME

GRENADINE TO TASTE

3/4 OUNCE CALVADOS OR
   APPLEJACK

1 1/2 OUNCES DRY GIN

Shake all ingredients with cracked ice and strain into stemmed cocktail glass. Makes 1 drink.

If you happen to like applejack or Calvados (actually Calvados is far superior to domestic applejacks because it is aged considerably longer), here is a fine old favorite from the Savoy Hotel in London.

SAVOY TANGO COCKTAIL

1 OUNCE SLOE GIN

1 OUNCE CALVADOS OR
APPLEJACK

SEVERAL DASHES OF LIME JUICE
TO TASTE

Shake ingredients well with ice and strain into stemmed cocktail glass. Makes 1 drink.

Here is an interesting variation of the famous tropical drink that was invented at the Caribe Hilton Hotel in San Juan, Puerto Rico.

PIÑA COLADA ALMENDRA

1 1/2 OUNCES LIGHT RUM

1 OUNCE COCONUT MILK

2 OUNCES PINEAPPLE JUICE

SEVERAL DASHES ORGEAT
SYRUP

PINEAPPLE SPEAR (FOR
GARNISH; OPTIONAL)

Mix all ingredients with a little ice in an electric blender and serve in 10-ounce glass with plenty of shaved ice. You may garnish with a pineapple spear if you wish. Makes 1 incredibly delicious drink.

Sometimes Champagne cocktails are nothing more than a means of adulterating a fine wine. However, a really good Champagne cocktail comes from the Coq Hardy restaurant near Paris. The proportions involved are minuscule, and you can vary them according to your taste. Perhaps this explains the drink's subtle charm.

COQ HARDY CHAMPAGNE COCKTAIL

1 SUGAR CUBE	1 DROP OF GRAND MARNIER
2 DROPS OF ANGOSTURA	1 DROP OF COGNAC
BITTERS	CHAMPAGNE
1 DROP OF	MARASCHINO CHERRY
FERNET-BRANCA	SLIVER OF ORANGE PEEL

Make certain sugar cube is well saturated with all ingredients except Champagne and garnishes. Place cube in chilled Champagne glass and fill with Champagne. Garnish with maraschino cherry and sliver of fresh orange peel. Makes 1 drink.

We don't hold much with sweet drinks, but this one is good, by Jupiter! Here's the old original recipe.

JUPITER COCKTAIL

1 TEASPOON ORANGE JUICE

1 TEASPOON Parfait Amour
  LIQUEUR OR CRÈME DE
  VIOLETTE

3/4 OUNCE FRENCH VERMOUTH

1 1/2 OUNCES DRY GIN

Shake all ingredients well with cracked ice and strain into cocktail glass. As with any gin-vermouth combination, feel free to change the proportions to suit your taste. Makes 1 drink.

Hot Tips—No. 20

It is difficult to believe how much better things taste if they are aerated. For this reason, electric blenders have provided the greatest flavor dividend to mixed drinks (and everything else liquid for that matter) in recent history. If you use a blender for all drinks that are to be shaken, you will be astounded how flavors come alive. This works equally well with nonalcoholic drinks. The next time you want to put a little life in your morning fruit juice, just dump it in the blender, whip it up, and see how much better it tastes. A good motto seems to be, "If the flavor has abated, it'll snap back when aerated."

This one is for expensive-car buffs.

ROLLS-ROYCE COCKTAIL

1 OUNCE COGNAC   1 OUNCE ORANGE JUICE

1 OUNCE COINTREAU

Shake all ingredients well with cracked ice and strain into cocktail glass.
Makes 1 very tasty and very mobile drink.

The remaining recipes in this chapter come under the heading of "orig-
inals." The word is used advisedly and most humbly, for it is highly
doubtful that there is any so-called original drink that has not somewhere, at some time, been approximated by someone. So drink them in
the spirit in which they are offered: to spread joy and warmth to all who
gather in goodwill around the Bacchic bowl.

THE WHISKY HOUND

1 OUNCE LEMON JUICE

1 TABLESPOON SUGAR OR
   SIMPLE SYRUP

1 1/2 OUNCES 100-PROOF
   BOURBON

1/2 OUNCE 86-PROOF
   DEMERARA RUM (OR
   151-PROOF IF YOU FEEL
   DARING)

1/2 OUNCE ORANGE JUICE AND
   1/2 OUNCE GRAPEFRUIT
   JUICE, OR
   1 OUNCE ORANGE JUICE

DASH OF MARASCHINO CHERRY
   JUICE

Mix all ingredients with ice in electric blender and serve in double Old-Fashioned glass. Makes 1 drink.

SEWICKLEY HEIGHTS GUN CLUB PUNCH

(Also known as the Skeet Shooter's Special, an après-shooting bracer for winter or summer)

1¹/₂ OUNCES PINEAPPLE JUICE

1¹/₂ OUNCES GRAPEFRUIT JUICE

1¹/₂ OUNCES ORANGE JUICE

1 OUNCE LEMON SODA

1¹/₂ OUNCES DARK JAMAICA
   RUM

³/₄ OUNCE LIGHT PUERTO
   RICAN RUM

3 OR 4 WHOLE MARASCHINO
   CHERRIES

PINCH OF GROUND CINNAMON

Mix all ingredients well in electric blender with cracked ice and serve in 14-ounce glass. Makes 1 hearty draught—good for celebration or consolation, whichever the case may be.

THE GILDED ORANGE, NO. 1

2 OUNCES ORANGE JUICE

2 OUNCES DRY GIN

$^1/_2$ OUNCE DARK JAMAICA RUM

1 TEASPOON GRANULATED
   SUGAR

$^1/_2$ TEASPOON ORGEAT SYRUP

DASH OF LEMON JUICE

ORANGE PEEL

Mix all ingredients except orange peel well with cracked ice in electric blender and serve in double Old-Fashioned glass. Garnish with orange peel. Makes 1 drink.

THE GILDED ORANGE, NO. 2

2 OUNCES ORANGE JUICE

2 OUNCES DARK JAMAICA RUM

$^1/_2$ OUNCE 151-PROOF
   DEMERARA RUM

$^1/_2$ OUNCE GRENADINE OR TO
   TASTE

1 TEASPOON LEMON JUICE

DASH OF LIME JUICE

ORANGE SLICE

Mix all ingredients except orange slice with cracked ice in electric blender and serve in double Old-Fashioned glass. Garnish with orange slice. Makes 1 drink.

This is an original picker-upper for downtrodden huntsmen.

THE PINK PEARL

4 OUNCES GRAPEFRUIT JUICE

1 OUNCE MARASCHINO CHERRY
  JUICE

1½ OUNCES ROSE'S LIME
  JUICE

2½ OUNCES VODKA

MARASCHINO CHERRY

Mix all ingredients except cherry with ice in electric blender. Pour into 12-ounce Collins glass and garnish with maraschino cherry. Makes 1 drink.

HABIT ROUGE

1½ OUNCES GRAPEFRUIT JUICE

1½ OUNCES CRANBERRY JUICE

1 TEASPOON MAPLE SYRUP OR
  HONEY

1½ OUNCES DRY GIN

Place all ingredients in electric blender and frappé with ice. Serve in 6-ounce Champagne saucer or cocktail glass. Makes 1 drink.

And here's a beautiful prebrunch drink.

THE SPICED ORANGE BLOSSOM

4 OUNCES FRESHLY SQUEEZED
    ORANGE JUICE
DASH OF MARASCHINO CHERRY
    JUICE
2 MARASCHINO CHERRIES

DASH OF ANGOSTURA BITTERS
PINCH OF GROUND CINNAMON
DASH OF LEMON OR LIME JUICE
2 OUNCES GIN OR VODKA

Mix all ingredients with ice in electric blender and serve in double Old-Fashioned glass. Makes 1 drink.

Here's a variation on the above.

MORNING SUN

2 OUNCES GRAPEFRUIT JUICE
2 OUNCES ORANGE JUICE
$1/2$ TEASPOON MARASCHINO
    CHERRY JUICE

DASH OF ANGOSTURA BITTERS
2 OUNCES VODKA OR GIN
MARASCHINO CHERRY

Mix all ingredients except cherry with ice in electric blender and serve in double Old-Fashioned glass. Garnish with maraschino cherry. Makes 1 drink.

BIG JOHN'S SPECIAL

1 OUNCE ORANGE JUICE

3 OUNCES GRAPEFRUIT JUICE

DASH OF MARASCHINO CHERRY
    JUICE

1 1/2 OUNCES DRY GIN

1 OUNCE VODKA

4 MARASCHINO CHERRIES

1 WEDGE PRESERVED COCKTAIL
    ORANGE

DASH OF ORANGE-FLOWER
    WATER

Mix all ingredients in electric blender and frappé. Serve in double Old-Fashioned glass or large Collins glass. Makes 1 marvelous before-lunch drink.

MIXED BLESSING

4 OUNCES PINEAPPLE JUICE

DASH OF LIME JUICE

2 TABLESPOONS CRUSHED
    PINEAPPLE

1 TABLESPOON FALERNUM
    (A COMPOUND SWEET SYRUP
    FROM BARBADOS), OR
    SWEETEN TO TASTE

1 1/2 OUNCES GOLD LABEL
    PUERTO RICAN RUM

1/2 OUNCE 151-PROOF
    DEMERARA RUM

MARASCHINO CHERRY

Mix all ingredients except cherry with plenty of ice in electric blender and frappé. Garnish with maraschino cherry in double Old-Fashioned glass. Makes 1 drink.

52ND STREET

1 OUNCE LEMON JUICE

1 TEASPOON GRENADINE OR TO
    TASTE

1 1/2 OUNCES DARK JAMAICA
    RUM

1 TABLESPOON COGNAC

1 TABLESPOON CURAÇAO

Mix all ingredients with plenty of ice in electric blender and frappé. Serve in 6-ounce Champagne saucer or stemmed cocktail glass. Makes 1 drink.

12-GAUGE GROG

1 OUNCE LEMON JUICE

1 TABLESPOON SUGAR OR TO
    TASTE

2 OUNCES ORANGE JUICE

DASH OF ANGOSTURA BITTERS

1 1/2 OUNCES DARK JAMAICA
    RUM

3/4 OUNCE 151-PROOF
    DEMERARA RUM

GRAPEFRUIT SODA

MARASCHINO CHERRY

ORANGE SLICE

Shake well all ingredients, except grapefruit soda and garnishes, with ice. Strain and pour into 14-ounce glass with 2 ice cubes. Fill up with grapefruit soda. Garnish with maraschino cherry and orange slice. Makes 1 drink.

THE BOURBON CARDINAL

1 OUNCE GRAPEFRUIT JUICE

1 OUNCE CRANBERRY JUICE

2 OUNCES 100-PROOF STRAIGHT
    BOURBON

1/2 OUNCE LEMON JUICE

1 TABLESPOON SUGAR OR TO
    TASTE

DASH OF MARASCHINO CHERRY
    JUICE

2 MARASCHINO CHERRIES

Mix all ingredients with ice in electric blender. Strain and serve in whisky sour glass. Makes 1 drink.

SUTTON PLACE SLING

2 OUNCES ORANGE JUICE

DASH OF MARASCHINO CHERRY
    JUICE

DASH OF ANGOSTURA BITTERS

DASH OF LIME JUICE

2 OUNCES DARK JAMAICA RUM

BITTER LEMON SODA

1 TEASPOON 151-PROOF
    DEMERARA RUM

Shake all ingredients except bitter lemon soda and rum with ice. Strain and pour into 12-ounce glass with several ice cubes. Fill with bitter lemon soda and stir. Float 1 teaspoon Demerara rum on top. Makes 1 drink.

THE RANGIRORA MADNESS

2 OUNCES ORANGE JUICE

2 OUNCES PINEAPPLE JUICE

2 OUNCES DARK JAMAICA RUM

BITTER LEMON SODA

1/2 OUNCE 151-PROOF
   DEMERARA RUM

MARASCHINO CHERRY

PINEAPPLE SPEAR

Shake juices and Jamaica rum with ice. Pour into 12-ounce glass with several ice cubes. Fill up with lemon soda, stir, and float Demerara rum on top. Garnish with maraschino cherry and pineapple spear. Makes 1 mad drink.

J.P.'S PUNCH

2 OUNCES ORANGE JUICE

1 OUNCE PINEAPPLE JUICE

1/2 OUNCE LIME JUICE

1/2 SLICED RIPE BANANA

DASH OF GRENADINE OR TO
   TASTE

1 1/2 OUNCES PUERTO RICAN
   RUM

1 OUNCE DARK JAMAICA RUM

MARASCHINO CHERRY

Mix all ingredients except cherry with ice in electric blender. Serve in 14-ounce glass. Garnish with maraschino cherry. Makes 1 drink.

We earnestly hope that this array of potions, both common and peculiar, will provide you with many hours of mental and physiological stimulation and move you to try a little original drink-building on your own. When experimenting, if you succeed in creating a concoction that looks like something that you might want to rush home from work and make again someday, be sure to keep a note of the ingredients and the precise measurements. It's amazing how these little details will slip away from you, particularly after you have had more than one of your own creations.

There's this much to be said for making your own. If the drink is no good, you usually know what went wrong and you have only yourself to blame. And if the drink went well, you have reason to rejoice and have another. When you've run out of patience, money, and exotic liqueurs to mix drinks with, you can always go back to the highball. Now there's a drink anybody can make—well, almost anybody.

FIVE

How to Fire Up the Party

$\mathcal{P}$eople make the party. Thus the seal of success—or doom—often is stamped inexorably on the best-laid plans when the invitations are sent out. But even a dull party can be fired up, if not salvaged completely; and a good people mix can be turned into a real swingin' affair or, as fire lovers are wont to say: a gasser!

Everyone has his own convictions about what makes a party a smashing success or a crashing bore. Here we are wholly committed to the unusual, and we hope the exotic, not for its own sake, but to inspire (or prod) you to draw upon your own creative resources and move onward and upward to new heights of flamboyancy. You will have a great sense of achievement—and your friends will love you for it.

Let us begin by reexamining your basic attitudes toward entertainment. There are many reasons for throwing a party, but it is the end result that really counts. What do you usually give your guests to remember you by—besides a monumental hangover? Was your cocktail party any different from all the other dead-tired affairs that memory has blurred into a hazy, kaleidoscopic mélange of endless standing, frenetic small talk, soggy canapés, the same old "something and tonic," drab highballs, "the usual" on-the-rocks and the old reliable skull-cracker twins: the little brown one with the cherry and the little white one with the olive? Was your buffet supper something special, or in retrospect would everyone have gratefully settled for Blimpie's, or for that matter had more fun at P. J. Clarke's pub? If you really have to ask yourself the next day whether your guests had a good time, chances are they didn't. And don't be fooled by the few diehards who were good till the last drop. They'd be the last to leave a flood as long as there was something around to mix it with.

A social affair should be approached as an *event*, not a chore. A good party—even for two (perhaps we should say *especially* for two)—should be planned. Whom to invite—well, that's pretty much up to you. But the important thing is, what happens after they get there? As a general rule, what we choose to call "the focal point" rule seems to work out best. It is quite simple. Have an important point of interest in every aspect of your party. This applies to decorations, table settings, hors d'oeuvres, cocktails, and, of course, the food. Each area of interest need not be an overwhelmer or elaborate or expensive. Call it conversation piece, point of interest, or tour de force, but be there it must.

Decorations are a good place to start. When you order the flowers (and what party doesn't need a few?), rather than busy up the place with lots of similar little flower arrangements, pick out an important location and make a real splash. If you're on a budget, better to blow it all on a few dozen long-stemmed roses to be displayed in a place of honor than to try to cover every table with fussy little posies. The point is, it's better to have one important thing (such as a Christmas tree) conspicuously present than a lot of insignificant festoons strewn around the room.

When your guests arrive, naturally they will be thirsty; therefore liquid refreshments are a first consideration. You will be faced immediately with the problem of keeping old George from having his usual exciting bourbon and water and old Martha from having her regular dusty-dry martini. But the justification is crystal clear: Your reputation as a host is at stake. Not only must you have an alternate potation to recommend, but you must lure them, even entrap them, so that they will be hard put to refuse "just a small glass" as a gesture of courtesy. Whether it remains merely a gesture or becomes a blessed moment of gustatory revelation depends entirely on you. You cannot expect to win over everyone, but some imaginative concoctions will be eagerly accepted by a surprisingly high percentage of your guests who yearn for something enticingly new to titillate their tired taste buds.

Punches are back in style again. Actually they were never out. It's just that we have all had unpleasant experiences with punches so ill conceived and ineptly made that we were sure that the resulting mixtures were intended for batteries, not stomachs. The following five recipes for punches have stood the test of many a high time and turned more than one gathering into a genuine celebration. In preparing them, please follow these simple rules for punch making: Use only the best ingredients, follow recipes exactly and in sequence, chill all ingredients in advance, and use only a large block of ice for cooling to minimize ice meltage and excessive dilution.

Here is a genuine American classic, born near Philadelphia well over two hundred years ago—and this is the genuine recipe.

FISH HOUSE PUNCH

3/4 POUND SUGAR

2 QUARTS SPRING WATER

1 QUART FRESHLY SQUEEZED
    LEMON JUICE

1/2 CUP PEACH BRANDY

1 QUART COGNAC

2 QUARTS FINE JAMAICA RUM

In punch bowl, dissolve most of the sugar (granulated or brown) in water. Stir in lemon juice and add peach brandy, cognac, and Jamaica rum. Taste, and add more sugar if necessary. Brown sugar was used originally but, again, this is a matter of taste. Makes a little more than 6 quarts.

There are many variations of this grand old favorite. Here is a fine English recipe.

CHAMPAGNE PUNCH

1/2 POUND SUGAR

1 CUP COGNAC

1 CUP MARASCHINO LIQUEUR

1 CUP CURAÇAO

2 FIFTHS EXTRA-DRY
    CHAMPAGNE

SPARKLING WATER (OPTIONAL)

SLICED FRESH OR BRANDIED
    PEACHES

RED AND GREEN MARASCHINO
    CHERRIES

In punch bowl, stir sugar in enough water to dissolve completely. Add cognac, maraschino liqueur, and Curaçao, and mix well. Just before guests arrive, pour in Champagne and stir carefully to preserve carbonation. Sparkling water can be added to reduce potency and increase fizziness. Garnish with sliced fresh or brandied peaches and red and green maraschino cherries. Makes slightly more than 2 quarts.

This is another old favorite and due for a revival.

BRANDY PUNCH

1 DOZEN LEMONS	2 FIFTHS COGNAC
4 ORANGES	1 QUART SPARKLING WATER
GRANULATED SUGAR	OR CHAMPAGNE
1 CUP GRENADINE	ORANGE PEEL SPIRALS
$^1/_2$ PINT TRIPLE SEC	

In punch bowl, squeeze juice from lemons and oranges and mix with enough sugar to sweeten. Add grenadine, triple sec, and cognac and stir well. Just before guests arrive, gently stir in sparkling water or Champagne. Garnish with spirals of orange peel. (Champagne substituted for sparkling water makes this a marvelous punch for brunch.) Makes about 4 quarts.

This is an English classic with old colonial overtones. The original recipe omitted lemon juice, which is included here as it seems more suitable for American palates.

BOMBAY PUNCH

1 DOZEN LEMONS

GRANULATED SUGAR

1 FIFTH COGNAC

1 FIFTH MEDIUM-DRY SHERRY

$^1/_4$ PINT MARASCHINO LIQUEUR

$^1/_4$ PINT CURAÇAO

4 FIFTHS EXTRA-DRY
  CHAMPAGNE

2 QUARTS SPARKLING WATER

In punch bowl, squeeze juice from lemons and mix with sufficient sugar to sweeten. Add cognac, sherry, maraschino liqueur, and Curaçao, Champagne, and sparkling water. As in all punches, stir in sparkling ingredients carefully just before serving. Makes a little less than 8 quarts.

Here is a hot drink that is great après-ski or après anything else and was once popular with the White Russian colony in Shanghai.

SHANGHAI PUNCH

2 QUARTS HOT BLACK TEA

2 CUPS LEMON JUICE

3 TABLESPOONS ORGEAT SYRUP

2 TABLESPOONS ORANGE-
  FLOWER WATER

1 FIFTH COGNAC

1 PINT TRIPLE SEC

1 PINT JAMAICA OR DEMERARA
  RUM

ORANGE AND LEMON PEEL

CINNAMON STICKS

To hot black tea in punch bowl add lemon juice, orgeat syrup, orange-flower water, cognac, triple sec, and Jamaica or Demerara rum (90-proof Demerara is preferred—or if your guests are strong and the night is frosty, you can use 151 proof). Garnish with orange and lemon peel, and serve steaming hot in mugs each containing stick of cinnamon. Makes approximately 4 quarts.

If we look upon the punch bowl as a community cocktail glass, it takes on an entirely new aspect and the possibilities for innovation are limitless. We can, for example, scrap the old custom of serving punch in tiny little cups. Glasses are more in keeping with modern drinking habits; your guests can pace themselves more easily and can have their punch straight or on the rocks.

An extension of "the group cocktail concept" will simplify your next Mint Julep party by doing away with the tedious business of crushing ice and trying to keep silver tumblers frosted. Why not a mass Mint Julep? Here's how it works.

PARTY MINT JULEP

MINT SPRIGS

GRANULATED SUGAR

CRUSHED ICE

2 FIFTHS 100-PROOF STRAIGHT BOURBON

Partially fill punch bowl with cracked ice and place large mixing bowl within it. Fill inner bowl with mint sprigs, being careful to select only small tender leaves from top. Sprinkle with sugar and, using muddler, bruise each leaf so mint essence will permeate bowl. Fill bowl completely with finely crushed ice and add copious amounts of your favorite straight bourbon. Garnish with more mint sprigs and ladle ice, bourbon, and mint into individual silver mugs.

Other old reliable standbys can be served in the same manner. It is ideal for French 75s, a great classic Champagne concoction that will quickly kindle a towering celebratory spirit amongst all who gather 'round the community cocktail bowl. Although made from noble ingredients—cognac and Champagne—this potation evolved from improbable beginnings: the battlefields of the First World War. American doughboys likened the kick of this drink to the recoil of that redoubtable French army field piece with a bore diameter of 75 millimeters, hence the name French 75. The unwary should be warned: it still packs a wallop.

THE COMPATIBLE FRENCH 75

1 DOZEN LEMONS	3 FIFTHS EXTRA-DRY
GRANULATED SUGAR	CHAMPAGNE
1 PINT COGNAC	LEMON PEEL

Squeeze juice from lemons into punch bowl and sweeten to taste with sugar. Add cognac and mix with Champagne. Garnish with lemon peel and serve in 12-ounce Collins glasses with cube of ice apiece. Makes about 3 quarts.

Here is another compatible drink that will buoy up any brunch.

PARK AVENUE ORANGE BLOSSOM

2 QUARTS FRESH ORANGE JUICE   3 FIFTHS EXTRA-DRY
6-OUNCE JAR MARASCHINO   CHAMPAGNE
    CHERRIES

Pour orange juice into punch bowl and add entire contents of jar of maraschino cherries. Mix well and then stir in Champagne. Ladle into 8-ounce Champagne tulips that have been thoroughly chilled. Makes a little over 4 quarts.

Glögg is a great traditional Swedish festive drink that is served during the *Jul*, or Christmas season, but is appropriate any time that the weather is nippy. The word *glögg* means "glow"; whether it takes its meaning from the fact that sugar is flamed during its preparation or from the magical warmth it brings to a gathering on a cold winter's night is unimportant. But it is vital that it be made meticulously. Like many another celebrated cheering cup, this traditional Swedish punch has been sorely violated and abused by those who do not understand its subtle charms. Here is an authentic Swedish recipe.

GLÖGG

1 CUP BLANCHED ALMONDS

1 CUP RAISINS

1/2 CUP DRIED FIGS OR
    APRICOTS

1/4 CUP DRIED ORANGE PEEL

3 CINNAMON STICKS

1 TABLESPOON CARDAMOM
    SEEDS

1 TEASPOON WHOLE CLOVES

1 FIFTH 100-PROOF VODKA

1 FIFTH RED BORDEAUX WINE

1/2 POUND SUGAR CUBES

In large saucepan or chafing dish place almonds, raisins, figs or apricots, orange peel, cinnamon sticks, cardamom seeds, and cloves and mix with vodka and wine (preferably a good full-bodied Médoc). Cover pan and heat gradually until mixture reaches boiling point. While allowing glögg to steep for a few minutes, put sugar cubes in ladle or sieve, dip into hot glögg, and ignite. Add some additional vodka to ladle to ensure a festive flare-up. Keep dousing ladle into mixture until all sugar is dissolved. Serve in mugs or wineglasses with a little of the fruit and almonds. Makes a bit less than 2 quarts.

At its original and authentic best, glögg was made with an *unflavored* aquavit called Renat Brännvin. Somewhere along the line someone must have said, "Funny thing, everywhere else in the world, *Renat Brännvin* is called VODKA." "Are you sure?" "Absolutely." "Then that's what we'll call it: 'ABSOLUT VODKA.'"

A prepared glögg mix consisting of spices and dried fruits can be obtained at most stores specializing in Scandinavian delicacies. It is quite satisfactory and will save some time for the busy party maker, but you'll have more fun if you make your own.

Here is another authentic Swedish glögg formula, with a little more authority, that will positively turn any affair into a full-blown rally.

SVEN'S GLÖGG

$^1/_2$ GALLON DRY RED WINE

1 PINT PORT WINE

$^1/_2$ CUP DRY VERMOUTH

1 CUP BLANCHED ALMONDS

1 CUP SEEDLESS RAISINS

$^1/_4$ CUP DRIED BITTER ORANGE
PEEL

4 CINNAMON STICKS

$1^1/_2$ TABLESPOONS CARDAMOM
SEEDS

1 TABLESPOON WHOLE CLOVES

1 TEASPOON ANISEED (ANISE)

1 TEASPOON FENNEL SEED

$^2/_3$ CUP GRANULATED SUGAR OR
TO TASTE

1 PINT VODKA

1 PINT COGNAC

1 PINT RYE

Pour dry red wine, port, and vermouth into large bowl. Add almonds and raisins. Place orange peel, cinnamon sticks, cardamom seeds, cloves, aniseed, and fennel seed in cloth bag and add it to wine mixture. Cover and let soak overnight. The next day, pour mixture into large saucepan. Slowly heat, then add sugar to taste (depending on sweetness of wines and raisins). Let simmer for several minutes. Remove from heat and add vodka, cognac, and rye. Cover pan and heat gradually until mixture reaches boiling point. Take out cloth bag and pour glögg into chafing dish over low heat. Put chafing dish on large tray and arrange glögg mugs, spoons, and gingersnaps around it. Bring the whole tray to your guests. Just before serving, remove lid and ignite. Extinguish flames and ladle glögg, almonds, and raisins into mugs. Makes about 1 gallon. Store leftover glögg in refrigerator, where it will keep for weeks. Actually, the flavor improves with a little aging.

Glögg should always be drunk to the accompaniment of lusty old drinking songs intermingled with loud shouts of *"Skål!"*

Hot Tips—No. 21

When serving hot drinks that require the use of boiling water or the addition of extremely hot liquors (alcohol should never be boiled where drinks are concerned), remember to place a long knife or spoon in the glass to prevent cracking. Preheating glasses by rinsing with hot water will help keep hot drinks hot. Metallic mugs and goblets are not recommended for drinks intended to be served and drunk piping hot.

The traditional American counterpart to glögg is another widely misunderstood cold-weather bracer: hot buttered rum. It also has been subjected to fearsome misuse—at one extreme, appearing as a tepid, slightly rancid mixture resembling diluted motor oil, and at the other, as an acrid, greasy grog, powerful enough to sear the gullet of a sword-swallower. The secret to building this fine old American hand-me-down lies in neither strength nor weakness, but in carefully combining the proper ingredients to produce the effect that our colonial ancestors intended: a delectable combination of dark rum, spices, and butter, a concoction to be savored for its delicate aromatic qualities and flavor as well as for its great restorative powers.

Here is a traditional recipe.

HOT BUTTERED RUM

BOILING WATER

2 HEAPING TEASPOONS BROWN
   SUGAR

1 CINNAMON STICK

LEMON PEEL

CLOVES

$2^1/_2$ OUNCES DARK JAMAICA
   RUM

1 TABLESPOON BUTTER

FRESHLY GRATED NUTMEG

Preheat large mug by rinsing with boiling water. Add brown sugar, cinnamon stick, and small piece of lemon peel that has been studded with cloves. Pour in just enough boiling water to dissolve sugar, and add dark Jamaica rum. Add more boiling water, mix well, and place butter on top of mixture. Sprinkle with nutmeg and serve steaming hot. Makes 1 drink.

The last recipe can be varied in many ways, but a dark, heavy-bodied rum works best to produce the mellow butter-rum flavor that is so highly treasured in this drink. The use of maple sugar (or syrup) and certain aromatic varieties of honey as sweeteners is worth investigating. If the night is especially dreary and it begins to look as if the high point of your party will occur when everybody starts putting on his hat and coat, you may as a last resort try flaming your hot buttered rum. If this doesn't help, then nothing will, but then you can console yourself with this mighty fine grog.

FLAMING HOT BUTTERED RUM

2 HEAPING TEASPOONS BROWN
SUGAR
1 CINNAMON STICK
LEMON PEEL
CLOVES
BOILING WATER
2 1/2 OUNCES DARK JAMAICA
RUM

GRANULATED SUGAR
1/2 OUNCE 151-PROOF
DEMERARA RUM
1 TABLESPOON BUTTER
PINCH OF FRESHLY GRATED
NUTMEG

Follow the directions for Hot Buttered Rum, above. Before adding butter, place a little sugar and Demerara rum for each serving in ladle. Warm by partially immersing bowl of ladle in very hot water. Ignite rum and pour flaming into each mug. Add butter and nutmeg and serve immediately. Makes 1 drink.

For impromptu gatherings when friends drop in after football games or just drop in, here are two spectacular blazers that can be made on short notice. Those in your inner circle who are addicted to the habit of re-freshing themselves with icy drinks no matter what the season will be gratified (perhaps even stunned) to discover how quickly and efficiently hot spirits will do their work.

JACK-THE-GRIPPER

1 FIFTH (750 ML) APPLEJACK

1 CUP GRANULATED SUGAR

JUICE OF 1 LEMON, PEEL
    RESERVED

2 TABLESPOONS ANGOSTURA
    BITTERS

CINNAMON STICKS

2 CUPS BOILING WATER

Heat applejack with sugar, juice of lemon, and Angostura bitters in flam-ing pan of chafing dish over direct heat. Add several cinnamon sticks and garnish with peel of lemon. Ignite and then quickly add just enough boiling water to extinguish flames. Serve scalding hot in mugs. Makes about ten 4-ounce servings.

The Blue Blazer is included in deference to that ever-growing horde of Scotch devotees who have spent so many happy hours carefully acquir-ing their taste for Highland malt whisky in all of its many blends and variations. This potation will satisfy the most fastidious Scotch drinker—particularly if he or she has spent a cold winter's day out of doors. The Blue Blazer was reputedly the invention of a legendary bar-tender by the name of Jerry Thomas who held court at the old Metro-politan Hotel, a renowned New York City watering place of the 1850s. The adventurous host is warned to practice privately with a little cold water before scheduling a public performance.

THE BLUE BLAZER

HOT WATER   SCOTCH

1 TEASPOON HONEY OR SIMPLE

SYRUP (SEE INDEX)

Two sturdy mugs are required: one barely half filled with hot water in which honey or Simple Syrup has been dissolved, the other less than half filled with warmed Scotch. Ignite whisky and pour back and forth from one mug to the other until thoroughly mixed. If done with aplomb, in a dimly lit room, the effect will be that of a continuous stream of blue fire.

Since hors d'oeuvres are the low point of most cocktail parties, they are worth special attention on your part. Counterfeit canapés and the usual assorted offal that is served perfunctorily during the cocktail hour have ruined more promising dinners than anything else save those extra-extra-dry martinis. Again "the focal point rule" suggests a happy solution. Have two or three selections of quality and in quantity and feature them importantly on your buffet or sideboard. An elegant threesome might consist of a really fine block of aged Cheddar, Port du Salut, or English Stilton cheese, a Smithfield ham, and a large bowl of jumbo Gulf shrimp. Instead of the usual assortment of packaged crackers, purchase two or three kinds of dark bread of the type made by small local bakeries, which is readily obtainable in all Swedish, Kosher, and Italian delicatessens. Punch out bread rounds with a cookie cutter and serve toasted and as is, in baskets, and let your hungry guests make their own canapés—fresh. The hors d'oeuvres selection can be varied endlessly: king or Dungeness crab in big chunks, thinly sliced Italian Prosciutto ham, smoked salmon, cold roast beef, sautéed chicken livers, smoked turkey, and, of course, an endless variety of cheeses and sausages available wherever fine foods are sold. You may wish to simplify matters and settle on just one important appetizer. An iced bowl of caviar needs no explaining. The Iranian variety is excellent, is frequently cheaper than Russian caviar, and can be found at fine food stores either fresh or preserved. Pâté de foie gras from Strasbourg is also in the blue-ribbon class, and while the pure goose liver is expensive, there are many forms of the pâté that are highly recommended and moderately priced.

Those who prefer a potpourri can take inspiration from the Dutch *riestaffel* and serve a variety of delicacies to be mixed and matched by guests in accordance with their own imagination and taste.

A table with do-it-yourself hors d'oeuvres is guaranteed to be a focal point. While many selections are offered, it is, in effect, a single unit, for the challenge of experimentation is indeed a unifying force not to be underestimated—particularly when aided by the effects of an inspired punch. Take a dozen soup or salad bowls and strike out in bold new directions. It is entirely possible that your soirée may turn out to be a time of revelation and discovery. The selection, the variety, the contrasts are up to you. Here are some possibilities: deviled ham, Cheddar cheese puréed with port wine, Major Grey's Chutney, ground beef tartare, smoked salmon, chopped tongue, chopped gherkins, ground chicken livers, potted meat, piñon nuts, cream cheese, chopped onions, pâté de foie gras, chopped egg, salmon pâté, chopped olives, minced ham, pâté of smoked turkey, minced clams, lobster pâté, thinly sliced Vienna sausages, smoked sturgeon, herring fillets, and minced canned chicken. All the ingredients in this microcosmic smorgasbord (and many others that will occur to you) when massed together provide a dramatic solution to the appetizer problem. Baskets of toast points, bread rounds, and Swedish crisp bread will complete the ensemble. Now stand back and watch your guests go to work making the hors d'oeuvres that you would have spent hours assembling—hours before the party.

You will need some sauces, lively and piquant, for meat, seafood and fowl. Here are three basic and indispensable liquid condiments that are *de rigueur* for any well-graced hors d'oeuvres board.

BASIC COCKTAIL SAUCE

1 BOTTLE KETCHUP

1 TABLESPOON LEMON JUICE

1 TABLESPOON
WORCESTERSHIRE SAUCE

DASH OF TABASCO SAUCE

2 TABLESPOONS FRESHLY
GROUND HORSERADISH OR
TO TASTE

1 TEASPOON CRACKED
PEPPERCORNS

DRIED DILL, TARRAGON,
OREGANO, OR THYME
(OPTIONAL)

Pour bottle of your favorite ketchup into mixing bowl, add lemon juice, Worcestershire sauce, dash or two of Tabasco sauce, horseradish (amount depends on freshness and strength), and cracked peppercorns. Mix thoroughly and let stand in refrigerator for at least 4 hours. Accent herbs can be used at your option.

REMOULADE SAUCE

1 TABLESPOON CHOPPED FRESH
   TARRAGON

1 TABLESPOON CHOPPED
   CAPERS

1 TABLESPOON CHOPPED FRESH
   PARSLEY

1 TABLESPOON CHOPPED SWEET
   GHERKINS

1 TABLESPOON CHOPPED FRESH
   CHERVIL

2 ANCHOVY FILLETS

3 TEASPOONS PREPARED
   MUSTARD

$^1/_2$ TEASPOON LEMON JUICE

1 CUP MAYONNAISE

BLACK PEPPER

PINCH OF CELERY SALT

Place tarragon, capers, parsley, sweet gherkins, and chervil in mixing bowl. Add anchovy fillets and, with spoon, mash into other ingredients. Add prepared mustard and lemon juice. Blend mixture into mayonnaise and beat well. Season with several grinds of pepper and celery salt.

ENGLISH MUSTARD

3 TABLESPOONS DRY MUSTARD

1 TEASPOON SALT

$^1/_2$ TEASPOON WHITE PEPPER

4 TABLESPOONS FIRMLY PACKED
   BROWN SUGAR

CIDER VINEGAR

To dry mustard, add salt, white pepper, and brown sugar. Mix thoroughly with just enough hot vinegar to make thick and creamy. Prepare at least a day in advance so that mustard has an opportunity to age.

Cover and let stand at room temperature. If you like your mustard with a little more bite, simply reduce amount of brown sugar.

The ultimate refinement of the community cocktail hour depends on optimum involvement, which means simply that the more you can get your guests to do in the way of serving themselves, the more they will enjoy your party. The psychology is unbeatable, for your friends are being given an opportunity to participate actively, to contribute importantly, and to further their own enjoyment all at the same time. A fine example of social byplay in action is the "cook-in," the indoor version of the cookout. It works its special magic so well that we will extend it beyond the happy sanctuary of the cocktail hour and make it the pièce de résistance of our party supper as well. There is, literally and figuratively, no better way to fire up the party.

As for the cocktail hour, make it a point to include in your selection of appetizer fixin's some tiny frankfurters, Swedish meatballs, thin tender sirloin strips, parboiled chicken livers, and any other viand that lends itself to quick cooking over an open flame. Provide a number of long fondue forks or ordinary meat skewers as toasting tools and then take a small hibachi, fondue pot, or other suitable metal container, fill it with a generous glop of canned heat, ignite, and turn your guests loose on their cook-in. They will love broiling their little hors d'oeuvre kabobs over the open fire and you may find that you are well on your way to cornering the market for Sterno in your neighborhood.

Hot Tips—No. 22

For protracted cooking with canned heat, you will find that some porous stones, slag, cinders, small pieces of cement block, certain kinds of porous brick, or whatever, will extend the cooking life of

your fire. The porous material absorbs the alcohol during the com-
bustion process and delivers a more constant, even heat. Charcoal and
other materials are taboo for indoor cooking (except in the fireplace)
because they release an excessive amount of carbon monoxide.

Dinner should be a cooperative affair. Now that you have collectively conquered anemic highballs, sleazy snacks, and the other deadfalls that comprise many a lackluster cocktail convocation, it would be anticlimactic to settle for the formula buffet or settle down to the same old sit-down dinner. Having fired up the party by taking advantage of the irresistible "herd instinct," we must forge on relentlessly to our culinary denouement like characters caught up in a classic Greek drama, which in this instance will not be Greek but rather a pleasant combination of Swiss and American.

Fondue Bourguignonne is a Swiss innovation that reaches its apogee when prepared with fine American cuts of beef. The recipe is amazingly simple. It consists of cooking pieces of tender beef in a pot of boiling cooking oil, each diner cooking his own portion to suit his taste. You will need a *caquelon*, or fondue pot, which is obtainable at moderate cost in the housewares section of most department stores. It is simply a deep cooking pot with handle and lid that can usually be purchased with or without burner and stand. You could, of course, use your chafing dish, but this may be pressed into service for other needs so a separate and complete fondue unit is recommended. The beef tenderloin you select should be the finest available, aged, tender, and prime. Tell your butcher how it will be cooked so that he will be duly impressed by the fact that if the cuts he supplies are less than magnificent, you may suffer an embarrassment from which he may never be allowed to recover. The beef should be cut into 1-inch cubes. Before the cooking begins, you will want to prepare dishes of various condiments and sauces into which the cubes of hot beef can be dipped. Place these around the fondue pot so that they are easily accessible.

Condiments should include generous portions of cracked pepper-corns, salt, paprika, onion powder, hickory-smoked salt, ground ginger, and any other herbs or spices you fancy. In addition to prepared sauces such as Worcestershire, A-1, Escoffier Sauce Diable, and Sauce Robert, you will want to make a good tangy meat sauce, mustard mayonnaise, curry sauce, and Béarnaise sauce. In case you don't have closely guarded family recipes for these sauces, here are some designed to complement the best Fondue Bourguignonne imaginable.

HUNTER'S MEAT SAUCE

5 OUNCES PREPARED MUSTARD

1 TABLESPOON
    WORCESTERSHIRE SAUCE

2 TEASPOONS A-1 SAUCE

2 TEASPOONS HICKORY-SMOKED
    SALT

1/2 TEASPOON CELERY SALT

1/2 TEASPOON WHITE PEPPER

1/2 TEASPOON CRACKED OR
    FRESHLY GROUND BLACK
    PEPPER

Combine all ingredients and mix well.

MUSTARD MAYONNAISE

1/2 CUP MAYONNAISE

1/3 CUP PREPARED MUSTARD

2 TEASPOONS LEMON JUICE

To mayonnaise add prepared mustard (or you can use recipe for English Mustard—see Index) and beat well, adding lemon juice as you mix. Proportions can be varied according to whether a mild or spicy sauce is desired.

CURRY SAUCE

4 TABLESPOONS BUTTER

1 MEDIUM ONION, FINELY
   CHOPPED

1 BAY LEAF

PINCH OF PULVERIZED SAFFRON

PINCH OF DRIED THYME

1 TO 3 TABLESPOONS FINEST
   IMPORTED MADRAS CURRY
   POWDER (DEPENDING ON
   ZESTINESS)

2 TABLESPOONS
   ALL-PURPOSE FLOUR

1/2 CUP CHICKEN STOCK OR
   CONSOMMÉ

1/4 TO 1/2 CUP CREAM
   (DEPENDING ON RICHNESS
   WANTED)

Melt butter in saucepan and add onion, bay leaf, saffron, thyme, curry powder, and flour. Blend well over low heat. Add chicken stock or consommé. Boil for 15 minutes, strain through fine sieve, and blend in cream.

BÉARNAISE SAUCE

2 TABLESPOONS CHOPPED
FRESH TARRAGON

1 TABLESPOON FINELY MINCED
SHALLOTS OR GREEN ONIONS

2 TABLESPOONS FINELY MINCED
FRESH CHERVIL OR PARSLEY

4 OR 5 CRUSHED PEPPERCORNS

2 TABLESPOONS WHITE WINE
VINEGAR

$^1/_4$ CUP DRY WHITE WINE

3 EGG YOLKS

$^1/_2$ POUND BUTTER

1 TABLESPOON WATER

SALT

In saucepan, mix 1 tablespoon tarragon, shallots or green onions, 1 tablespoon chervil or parsley, and peppercorns with wine vinegar, and wine. Boil mixture over medium heat until reduced to a thick paste. Set aside to cool. Strain mixture, add egg yolks, and beat until light and fluffy. Divide soft butter into three equal portions. Place pan over hot water, add water and first portion of butter, and stir briskly. Stir constantly until mixture is smooth. Add remaining portions of butter *gradually* until it all has been blended into sauce. When thick, beat in remaining 1 tablespoon each of tarragon and chervil or parsley. Season to taste with salt and cayenne pepper. The secret of making this sauce is to cook eggs very slowly and incorporate butter very gradually.

When ready to begin the fondue, pour enough cooking oil into your fondue pot to fill it to the halfway mark, and heat it on the stove. When the oil reaches the boiling point, place it on the burner at table, hand guests fondue forks, and turn them loose. Fondue Bourguignonne should be accompanied by a tossed salad, French bread, and a good full-bodied Burgundy.

Some thought should be given to the selection of a good cooking oil. Coconut fat is frequently used in Switzerland because of its good cooking qualities (it doesn't foam when boiled) and absence of aftertaste, but it is loaded with saturated fats. Peanut oil or a mixture of half peanut oil and half butter is also popular. Any good commercial oil is acceptable if it does not take on a strong flavor when boiled or smoke or spatter excessively when subjected to high heat.

People concerned with saturated fat should investigate cooking oils such as canola, olive, corn, sunflower, and macadamia, which are low in saturated fats and high in polyunsaturated and monounsaturated fats.

Another and perhaps better-known version of the cook-in invented by the Swiss is Cheese Fondue. It is also a community activity requiring happy social involvement. Here is a basic recipe utilizing the foregoing setup but sans sauces and condiments.

CHEESE FONDUE

2 GARLIC CLOVES	SALT
2 CUPS DRY WHITE WINE	BLACK PEPPER
3 CUPS GRATED IMPORTED	PINCH OF GRATED NUTMEG
SWISS CHEESE	2 OUNCES KIRSCH
2 TABLESPOONS FLOUR	CREAM (OPTIONAL)
2 TABLESPOONS BUTTER	BREAD CUBES

Rub inside of fondue pot thoroughly with garlic and add Chablis, Riesling, or any other dry white wine. Reduce by boiling on stove until about $1^1/_3$ cups remain. Mix Swiss cheese and flour that has been made into a paste with a little cold water and add to pot. Stir in butter, season with salt and pepper to taste, and add nutmeg and kirsch. Simmer over low heat. Add additional kirsch or cream if fondue becomes too thick. Supply large basket of 1-inch bread cubes with a lot of crust to be dipped into fondue with long forks and eaten directly from pot. (If you are lucky enough to own a fondue set, the Sterno flame will keep cheese from congealing. If not, and cheese begins to get sticky, simply return the pot to the stove and warm the contents over low heat.) Serves 6.

Care should be taken in eating cheese fondue. Traditionally, if a gentleman loses his piece of bread in the fondue pot, he must pay for his carelessness by buying a bottle of wine for the table; and if a woman loses her piece, she must pay another kind of penalty—a kiss to the man on her immediate right or left.

What to serve at the increasingly popular American custom of brunch parties is always a problem. The menu obviously should be light in order to accommodate the considerable amount of drinking that usually precedes the brunch itself. This is a convenience not only for the guests but for the host or hostess as well, who will want to feel (and look) competent enough to prepare this unusual sausage and eggs duo personally.

EGGS J.P.

EGGS	CHOPPED FRESH DILL
TABASCO SAUCE OR DRY MUSTARD	WHITE PEPPER
	BLACK PEPPER
HICKORY-SMOKED SALT	PAPRIKA
CELERY SALT	CHOPPED FRESH PARSLEY

Soft boil enough large eggs to provide each guest a serving of 2. Preheat egg cups (teacups will do) by rinsing with very hot water. In each cup place the following: dash of Tabasco sauce (or pinch of mustard powder), $1/4$ teaspoon hickory-smoked salt, and generous pinch each of celery salt, dill weed, white pepper, and freshly ground black pepper. Place shelled eggs unbroken into cups and garnish with pinch of paprika and parsley. Guests chop up their own eggs and mix them with ingredients at bottom of cup.

KARSTIN SAUSAGE

1 POUND LITTLE PORK
SAUSAGES

BUTTER

$^1/_4$ CUP PURE MAPLE SYRUP

$^1/_3$ CUP 100-PROOF STRAIGHT
BOURBON

Place sausages in water that barely covers bottom of flaming pan of chafing dish. Place over direct heat and cover. Remove cover after 5 minutes and continue cooking until brown. When almost cooked, pour off all excess fat and add enough butter to cover bottom of pan lightly. When butter begins to froth, pour maple syrup over sausages and add bourbon. Ignite and serve flaming portions to each guest. Serves 3.

The cooking process can be speeded up if the initial steps are performed in the kitchen. After pouring off fat, bring pan to table and add butter, maple syrup, and bourbon, and complete on chafing-dish burner.

Hot Tips—No. 23

When flaming dishes in a brightly lighted room (as at a brunch), it is important at the moment of ignition to dim the lights and draw the draperies, or whatever, in order to achieve the proper effect. Alcohol flames are practically invisible in broad daylight. In any case, the display is far more dramatic in subdued light, and after all, one of the true joys of the flaming is in the watching, as any fire lover knows.

For more stately brunches you may wish to substitute a more regal egg dish. Here is a recipe with a devilish twist that you can prepare in your chafing dish, in its entirety, at the table.

EGGS OPORTO
(Formerly Eggs Portugaise)

1 TABLESPOON BUTTER	BLACK PEPPER
4 EGGS	2¼ OUNCES DEVILED HAM
2 TEASPOONS WATER	3 TABLESPOONS PORT WINE
DRY MUSTARD	TOAST (OPTIONAL)
CELERY SALT	

Fill double-boiler pan of chafing dish with enough hot water to barely touch bottom of flaming pan. Add butter to flaming pan. When it bubbles, pour in eggs that have been whipped with a fork with water. Season to taste with pinches of dry mustard, celery salt, and freshly ground pepper. Fold deviled ham into partially cooked eggs. When eggs are nearly ready for serving but still moist, add wine. Allow time for wine to heat but do not overcook. Serve on hot plates, plain or on toast that has been lightly brushed with browned butter. If your taste runs to a lighter wine with eggs, you may wish to substitute a light red wine such as Châteauneuf-du-Pape. Serves 2.

And finally, here is a flaming version of an old late-night favorite that can be prepared quickly to sustain your departing guests for their journey home.

BLAZING HOLE-IN-ONE

1 SLICE BREAD	1 EGG
BUTTER	1 TABLESPOON AQUAVIT

For each serving tear out a hole in center of slice of bread (or use cookie cutter) and butter lightly on both sides. Place bread slices in skillet, chafing dish, or crêpe pan. Break egg carefully and drop in hole without breaking yolk. Sauté as desired, on both sides or sunnyside up. Immediately before serving, pour aquavit in skillet around bread and blaze. Have plenty of eggs and bread on hand, as this is a cinch for seconds.

Successful party-giving is largely a matter of point of view, like cooking, making love, giving a speech, playing bridge, or any other activity involving the interaction of people. In a real sense it reflects your approach to life in general. It's no accident that interesting people seem to have the best parties. If what you serve in the way of food and drink is imaginative, then the rest is simply a matter of blending the best ingredients (including people) plus your personal touch. So, be daring! Get things fired up! Make a firm resolution that your next affair is going to be more than just a blowout (a bad word for pyromaniacs) but a real blast and a night to remember.

SIX

Light Up the Sky!

$\mathscr{O}$utdoor cooking is not simply a matter of moving the kitchen into the backyard; for cooking over an open fire requires an entirely new orientation on the part of the chef, as any outdoorsman who has camped for a time in the bush can attest. Anyone can have a go at a cookout. The setup can be as simple as a campfire or as elaborate as a deluxe chrome-plated, balloon-tired rotisserie complete with motorized spits, smoking oven, warming compartments, and electric lights. But the results will depend almost entirely on the observance of a few basic principles that may seem unorthodox by indoor-kitchen standards but nevertheless will prove out in the glowing embers of the countless cooking fires that nightly light up the sky.

Of first importance is the fuel to be used. Charcoal is universally popular, whether in its natural form or compressed into briquets, since it burns slowly and gives off great heat. Contrary to widely accepted belief, charcoal does not add flavor to food of itself. Flavor is produced almost entirely by the searing effect of direct flame and the prolonged exposure of food to aromatic smoke resulting from fat, natural juices, and various seasonings that drip down upon and are ignited by the hot coals. Certain peculiar notions that have grown up around the lore of the open fire not only are erroneous but seem to be shrewdly calculated to keep people indoors cooking by conventional means on good old reliable gas or electric ranges. One of the misconceptions perpetrated by traditional indoor cooks who write outdoor cookbooks is the stern admonition that the flame must never touch the meat. Actually, the most highly prized flavor in a charcoal-broiled steak is brought about by charring the outside of the meat by the direct application of fire. While this searing process must be done deftly, it is a prime requisite for a properly grilled steak as it not only accents the flavor but seals in the natural juices of the meat. Another popular old wives' tale has to do with the business of seasoning meat before it is grilled. Dire results are threatened as if some arcane alchemy occurs in the mating of fire and condiment. Practically speaking, the burning of condiments mixed with meat drippings makes the smoke that makes the flavor. This synergetic action produces flavor to a far greater degree than can be achieved by conventional kitchen broiling.

Wood is also an excellent outdoor cooking fuel. Hickory is perhaps the best known. Its reputation is well earned, for only after you have seared a fine, aged sirloin in a hickory fire and then finished it slowly over a bed of glowing coals can you appreciate the enormous flavor potential of outdoor cookery. Mesquite, a scrub tree that grows in the

Southwest, has become popular in recent years. It imparts a woody, herbal flavor to food on the grill. Other woods recommended are any slow-burning hardwood such as sugar maple or oak and especially the fruit woods: apple, peach, cherry, orange, and lemon. Conifers such as pine, spruce, yew, and juniper should be avoided as they impart a strong flavor akin to turpentine.

The type of outdoor cooking equipment you select is largely a matter of personal choice, but be certain that your grill is adjustable so that the distance between the broiling surface and the fire can be regulated easily. This gives you complete control over the temperature and thus over the speed at which food is cooked. Also desirable, but not mandatory, are air intake holes in the firebox of your grill that can be opened or closed to provide the right amount of draft. If your grill does not have this feature, then partially fill the firebox with coarse gravel or stones as a base upon which charcoal will be laid. A hibachi is ideal since it is designed to provide concentrated heat in a small, compact area, and the newer models are fully adjustable.

Hot Tips—No. 24

A few handfuls of wet hickory or mesquite chips thrown on the fire will impart a matchless outdoor flavor to almost anything that can be grilled. They should be well soaked in a can of water so that they will burn slowly. The resulting aroma, which permeates the air as well as the food, is one of the world's great appetite energizers.

When preparing the firebed in your grill, remember that a single layer of charcoal briquets is adequate for most cooking chores. Start with just enough charcoal to approximate the dimensions of whatever is to be cooked. More charcoal can be added after the fire is under way by placing additional briquets around the periphery of the firebed and pushing them in toward the center as the fire burns down. Lighting charcoal is a problem that can be virtually eliminated by the use of an electric fire lighter. A fire chimney is also very effective and can be made easily from a No. 10-size can. Remove both ends with a can opener and punch holes or cut slots in one end. Place the ventilated end down in the firebox, add eight or ten briquets that have been soaked in a commercial liquid charcoal lighter, and ignite. Add additional dry briquets, and when the fire is under way, remove the chimney and spread charcoal under the cooking area. Wait until the charcoal is thoroughly lit before starting to cook. When each briquet is covered with a light gray ash, you are ready. For optimum heat, whisk off ashes, as they act as an insulating layer. Cooking too fast and overcooking are the most common causes of failure on the patio. Proper control of the fire will eliminate the former, but only experience can remedy the latter.

Hot Tips—No. 25

As a rule, don't marinate beef that you intend to broil—whether in the kitchen or out on the patio. This vestige of barbarism dates back to a day when beef was boiled, baked, and roasted to a dull, drab gray. Tastes have changed. Today people want their beef juicy and with a wholesome, natural flavor. The use of meat tenderizers is another matter. Some of the best-tasting cuts of beef are not the tenderest. Meat tenderizers that make meat more edible without affecting the flavor are invaluable.

Since beefsteak is undoubtedly one of the most "cooked out" of all viands, here is a good basic recipe that will enhance your status as a proficient *chef de bois* all in the short space of a single summer's eve. Whatever cut of beef you choose—sirloin, T-bone, porterhouse, or club—buy the best and be sure it is properly aged. Look for beef that is bright red and well marbled with light cream-colored fat. Aging gives the outer layer of fat a hard, waxy texture. A good butcher is your best guarantee of good meat. He is worth cultivating.

ALL-AMERICAN STEAK

1 STRIP SIRLOIN STEAK	WHITE PEPPER
(1½ TO 2 INCHES THICK)	A-1 SAUCE
SALT	WORCESTERSHIRE SAUCE
HICKORY-SMOKED SALT	2 TEASPOONS PREPARED
CELERY SALT	MUSTARD
BLACK PEPPER	

On thick, individual strip sirloin steak, add a sprinkling of the following ingredients *before* broiling, in order listed: salt, hickory-smoked salt, celery salt, generous grinds of black pepper, and pinch of white pepper and rub into steak. Add 3 or 4 dashes of A-1 Sauce. Sprinkle well with Worcestershire sauce. Cover with thin layer of prepared mustard. Place on grill close to firebed with condiment side down. When well seared by flames from drippings, raise grill and finish slowly. Repeat procedure on uncooked side. Serve sizzling on hot plate. Steak should be accompanied by a California pinot noir.

A good barbecued steak deserves an equally distinguished salad. This recipe is made for those who lean toward a tart rather than an oily dressing, and was inspired by a highly respected Chicago restaurant that helped make the Windy City justly famous for robust steaks and hearty salads.

CORONA DRESSING

1 GARLIC CLOVE

1/4 TEASPOON SALT

1/4 TEASPOON CELERY SALT

PINCH OF DRY MUSTARD

BLACK PEPPER

1/4 TEASPOON DRIED
   TARRAGON

1/4 TEASPOON WHITE PEPPER

PINCH OF PAPRIKA

3 TABLESPOONS RED OR WHITE
   WINE VINEGAR

2 TABLESPOONS LIGHT OLIVE
   OIL

This will take some practice as the proportions can only be approximated. Finely mince garlic clove in bottom of wooden salad bowl. Add salt, celery salt, dry mustard, several generous grinds of black pepper, tarragon, white pepper, and paprika. Mash dry ingredients into garlic with fork until completely pulverized. Add wine vinegar and mix well until all salt is dissolved, then pour in olive oil and blend thoroughly. If too tart, adjust by adding oil. Makes about 1/2 cup.

Corona dressing should be made well in advance, for the longer it stands the better the flavor.

Hot Tips—No. 26

Always salt meat before barbecuing, then add pepper. Salt draws some of the juice to the surface, and this enables the salt and pepper to stick more readily to the meat. If pepper is sprinkled on first, the salt will not adhere. A certain amount of any seasoning will fall into the fire with the drippings, so be generous.

In the volatile world of flambé cookery, we are not satisfied only with the use of fire as a cooking source, but rather with its application in other ways to further enhance the flavor of our fare. This opens a whole new dimension of outdoor cookery, and we are obliged to call upon the spirits to aid us in this worthy cause. As a general rule, anything that can be flamed indoors can be fired successfully at grillside. Bourbon Steak is a case in point.

BOURBON STEAK

2 POUNDS PRIME SIRLOIN (CUT THICK)

$^1/_2$ TEASPOON SALT

$^1/_2$ TEASPOON HICKORY-SMOKED SALT

BLACK PEPPER

3 TABLESPOONS BUTTER

1 TABLESPOON CHOPPED FRESH PARSLEY

1 TABLESPOON CHOPPED SHALLOTS

$^1/_3$ CUP BOURBON, WARMED

Cover sirloin with salt, hickory-smoked salt, and generous layer of freshly ground black pepper well in advance of cooking. While grilling steak, place a sturdy oval flaming pan over coals until it is very hot. Just before steak is done, melt butter in pan with parsley and shallots. Place steak in pan and cover both sides with butter mixture. Pour on warmed bourbon and blaze. Serve immediately with a good Médoc or California cabernet sauvignon. Serves 4.

Even the humble hamburger can benefit from a little backyard bour-
bonizing. In the following recipe, cognac can be used in place of bourbon, since some will find that the latter is more harmonious with the
Roquefort cheese mixture.

HAMBURGER ROYALE

$1^1/_2$ POUNDS GROUND BEEF

$1^1/_2$ TABLESPOONS MINCED
    ONION OR SHALLOTS

$1^1/_2$ TEASPOONS HICKORY-
    SMOKED SALT

1 TABLESPOON
    WORCESTERSHIRE SAUCE

BLACK PEPPER

$1/_3$ CUP BOURBON OR COGNAC

2 TABLESPOONS BUTTER

3 TABLESPOONS ROQUEFORT
    CHEESE

TOASTED BUNS OR DARK RYE
    BREAD

To ground beef add onion or shallots, hickory-smoked salt, Worcestershire sauce, and generous amount of freshly ground pepper. Mix thoroughly, form into individual patties, and sear well on grill to keep in
juices. When ready to serve, ladle small amount of blazing bourbon or
cognac on each patty. Blend butter and Roquefort cheese well, until
creamy mixture. Spread on each burger. Place hamburgers on toasted
buns or dark rye bread. Serves 2 to 3. A bright Côtes-du-Rhône or a
stein of full-bodied English ale makes this royal fare indeed.

This recipe is equally delicious for regular cuts of beef and when
used thus becomes known as *Steaks au Roquefort flambés*. The only basic
change is the omission of the minced shallots. Charcoal-broiled hamburgers, whether flambéed or plain, benefit from the use of various
kinds of stuffing. Diced Cheddar, Swiss, or Mozzarella cheese sealed inside hamburgers before broiling makes a kind of "hidden cheeseburger"

that is easy to prepare in advance and more toothsome than the original slab-on-patty version. Other stuffings such as pickle relish, chopped peppers, beets, or even diced frankfurters make combinations that are particularly good when barbecued.

Flank steak is cheap in price and rich in taste. In its most popular form, it is known as London broil, which is tender although coarse-grained, but possessed of far more natural flavor than the best filet. It's at its beefy best when broiled over charcoal and flambéed.

FLANK STEAK FLAMBÉ

SALT	1 POUND FLANK STEAK
HICKORY-SMOKED SALT	1 TABLESPOON SPICY BROWN
BLACK PEPPER	MUSTARD
2 TEASPOONS WORCESTERSHIRE	$^1/_3$ CUP RYE OR AQUAVIT,
SAUCE	WARMED

Sprinkle salts and pepper to taste, plus Worcestershire sauce, over entire steak, then spread with thin layer of mustard. Place on grill close to coals with prepared side down, and repeat seasoning process on top side of steak. When cooked, remove to heated flameproof platter, pour on warmed rye or aquavit, and blaze. Meat should be sliced in thin strips across grain. Serves 2. Serve with a good Beaujolais such as a Moulin-à-Vent.

If old Dad, who sallies forth onto the patio once a week to torture some meat on the grill, is hard put to make a presentable barbecue sauce, maybe he needs a new recipe to build his confidence. These three sauces are tested and guaranteed to be fireproof.

EASY BARBECUE SAUCE

$^3/_4$ CUP BUTTER

$^1/_4$ CUP WORCESTERSHIRE

    SAUCE

Mix butter with Worcestershire sauce and heat in saucepan. Keep warm on side of grill and douse steaks, hamburgers, chicken, and seafood liberally as you cook. A pastry brush makes the task easy. Makes 1 cup sauce.

Skokie Valley Barbecue Sauce requires no cooking and can be made well in advance. The proportions are approximate and should be varied to suit individual tastes.

SKOKIE VALLEY BARBECUE SAUCE

8-OUNCE JAR SPICY BROWN
    MUSTARD
2 TABLESPOONS
    WORCESTERSHIRE SAUCE
1 TABLESPOON A-1 SAUCE
1 TEASPOON HICKORY-SMOKED
    SALT

$^1/_2$ TEASPOON WHITE PEPPER
1 TABLESPOON GRATED
    HORSERADISH
DASH OF TABASCO SAUCE
BLACK PEPPER
3 TABLESPOONS KETCHUP OR
    CHILI SAUCE (OPTIONAL)

To contents of jar of mustard add Worcestershire sauce, A-1 Sauce, hickory-smoked salt, white pepper, horseradish, Tabasco sauce, and several generous grinds of black pepper. Mix well. Can be spread on meat before, during, and after grilling. Great on steaks, hamburgers, and hot dogs. A good slug of ketchup or chili sauce can be added as an option. Makes a little over $1^1/_4$ cups of sauce.

Hot Tips—No. 27

Before cooking on your grill, grease the grid well with a piece of bacon or suet. This will prevent food from sticking and will materially reduce your cleaning chores after the ball is over. One cause of food sticking is too much heat and flame. Experienced chefs keep a clothes sprinkler, water pistol, bulb syringe, or similar water dispenser at hand to dampen the fire when it gets too rambunctious.

Feel free to vary the proportions in this recipe until it is custom-made to your taste.

ALL-PURPOSE BARBECUE SAUCE

$^1/_2$ CUP BUTTER

1 MEDIUM ONION, CHOPPED

1 GARLIC CLOVE, MINCED

BOUQUET GARNI: 2
TABLESPOONS TOTAL DRIED
PARSLEY, TARRAGON, AND
THYME

1 TABLESPOON LEMON JUICE

$^1/_2$ CUP DRY WHITE WINE

$^2/_3$ CUP KETCHUP

2 TABLESPOONS FIRMLY PACKED
BROWN SUGAR

1 TABLESPOON
WORCESTERSHIRE SAUCE

$^1/_2$ TEASPOON CHILI POWDER

$^1/_2$ TEASPOON DRY MUSTARD

$^1/_2$ TEASPOON CELERY SALT

2 OR 3 DASHES OF TABASCO
SAUCE

BLACK PEPPER

1 CUP WATER

In saucepan, melt butter. Brown onion with garlic. Add bouquet garni, lemon juice, wine, ketchup, brown sugar, Worcestershire sauce, chili powder, dry mustard, celery salt, Tabasco sauce, and several generous grinds of pepper to taste. Stir in water and simmer gently for 1 hour. Remove bouquet garni. Can be used for all meats, chicken, and shellfish. Makes approximately 2 cups.

Lobster takes on an entirely new aspect when broiled over charcoal and flambéed. Here are two recipes adapted for outdoor cooking that had their genesis in more genteel surroundings.

HOMARD FLAMBÉ

1 LOBSTER

LEMON BUTTER (SEE NEXT
    RECIPE)

BUTTER

1 TEASPOON CHOPPED FRESH
    PARSLEY

1 TABLESPOON CHOPPED FRESH
    TARRAGON

1 TABLESPOON COGNAC

$^1/_4$ CUP PERNOD, WARMED

Select medium ($1^1/_2$-pound) lobster for each person. Split lobster, remove intestinal vein and sac behind eyes, and save green tomalley and coral. Rinse lobster in cold water, spread lemon butter on meat, place on grill, and broil until meat is opaque. In small saucepan, melt enough butter (about 2 tablespoons) to make a creamy mixture when combined with tomalley and coral. Add parsley, tarragon, and cognac to butter mixture and cook on grill for 5 minutes. When lobsters are done, spread hot sauce over meat. Flame lobster with warmed Pernod and eat with your favorite beer or a fine Montrachet. Serves 1.

LEMON BUTTER

$^1/_3$ CUP BUTTER

2 TABLESPOONS LEMON JUICE

1 TABLESPOON FINELY
    CHOPPED FRESH PARSLEY

$^1/_2$ TEASPOON SALT

PINCH OF BLACK PEPPER

Cream butter and stir in lemon juice, parsley, salt, and freshly ground pepper. Beat mixture until light and fluffy. Makes slightly less than $^1/_2$ cup.

The following recipe is designed for use with lobster tails since there is no tomalley sauce involved.

LANGOUSTE FLAMBÉE AU FENOUIL

4 LOBSTER TAILS

2 TABLESPOONS CHOPPED
FRESH TARRAGON

1 CUP VODKA, WARMED

6 TO 8 DRIED FENNEL STALKS
(CAN BE FOUND AT FOOD
SPECIALTY STORES)

1 CUP LEMON BUTTER (SEE
PRECEDING RECIPE)

If frozen lobster tails are used, thaw before grilling. An hour in advance, place tarragon in covered container with vodka to be used for flaming. Remove under shell and slit back of shell partially so lobsters will lie flat. Grill over medium heat for 5 minutes shell down. Turn, baste and grill 5 minutes more. Check for doneness. Meat should be juicy and opaque. Just before lobsters are done, throw stalks of dried fennel on coals and pour on about half the warmed vodka-tarragon mixture. After it has blazed for a minute, turn lobster, meat side up, and blaze with remainder of vodka. Serve with melted Lemon Butter. Serves 4.

Cooking seafood in a rack over a bed of fennel is common in southern France. It is recommended for several different kinds of fish, including trout, striped bass, and bluefish.

POISSON FLAMBÉ PROVENCALE

1 LARGE BLUEFISH

OLIVE OIL

SALT

BLACK PEPPER

BOUQUET GARNI: 1
TABLESPOON TOTAL DRIED
PARSLEY, BAY LEAF, AND DILL

4 STALKS DRIED FENNEL
(FOUND AT SPECIALTY FOOD
STORES)

$1/2$ CUP ARMAGNAC OR
COGNAC, WARMED

Clean bluefish but do not remove head. Brush with olive oil, season with salt, pepper, and bouquet garni. Place fish on grill in a hinged broiling rack. Broil on both sides. Before serving, throw stalks of dried fennel on coals and blaze with $1/4$ cup heated brandy, which should be poured directly on fennel. After exposing both sides of fish briefly to blazing fennel, remove to heated serving platter, pour on remainder of brandy, and flame. Serve with lemon wedges, melted butter, and French-toasted bread with Anchovy Butter (see next recipe). Serves 4.

ANCHOVY BUTTER

BUTTER

ANCHOVY PASTE

LEMON JUICE

To every 3 tablespoons butter, add 1 tablespoon anchovy paste. Blend well until smooth and creamy. Add dash of lemon juice for accent.

This recipe works equally well whether with scallops cooked *en brochette* or *en masse* in a rack. For esthetic reasons as well as for ease of handling, we have elected *en brochette*.

SCALLOPS EN BROCHETTE FLAMBÉ

2 POUNDS LARGE FRESH
    SCALLOPS

1/2 CUP LIGHT OLIVE OIL

1/4 CUP LEMON JUICE

2 TEASPOONS SALT

1/2 TEASPOON WHITE PEPPER

DASH OF BLACK PEPPER

BACON SLICES

PAPRIKA

VODKA, WARMED

Select choice fresh scallops, rinse in cold water, and drain. Place in bowl with light olive oil, lemon juice, salt, white pepper, and freshly ground black pepper. Let stand for 45 minutes. Wrap scallops in lean bacon strips cut to size and place on skewers. Save sauce for basting. Place skewers on grill and sprinkle with ground pepper and paprika. Broil for 10 to 15 minutes, or until bacon is crisp. Immediately before serving, pour warmed vodka along length of each skewer, ignite, and bring to table blazing. Serves 4. A well-chilled Chablis, Sancerre, or California sauvignon blanc will make beautiful music with this dish.

The quiet clam (whether it is the petite littleneck or the larger cherrystone or quahog) can be grilled but blazing is unnecessary, since flambéing would not enhance the natural juices of these benevolent bivalves.

GRILLED CLAMS

CLAMS   LEMON JUICE
BUTTER   CRACKED PEPPERCORNS

Scrub clams thoroughly in cold water, making certain to remove *all* sand. Place on grill and broil until shells are open. Remove after a minute or two and serve with little cups of melted butter to each of which has been added dash of lemon juice and a pinch of cracked peppercorns. A well-chilled bottle of Chablis is the classic accompaniment.

A little pyrotechnical magic will even add a touch of glamour to that all-time backyard favorite, the Great American Hot Dog.

FRANKFURTERS FLAMBÉ

FRANKFURTERS   AQUAVIT OR BOURBON
BACON   HOT-DOG BUNS (OPTIONAL)

With a knife, score or make spiral cut from end to end on a pack of your favorite hot dogs. Wrap each frank with strip of bacon. Secure bacon strip with halved toothpicks and grill on all sides until bacon is cooked. Just before serving, pour on small amount of warmed aquavit and blaze. These are marvelous plain or in the traditional bun. If a more pronounced flavor is desired, bourbon can be substituted for aquavit. A tall cold stein of draft beer will help the cause.

Frankfurters flambéed, wrapped in bacon, stuffed with cheese, smothered with chopped onion and pickle relish, or served just plain cry out for the companionship of a palate-pulsating plateful of just one thing: baked beans! Baked beans are so much a part of outdoor eating that there is some question as to whether the world is ready for yet another recipe. But try this anyway.

UNCLE JOHN'S SPICY BAKED BEANS

4 CUPS BAKED BEANS

1/3 CUP KETCHUP

1/2 CUP CHOPPED ONION

1 TEASPOON DRY MUSTARD

2 TABLESPOONS
   WORCESTERSHIRE SAUCE

1/2 CUP FIRMLY PACKED BROWN
   SUGAR

1/4 TEASPOON CAYENNE PEPPER

TABASCO SAUCE

BLACK PEPPER

PINCH OF SALT

6 TO 8 SLICES BACON

Empty 2 cans of your favorite brand of baked beans into casserole and stir in ketchup, onion, mustard, Worcestershire sauce, brown sugar, cayenne pepper, several dashes of Tabasco sauce, several grinds of pepper, and salt. Top beans with strips of lean bacon, cut into thirds. Sprinkle on a little additional brown sugar and bake in a medium oven (350° F) for at least 2 hours. Remove from oven and place near coals or on cooking surface of outdoor grill, where beans will continue to simmer gently. Serves 4.

Charcoal broiling is one of the great traditional cooking methods for all upland game, such as pheasant, grouse, woodcock, and quail, and it does wonders for waterfowl. The following recipe has been field-tested on duck, both wild and domestic.

CANARD DE BOIS FLAMBÉ

2 DUCKS	BLACK PEPPER
ONION	MELTED BUTTER
LEMON JUICE	ONION JUICE
SALT	COGNAC, WARMED

Clean and halve ducks and rub well on all sides with a cut of onion and lemon juice. Season to taste with salt and freshly ground pepper, and broil on spit or directly on grill. While cooking, brush with melted butter that has been laced with dash of lemon juice and onion juice. Broil for about 20 minutes, depending on size of birds and heat of fire. Immediately before serving, pour warmed cognac over ducks and bring to table blazing. Serves 2 to 4, depending on size of birds. If you've been saving a precious bottle of Château Haut-Brion for some suitable occasion, this is it! Otherwise any good red Graves will do.

Pheasant, contrary to popular opinion, is not easy to cook properly. It is a lean bird, lacking the generous amounts of fat found in geese and duck. It is frequently overcooked and ends up on the platter dry, tasteless, and tough. Overcooking is no protection against toughness—at least not on the grill—but you can serve a flavorful and moist pheasant by watching your cooking time. As far as tenderness is concerned, when dealing with wildfowl, you must be prepared to accept nature's bounty as it comes.

FAISAN À L'ORANGE FLAMBÉ

1 PHEASANT

1/2 CUP VEGETABLE OIL

SALT

BLACK PEPPER

1 SMALL ONION, MINCED

1 TEASPOON TOTAL CHOPPED
   FRESH BAY LEAVES, JUNIPER
   BERRIES, AND THYME OR
   ROSEMARY (OPTIONAL)

BACON SLICES OR SALT PORK

1/4 CUP COGNAC, WARMED

1/4 CUP TRIPLE SEC, WARMED

2 TABLESPOONS ORANGE JUICE,
   WARMED

Split pheasant lengthwise and rub all sides well with vegetable oil. Sprinkle with generous amounts of salt and freshly ground pepper. Mix oil with onion, ground pepper, and, if desired, *herbes chasseur* (bay leaves, juniper berries, and rosemary or thyme). Secure several strips of bacon or salt pork on both sides of bird with toothpicks or small skewers, and grill over hot fire, turning frequently and brushing regularly with seasoned vegetable oil. Broil for 30 to 45 minutes, depending on size of birds and heat of fire. Just before serving, remove skewers and pour warmed mixture of cognac, triple sec, and orange juice over pheasant and blaze. Serves 2. A full-bodied Burgundy is the classic wine needed to complement the wonderful woodsy flavor of pheasant.

Some cooks surround the cooking of game with a strange mystique that calls for certain sacred and timeworn practices that, though hoary with the authority of the ages, in fact defy all logic and contemporary experience. It makes no more sense to marinate, for example, a fine cock pheasant before cooking than it does to desecrate a fine beefsteak similarly. Yet in kitchens daily, wildfowl, venison, and even prime sirloins are

subjected to the weird baptism of the marinade. It has been the ruination of more game than any other single cause. If the infusion of a sour, vinegar-and-spice flavor supposedly is needed to temper the "wild taste" of game, then it should not be served to begin with. The very civilized art of cooking is not intended to disguise the natural flavor of food but to complement it. There is a case for marinating certain very tough pieces of meat or meat that is pungent and fatty. The Mongolians and Chinese marinate mutton that comes from the wastes of northern China. It is laced with suet and is strong enough to stop a charge of Tartar bandits. It becomes edible only after a long bath in rice wine, soy sauce, and *épices variées* and bears little resemblance to its original form. Marinating is a defensive measure, to tenderize that which is not tender, to substitute flavor that is tolerable for that which is obnoxious. It should never be used for the more common types of game.

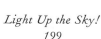

Good old everyday chicken basks in the glory of good seasoning and revels in the flames of the open fire. It can be cooked in a thousand delicious ways. Here are two of them.

POULET FLAMBÉ BONNE FEMME

2 YOUNG BROILING CHICKENS (2½ POUNDS EACH)

1 GARLIC CLOVE, FINELY CHOPPED

2 TEASPOONS DRIED PARSLEY

½ TEASPOON CRACKED PEPPERCORNS

½ CUP MELTED BUTTER

SALT

½ CUP COGNAC OR VODKA, WARMED

Split chickens in half lengthwise and brush well with basting sauce made of garlic, parsley, and cracked peppercorns in melted butter. Sprinkle birds with salt to taste and turn frequently, brushing with additional butter mixture as needed. Broil until thigh cuts easily and there is no pink showing near bone. Serve chickens on hot platter, then pour warmed cognac or vodka over each piece and blaze. Serves 4. A well-chilled Pouilly-Fuissé, Graves, or California pinot chardonnay makes a good companion.

CHICKEN GLENLIVET

2 BROILING CHICKENS   DASH OF LEMON JUICE
    (2$^1/_2$ POUNDS EACH)   PINCH OF DRIED ROSEMARY
$^1/_2$ CUP MELTED BUTTER   SALT
$^1/_2$ TEASPOON DRIED $^1/_2$ CUP GLENLIVET SCOTCH,
    TARRAGON   WARMED
$^1/_2$ TEASPOON DRIED THYME
$^1/_2$ TEASPOON CRACKED
    PEPPERCORNS

Split chickens in half lengthwise and brush well with basting sauce made of melted butter to which has been added tarragon, thyme, cracked peppercorns, lemon juice, and rosemary. Sprinkle generously with salt. Brush with additional basting sauce as needed while broiling. Grill chickens, skin side down, for 20 minutes. Turn, baste with sauce, and grill for 20 minutes more. Turn, baste, and grill from 10 to 20 minutes more. (These cooking times are approximate, depending on heat from grill.) Check for doneness. When done, remove to heated platter and pour over a warmed Glenlivet—or any *unblended*, all-malt Scotch—and blaze. If an unblended Scotch is not available, use your favorite blended Scotch. Serves 4. This is best accompanied by a Beaujolais, Châteauneuf-du-Pape or California cabernet sauvignon.

The perfect complement for all outdoor *grillées* is a well-prepared salad. A few basic rules should be observed. Select greens carefully for variety and freshness. The team concept works well here. If you select a bland leaf such as Boston lettuce, match it up with an accent green such as endive.

You can use a variety of greens, but make a point of having at least two that contrast in both flavor and texture. Greens should be crisped by washing carefully in cold water. Drying is essential, since salad dressing will not adhere to wet leaves. If you do not have a salad basket for drying greens, blot them carefully after washing with paper towels. They can be stored in the refrigerator in a plastic bag, in foil, or wrapped in a dry towel.

Ingredients are extremely important in the making of the dressing. A fine wine vinegar is used by most chefs, and the oil selected must be the very best. A light olive oil or French peanut oil is preferable to the heavier varieties of oils intended primarily for cooking. The classic dressing is Sauce Vinaigrette, which should be made immediately before the salad is served. Dressing should be used sparingly to avoid "drowning" the greens. And no dressing should ever be mixed with greens until the very last minute. This ensures freshness and crispness—two attributes highly prized by salad lovers the world over. Here is the basic French dressing recipe in case you've forgotten.

SAUCE VINAIGRETTE

2 TABLESPOONS WHITE WINE VINEGAR

1 TEASPOON SALT

SCANT ¼ TEASPOON BLACK PEPPER

6 TABLESPOONS SALAD OIL

1 OR 2 PINCHES OF DRY MUSTARD (OPTIONAL)

To wine vinegar add salt and freshly ground pepper. Beat with fork while very gradually adding salad oil. Continue beating or shake in glass jar until mixture becomes cloudy. For added zest, add dry mustard.

In making dressings, it is wise to dissolve the dry ingredients in the vinegar and then add the oil. Oil tends to coat condiments and thus retard the mixing process. White pepper can be used either with or in place of black pepper, as the former will blend with the dressing while the latter defies mixing.

After you have experimented with variations of Sauce Vinaigrette, both ancient and modern, you will enjoy making more elaborate salad dressing combinations. A fine addition to any barbecue is this true salad masterpiece, which lives up to its regal name.

CAESAR SALAD

ROMAINE LETTUCE

2 OR 3 GARLIC CLOVES

1 TEASPOON SALT

$^1/_2$ CUP LIGHT OLIVE OIL

1 CUP DICED FRENCH BREAD
CUBES

1 SMALL CAN ANCHOVY
FILLETS, DICED

$^1/_4$ TEASPOON DRY MUSTARD

$^1/_4$ TEASPOON FRESHLY GROUND
PEPPER

2 TEASPOONS WORCESTERSHIRE
SAUCE

1 EGG

$^1/_4$ CUP GORGONZOLA OR BLUE
CHEESE

2 TABLESPOONS PARMESAN OR
ROMANO CHEESE

JUICE OF $^1/_2$ LEMON

Wash and crisp romaine lettuce, trim core, and remove large ribs. Dry thoroughly and store in refrigerator for several hours. Crush garlic clove (or 2 if you like a strong garlic flavor), knead with salt into a paste, mix with olive oil, and let stand in jar for at least 2 hours in refrigerator. Sauté diced French bread cubes in small pan, using just enough garlic-oil mixture to barely cover bottom. Remove when well browned. To jar of garlic-oil mixture, add anchovy fillets, dry mustard, pepper, and Worcestershire sauce and shake well. Coddle egg by immersing in hot water for 1 minute and then allowing to cool. Prepare salad bowl by rubbing with halved garlic clove. Tear lettuce into easy-to-manage pieces and place in bowl. Shake dressing, pour over greens, and sprinkle on Gorgonzola or blue cheese and Parmesan or Romano cheese. Toss salad. Break coddled egg into salad, add lemon juice, and toss again. Finally, add sautéed bread cubes, toss a third time, and serve immediately. Serves 4.

Not too far from the village of Brewster, New York, is a charming, country hideaway called Whiteoaks where a creative New York advertising man relaxes by inventing good things to eat and drink. Here is one of his creations.

WHITEOAKS SALAD

BIBB LETTUCE AND FIELD
SALAD, OR RAW SPINACH AND
WATERCRESS, OR BOSTON
LETTUCE AND ENDIVE
1/2 CUP LIGHT OLIVE OIL
JUICE OF 1 LEMON

PINCH OF DRY MUSTARD
PINCH OF DRIED TARRAGON
SALT
BLACK PEPPER
1/2 BOTTLE CHAMPAGNE

Two kinds of greens are mandatory—one sharp and one mild. Suggested combinations are: Bibb lettuce and field salad, raw spinach and watercress, Boston lettuce and endive, or pick your own. Wash, dry thoroughly, break up into bite-size pieces, and store in refrigerator until needed. In jar, add olive oil, lemon juice, dry mustard, tarragon, salt, and freshly ground pepper to taste. Mix by shaking in jar. Store in refrigerator. When ready to serve, place lettuce in large salad bowl, pour on oil mixture, and toss. Open chilled Champagne and pour small amount on salad, toss, and serve. After individual plates are filled with salad, additional cold Champagne should be poured on salad without further mixing.

Note that no vinegar is used in the last recipe. The necessary (and subtle) substitute, which makes this salad so unusual and refreshing, is the combination of lemon juice and Champagne. This salad is ideal for a hot summer day and is a good foil for highly seasoned, charcoal-broiled entrées.

Occasionally a salad recipe comes to light that is so hearty and satisfying that it more than fills the bill of fare as a main course. Because of its Scandinavian origins, it is called:

VIKING SALAD

1 MEDIUM CHICKEN

1/2 POUND BACON

8 TO 10 SMALL MUSHROOMS

3 TABLESPOONS OLIVE OIL

3 TABLESPOONS WHITE WINE
    VINEGAR

1/2 TEASPOON LEMON JUICE

1/2 TEASPOON DRIED
    TARRAGON

PINCH OF SALT

2 PINCHES OF WHITE PEPPER

PINCH OF GARLIC SALT

1 TOMATO, CUT INTO WEDGES

1 PEACH, PEELED, CUT INTO
    WEDGES

3 GREEN ONIONS, SLICED

1 AVOCADO, DICED

6 PARSLEY SPRIGS, CHOPPED

12 RIPE OLIVES, SLICED

BOSTON LETTUCE

3/4 CUP MAYONNAISE

1/2-OUNCE PACKAGE GREEN
    ONION DIP MIX

3 TABLESPOONS GRATED
    ROMANO CHEESE

2 TABLESPOONS KETCHUP

1 TABLESPOON CHILI SAUCE

1/2 TEASPOON PAPRIKA

PINCH OF CELERY SALT

Broil chicken, remove meat, and cut into 1-inch cubes. Set aside. Fry bacon until crisp, drain, and reserve. Wash and slice mushrooms. Place in jar with marinade consisting of olive oil, vinegar, lemon juice, tarragon, and salt, pinch of white pepper, and garlic salt. Shake well and refrigerate until needed. Mix chicken cubes and bacon with tomato and peach, green onions, avocado, parsley, and ripe olives. Add mushrooms, discarding marinade. Serve on bed of Boston lettuce with dressing made of mayonnaise mixed with green onion dip, cheese, ketchup, chili sauce, paprika, and pinch of white pepper and celery salt. Serves 3 or 4.

Outdoor cooking has a timeless, primeval appeal, and whether through basic necessity or in the pure pursuit of pleasure, it has brought joy and satisfaction to food lovers everywhere. The principles of good cooking work their charms as much around the glowing coals of the wilderness campfire as they do in the chafing dish at the most hallowed precincts of haute cuisine. In the open air, the lure of the cooking fire is at its irresistible best. When the quiet hours of twilight settle upon the land and the soft, gray hickory smoke blends with the evening haze, appetites quicken and the gentle, mystical moments of *l'heure bleue* steal upon us to weave their spell. And once again, as in a millennium of evenings past, the time is at hand to celebrate our ritual of fire, to light up the sky!

SEVEN

The Fiery Finish

You're giving a party. So far things have only been so-so, and you're reluctantly coming to the conclusion that as a host or hostess you are not exactly setting the world on fire. This is your cue to trot out that flambé dessert you've been saving to top off your dinner in refulgent triumph. And if it doesn't, be philosophical and make up your mind that if you're going to go down, it is better to go down in flames.

Don't underestimate the advantages of a flaming sundae or a blazing crêpe to give a supernal aura to your menu. Some people find it fascinating just to sit around the table and watch the flames, and it is possible that weight watchers derive a certain Freudian satisfaction out of seeing a lot of calories go up in smoke. Most ignitable desserts are really very simple to prepare. Thus the goal of these recipes is to take the fussing, but not the fuming, out of flambé-dessert preparation.

The recipes are divided into four major classifications: first and most common are plain fruits flambé; the second group, and also very popular, are flaming sundaes; the third is a combination of omelets, crêpes, and pancakes; and the last group, which is sort of a catchall, is what a *chef de cuisine* might call *"spécialités."* So, ladies, light your tapers, and, gentlemen, don your blazer coats, for here is a pyrogenous parade of easily kindled *entremets* that will turn even a drab occasion into a fiery fête.

First, the fruits. The good thing about fruits flambé is that they can be prepared on very short notice—or no notice at all. Canned fruits do very nicely, since many are saturated in a sugar syrup that aids the flaming process. Here are some refulgent recipes that are guaranteed to add a warm touch to luncheon, dinner, or late supper.

FIERY FIGS

1-POUND CAN KADOTA FIGS IN LIGHT SYRUP	GROUND CINNAMON
	CINNAMON STICKS
2 TABLESPOONS FIRMLY PACKED BROWN SUGAR	$^1/_2$ CUP KIRSCH, WARMED
	$^1/_2$ CUP CREAM OR
1 TEASPOON LEMON JUICE	HOMOGENIZED MILK
6 OR 8 WHOLE CLOVES	

Pour a little syrup from figs into flaming pan of chafing dish over direct heat. Add brown sugar, lemon juice, cloves, and several pinches of cinnamon as well as several cinnamon sticks. Bring syrup to boil. Cook until it begins to thicken. Add figs and continue simmering until thoroughly heated. Pour in warmed kirsch, ignite, and blaze. Top with cream or milk. Serves 2 to 3.

$$\approx$$

There are innumerable ways of flambéing peaches. Here are three favorite recipes.

PÊCHES FLAMBÉES

2 TABLESPOONS BUTTER

1-POUND CAN SLICED PEACHES
   IN LIGHT SYRUP, DRAINED,
   SYRUP RESERVED

1/2 CUP FRAMBOISE OR COGNAC

1 CUP CREAM OR HOMOGENIZED
   MILK

PINCH OF FRESHLY GRATED
   NUTMEG

Melt butter in flaming pan of chafing dish over direct heat, but do not brown. Sauté drained peach slices, and when thoroughly heated, add framboise or cognac and blaze. Serve peaches in individual dishes. Leave sauce in pan. Pour in 3 tablespoons canned peach syrup, and add small amount of additional butter if needed. Bring to a boil, add cream or milk, and stir constantly until sauce reaches desired degree of thickness. Spoon over sliced peaches. Add nutmeg. Serves 2 to 3.

$$\approx$$

KENTUCKY PEACHES

1-POUND CAN PEACH HALVES IN
   LIGHT SYRUP
2 TABLESPOONS RED CURRANT
   JAM

$^1/_2$ CUP BOURBON, WARMED
GROUND CINNAMON

Pour small amount of peach syrup from can into flaming pan of chafing dish over direct heat. Add red currant jam and dissolve by bringing liquid to a boil. Add peach halves and simmer until thoroughly heated. Pour in warmed bourbon, ignite, and blaze. Add several pinches of cinnamon. Serves 2 to 3.

PÊCHES AU RHUM

1 TABLESPOON BUTTER
1-POUND CAN PEACH HALVES IN
   LIGHT SYRUP, DRAINED,
   SYRUP RESERVED
2 TABLESPOONS FIRMLY PACKED
   BROWN SUGAR
$^1/_2$ TEASPOON LEMON JUICE

GROUND CINNAMON
$^1/_2$ CUP JAMAICA RUM OR
   $^1/_4$ CUP 151-PROOF
   DEMERARA RUM, WARMED
VANILLA ICE CREAM
   (OPTIONAL)

Melt butter in flaming pan of chafing dish over direct heat. Add 1 tablespoon peach syrup, brown sugar, and lemon juice, and cook until butter foams. Then add peach halves, sprinkle with cinnamon, and continue simmering until thoroughly heated. Pour in warmed rum, ignite, and blaze. Serve with dollop of vanilla ice cream, if desired. Serves 2 to 3.

Here is an original recipe that might tempt your palate, because it is made with an excellent American liqueur that is highly recommended for a variety of cooking (as well as drinking) purposes. It's called Southern Comfort. It has a marvelous peach flavor, and its high proof (100°) makes it excellent for flambé cooking.

PRIDE OF PADUCAH

1 TABLESPOON BUTTER

$^1/_4$ CUP HONEY

1 TEASPOON GROUND
CINNAMON

1-POUND CAN PEACH HALVES IN
LIGHT SYRUP, DRAINED,
SYRUP RESERVED

$^1/_2$ CUP SOUTHERN COMFORT,
WARMED

1 CUP HEAVY CREAM OR
WHIPPED CREAM (OPTIONAL)

Melt butter in flaming pan of chafing dish over direct heat. Add honey, cinnamon, and 1 tablespoon peach syrup, if desired. Cook until sauce is smooth and thick. Add peach halves and simmer until heated through. Pour in warmed Southern Comfort, ignite, and blaze. Top peach halves with heavy cream, or whipped cream, if you wish. Serves 2 or 3.

The Dorchester on Park Lane overlooking Hyde Park has, almost from the day it opened in 1931, held the position as one of London's premier showplace hotels. It boasts a fine kitchen, and its Promenade is the place to be at teatime. There you can sip and sup with the upper echelons of

English society and catch a glimpse now and again of a member of the Royal Family. Peppered Peaches is a popular house recipe that has been served at The Dorchester for many years.

PEPPERED PEACHES

$^1/_2$ CUP FIRMLY PACKED BROWN
SUGAR

$^1/_4$ CUP UNSALTED BUTTER

1 GENEROUS CUP ORANGE JUICE

$^1/_4$ TO $^1/_3$ CUP LEMON JUICE

8 PEACH HALVES, FRESH OR
CANNED IN LIGHT SYRUP

$^1/_4$ CUP BROWN CRÈME DE
CACAO

$^1/_4$ CUP COGNAC

BLACK PEPPER

4 SCOOPS OF VANILLA ICE
CREAM

WHIPPED CREAM

In skillet or flaming pan of chafing dish, heat sugar over low heat until it begins to caramelize. Add butter and blend together. Add orange and lemon juices and blend with caramelized sugar and butter. Cook over medium heat until mixture is reduced by one-third. Reduce heat, add peaches, and cook for 3 minutes, turning occasionally. Add crème de cacao, blend with sauce, and spoon over peaches. Add cognac, and when warmed, tip pan slightly, ignite, and flambé, shaking pan until flames subside. Give one generous grind of pepper over each peach. Remove pan from heat. Serve two peaches on each warmed dessert plate and cover with sauce. Add a scoop of ice cream to each plate topped with a large dollop of whipped cream. Serves 4.

Apples are always available and can be flamed in rum, bourbon, vodka, or, perhaps best of all, Calvados or applejack. Here are two old reliable recipes.

POMMES AU CALVADOS

6 TART APPLES

1/4 CUP MELTED BUTTER

1/4 CUP FIRMLY PACKED BROWN
SUGAR

3 TABLESPOONS HONEY

1 LEMON

1/4 TEASPOON SALT

GROUND CINNAMON

DASH OF VANILLA EXTRACT

1/2 CUP CALVADOS OR
APPLEJACK, WARMED

4 SCOOPS VANILLA ICE CREAM
(OPTIONAL)

Peel, core, and slice apples, and place in flaming pan of chafing dish over direct heat with melted butter. Add brown sugar, honey, lemon juice, and some grated lemon peel to flaming pan, and sauté apples gently. Sprinkle with salt, cinnamon, and vanilla extract. After apples have simmered for at least 5 minutes and become tender and transparent, pour in warmed Calvados or applejack and blaze. Can be served plain or with vanilla ice cream. Serves 4.

APPLES FLAMBÉ

6 SWEET APPLES

2 TABLESPOONS LEMON JUICE

6 TABLESPOONS GRANULATED
SUGAR

CINNAMON STICKS, BROKEN

1 DOZEN WHOLE CLOVES

DASH OF VANILLA EXTRACT

1/2 CUP BOURBON OR JAMAICA
RUM

Peel, core, and quarter apples. In flaming pan of chafing dish over direct heat, place apples in mixture of lemon juice, sugar, several broken cinnamon sticks, cloves, vanilla extract, and 1/4 cup bourbon or rum. Simmer covered until apples are tender. Warm remainder of bourbon or rum, pour into apples, and blaze. Serve apples with hot sauce. Serves 4.

Lots of exciting new food ideas are being developed by Hawaiian chefs bringing together East-West culinary traditions. Amy Ferguson-Ota, Executive Chef of The Ritz-Carlton, Mauna Lani (on the Big Island of Hawaii), loves to blend her native Southwestern and Hawaiian regional cuisines. This combination of mangoes and tequila is an example.

BLAZING MANGOES

1/4 CUP BUTTER

1/4 CUP GRANULATED SUGAR

2 TABLESPOONS FIRMLY PACKED
    BROWN SUGAR

6 RIPE MANGOES, PEELED AND
    SLICED

JUICE OF 1/2 LIME

1/4 CUP TEQUILA OR DARK RUM

4 TO 6 SCOOPS VANILLA OR
    MACADAMIA NUT ICE CREAM,
    OR FRESH COCONUT SORBET

Melt butter in skillet, add sugars, and cook until dissolved. Add mangoes and lime juice and heat thoroughly. Add tequila or rum. When warmed, tilt pan slightly to ignite tequila. Shake pan until flames subside. Serve immediately by spooning over vanilla ice cream, fresh coconut sorbet, or macadamia nut ice cream. Serves 4 to 6 depending on size of mangoes.

Hot Tips—No. 28

Many fruits are more suitable for flambéing if poached. First pre-pare a Simple Syrup (depending on the number of fruits you are going to poach) consisting of 1 cup sugar for each 2 cups of water used. Add a little lemon juice and any spices that may be appropriate, depending on the fruit used. Simmer the syrup for a few minutes to make sure that all the sugar is dissolved. Fruits to be poached should be completely immersed in syrup and simmered until they are tender and translucent. If you have a large number of fruits to process, be sure you poach only a few at a time so that they are well covered. After all fruit has been poached, reduce syrup over high heat to about half its former volume, or until it reaches a desired degree of thickness, and then use this as a sauce to serve over the fruit. Reduced syrup makes an excellent base for flambé recipes.

Poaching materially improves the delicate flavor of pears. In the following recipe, it is recommended that you poach the pears in advance with a little bit of vanilla bean added to the syrup or, as an alternative, poach them in a dry red wine, such as a Bordeaux or a California sauvignon. Pears readily take on the flavors of spices and other ingredients, so use restraint when seasoning this subtle fruit.

PEARS FLAMBÉ

4 RIPE PEARS

1 CUP GRANULATED SUGAR

2 CUPS WATER

JUICE OF $1/2$ LEMON

VANILLA BEAN, HALVED

$1/2$ CUP KIRSCH OR FRAMBOISE, WARMED

Peel pears, slice in half, and remove cores and stems. In saucepan, dissolve sugar in water with lemon juice and half of vanilla bean. Simmer syrup slowly until all sugar is dissolved. Poach pear halves in syrup until quite tender. Remove pears and boil syrup until reduced by half. Place pears in flaming pan of chafing dish over direct heat, pour in a little syrup, and simmer until pears are heated through. Add warmed kirsch or framboise, ignite, and blaze. Serves 4.

PEARS AU PRINCE

4 RIPE PEARS

2 CUPS RED BORDEAUX WINE

JUICE OF $1/2$ LEMON

CINNAMON STICK

3 CUPS GRANULATED SUGAR

$1/2$ CUP TRIPLE SEC, COGNAC, OR FRAISE

Peel and halve pears, and remove cores and stems. Place in saucepan with wine, lemon juice, cinnamon, and sugar. Simmer until pears are tender. Remove from saucepan and set aside. Boil syrup until reduced by half. Place pears in flaming pan of chafing dish over direct heat, pour in a little syrup, and heat thoroughly. Warm triple sec, cognac, or fraise, ignite, and ladle blazing into flaming pan. Serve pears with sauce. Serves 4.

Two fruits that lend themselves well to flambéed dishes after being poached are plums and apricots. The flambé fuel recommended is a liqueur or brandy made of the fruits themselves, which substantially reinforces their flavor.

APRICOTS FLAMBÉ

1-POUND CAN PITTED
    APRICOTS IN SYRUP; OR 2
    CUPS DRIED APRICOTS,
    POACHED, LIQUID RESERVED
DASH OF LEMON JUICE
GRANULATED SUGAR

GROUND CINNAMON
$^1/_3$ CUP APRICOT LIQUEUR OR
    BRANDY
3 TABLESPOONS 100-PROOF
    VODKA (OPTIONAL)
ICE CREAM (OPTIONAL)

Pour small amount of syrup from canned apricots (if dried apricots are poached, use about $^1/_4$ cup juice) into flaming pan of chafing dish over direct heat. Add lemon juice and sugar to thicken syrup, if needed. Add apricots, sprinkle with cinnamon, and simmer in syrup until thoroughly heated. Heat liqueur or brandy (if under 80 proof, add 100-proof vodka to bring up to a higher flaming level), ignite, pour over apricots, and blaze. Can be eaten plain or with ice cream. Serves 2 or 3.

PLUMS FLAMBÉ

1-POUND CAN PITTED
    PRESERVED PLUMS IN SYRUP,
    OR 1$^1/_2$ POUNDS FRESH PLUMS
SUGAR OR ARROWROOT

DASH OF LEMON JUICE
$^1/_2$ CUP QUETSCH OR
    SLIVOVITZ, WARMED

Pour a little syrup from can of plums into flaming pan of chafing dish over direct heat. If using fresh plums, poach as in recipe for Pears Flambé (see Index), remove pits, and use syrup after reducing by half. Thicken canned syrup with sugar or very small amount of arrowroot mixed with a little cold water. Bring syrup to boil, add lemon juice, and place plums in flaming pan. When thoroughly heated, pour in warmed quetsch or slivovitz and blaze. Serves 2 or 3.

~

Citrus fruits make light, refreshing flambé desserts that are ideal for brunch.

ORANGES CURAÇAO FLAMBÉES

4 LARGE ORANGES	1/3 CUP COGNAC, WARMED
1/2 CUP CURAÇAO	GRATED COCONUT (OPTIONAL)
4 TABLESPOONS HONEY	

Peel oranges, slice into sections, and remove seeds. Squeeze 2 tablespoons juice from some sections and reserve juice. Place oranges in flat pan, pour in Curaçao, and let stand covered overnight in refrigerator. Melt honey with reserved orange juice in flaming pan of chafing dish over direct heat. When mixture reaches boiling point, add oranges and Curaçao and warm thoroughly. Pour warmed cognac over oranges, ignite, and blaze. Can be served with grated coconut. Serves 4.

There are several variations of this recipe, but one of the best utilizes brown sugar in place of honey and dark Jamaica rum in place of cognac, all the other ingredients and proportions remaining the same.

~

This pleasant and refreshing recipe, created by Bruno Lopez, Executive Chef of The Ritz-Carlton, Marina del Rey, California, is elegant in its simplicity.

FLAMBÉED ORANGES

6 ORANGES

1 POUND COARSE-GRAINED
 SUGAR

5 OUNCES WATER

3½ OUNCES GRAND MARNIER

Peel oranges, cut each into 8 segments, and remove seeds. In large saucepan make caramel by heating sugar and water together. Pick up each orange segment with fork and dip into caramel. Place caramelized orange segments in flameproof pan over low heat. Sprinkle with Grand Marnier. When heated, ignite, and flambé rapidly. When flames subside, arrange orange segments on individual plates. Pour remaining caramel over oranges. Serves 6.

If you like broiled grapefruit, you should enjoy it even more flambéed in your chafing dish.

GRAPEFRUIT FLAMBÉ

4 GRAPEFRUIT

¼ CUP FIRMLY PACKED BROWN
 SUGAR

½ CUP BARBADOS OR LIGHT
 PUERTO RICAN RUM

Peel grapefruit, slice into sections, and remove seeds. Squeeze 3 tablespoons grapefruit juice from some of the sections into flaming pan of chafing dish over direct heat. Add brown sugar and, when melted, place grapefruit sections in chafing dish. Simmer until thoroughly heated. Add warmed rum and blaze. Serves 4.

The burning of bananas has been a most popular pyromaniacal pastime, because they can be blazed with a wide range of spirits. Here is a new recipe for Bananas Flambé that makes use of flavored rums followed by several variations that should be included in your repertoire.

SPICED BANANAS FLAMBÉ

6 TO 8 RIPE BANANAS

3 TABLESPOONS BUTTER

3 TABLESPOONS FIRMLY PACKED
   BROWN SUGAR

1 TABLESPOON LEMON JUICE

$^1/_4$ CUP COCONUT RUM

FRESHLY GRATED CINNAMON
   STICKS

$^1/_4$ CUP SPICED RUM, WARMED

ICE CREAM (OPTIONAL)

Peel bananas, slice lengthwise, and cut into manageable sections. Melt butter in flaming pan of chafing dish over direct heat. Add brown sugar, lemon juice, and coconut rum. When butter begins to foam, put in bananas and sauté on both sides until tender but not mushy. Sprinkle with cinnamon, pour in warmed rum, ignite, and blaze. May be served with or without ice cream. Serves 4 to 6.

Smith & Wollensky's midtown Manhattan steak house is home for hungry beef-eaters. The steaks are big, scrumptious, and so tender some regulars claim you can eat them with a spoon. After you load up on Porterhouse steak and old-fashioned hash browns, the resident Viennese pastry chef, Hossien E. Khanloo (with a master's degree from Vienna's redoubtable Wirtschaftsfoerderungs Culinary Institute) has a treat for you: Blazing Bananas.

BLAZING BANANAS
SMITH & WOLLENSKY

2 LARGE RIPE BANANAS	1 PINT VANILLA ICE CREAM
1 TO 2 TABLESPOONS BUTTER	1/4 CUP GOLD OR DARK
1/3 CUP BROWN SUGAR	JAMAICA RUM

Peel and slice bananas. In small saucepan melt butter, dissolve brown sugar, and caramelize bananas until thoroughly covered on all sides. In deep dish, place scoop of ice cream for each serving. Carefully spoon bananas over ice cream, pour rum into saucepan, and heat (but do not boil). Then ignite. Pour blazing rum over bananas and ice cream, and serve immediately. Makes 2 to 3 servings. Note: This dessert can be prepared entirely at table using the blazer pan of a chafing dish over direct heat.

THE TOP BANANA

6 TO 8 BANANAS

3 TABLESPOONS BUTTER

3 TABLESPOONS FIRMLY PACKED
    BROWN SUGAR

1 TABLESPOON LEMON JUICE

2 CINNAMON STICKS

$1/2$ TEASPOON GROUND GINGER

2 TABLESPOONS ORANGE JUICE

$1/4$ CUP CURAÇAO OR TRIPLE
    SEC

$1/4$ CUP DARK JAMAICA RUM OR
    COGNAC, WARMED

Peel and slice bananas lengthwise and cut in half, or into thirds if you prefer smaller pieces. Melt butter in flaming pan of chafing dish over direct heat. Add brown sugar, lemon juice, cinnamon sticks, and ginger. When butter foams, add orange juice and Curaçao or triple sec. Sauté bananas quickly on all sides over high heat. Pour in warmed rum or cognac, ignite, and blaze. Serves 4 to 6.

Benedictine is one of the world's great liqueurs. Unfortunately it cannot be used with very many flambéed dishes because its intricate and exotic flavors do not endure the flaming process too successfully. Its use in cooking has been expanded somewhat through the combination of Benedictine with brandy. Here is a subtle and memorable delightful recipe using B and B liqueur.

BANANAS B AND B

6 TO 8 RIPE BANANAS

3 TABLESPOONS BUTTER

3 TABLESPOONS FIRMLY PACKED
 BROWN SUGAR

1 TABLESPOON LEMON JUICE

$^1/_2$ CUP B AND B LIQUEUR

Peel and slice bananas lengthwise and cut into smaller pieces if desired. Melt butter in flaming pan of chafing dish over direct heat. Add sugar and lemon juice. When butter begins to froth, place bananas in flaming pan. Sauté gently but do not overcook. Pour in heated B and B liqueur, ignite, and blaze. Serves 4 to 6.

The next recipe can be varied any number of ways, limited only by your taste for bananas and the size of your liquor cabinet. Bananas have been flambéed successfully with bourbon, rum, rye, Drambuie, kirsch, Irish Mist, Curaçao, mirabelle, framboise, gin, and Calvados. When you have tried all of these flamers, if you still wish to experiment, you can consult Chapter 9. Its comprehensive list of spirits and liqueurs may give you some additional ideas worth kindling.

If Brennan's French and Creole restaurant is not the best of its kind in New Orleans, it certainly is the best looking with its elegant patio and sprawling eighteenth-century-style mansion located at 417 Royal Street in the heart of the Vieux Carré, the city's French Quarter. Bananas Foster, perhaps more than any other culinary creation in Brennan's famous repertoire of extraordinary things to eat and drink, has become the quintessential signature *spécialité de la maison*. Created by Brennan's talented chef, Paul Blangé for Richard Foster, New Orleans civic leader and a Brennan's regular, this delectable dessert has become internationally famous.

BANANAS FOSTER

4 RIPE BANANAS

$^1/_4$ CUP BUTTER

1 CUP FIRMLY PACKED BROWN
   SUGAR

$^1/_2$ TEASPOON GROUND
   CINNAMON

$^1/_4$ CUP BANANA LIQUEUR

$^1/_4$ CUP DARK RUM

4 SCOOPS OF VANILLA ICE
   CREAM

Peel bananas and halve lengthwise, then halve horizontally. Combine butter, sugar, and cinnamon in flambé pan or skillet. Place pan over low heat on alcohol burner of chafing dish or on top of stove, and cook, stirring, until sugar dissolves. Stir in banana liqueur, then place bananas in pan. When banana sections soften and begin to brown, carefully add rum. Continue to cook sauce until rum is hot, then tip pan slightly to ignite rum. When flames subside, lift bananas out of pan and place four pieces over each portion of ice cream. Spoon warm sauce over bananas and ice cream and serve immediately. Makes 4 servings.

A Mélange of fruit is called a *macédoine* of fruit in France; in the United States it is simply referred to as a compote or fruit cup. Here is a quick out-of-the-can dessert, so skillfully disguised in flames that your guests won't realize what it is until they've had a chance to really think about it.

FLAMING FRUIT CUP

2 TABLESPOONS BUTTER

1 TEASPOON LEMON JUICE

1-POUND CAN FRUIT SALAD IN
  HEAVY SYRUP, DRAINED,
  SYRUP RESERVED

$^1/_2$ CUP TRIPLE SEC OR KIRSCH

1 CUP CREAM OR HOMOGENIZED
  MILK

Melt butter in flaming pan of chafing dish over direct heat. Add lemon juice and fruit from can, but only a very small amount of the syrup. Simmer fruit slowly for several minutes until thoroughly heated, then pour in triple sec or kirsch. When warmed, ignite and blaze. Serve fruit with sauce and cover with cream or milk. Serves 3.

When fresh fruits are in season try this *macédoine des fruits flambés*.

MACÉDOINE DES FRUITS AU KIRSCH

ASSORTED FRESH FRUITS
  (ENOUGH TO SERVE 4 PEOPLE
  GENEROUSLY)

$^1/_4$ CUP BUTTER

3 TABLESPOONS GRANULATED
  SUGAR

$^1/_4$ CUP ORANGE JUICE

1 TEASPOON LEMON JUICE

$^1/_2$ CUP KIRSCH, WARMED

Prepare fruits (dicing when necessary), such as pineapple, grapefruit, oranges, apples, pears, strawberries, or bananas, for cooking. Place butter in flaming pan of chafing dish over direct heat, and when it reaches foaming stage, add fruits, sugar, and juices, and simmer until thoroughly heated. Pour in warmed kirsch, ignite, and blaze. Serve over spongecake if you wish. For a change of pace, rum makes an excellent substitute for kirsch.

In the entire panoply of flaming desserts, there is nothing more satisfying than the sizzling sundae. A seemingly miraculous combination of fire and ice, it can best be described as splendid, succulent, and spectacular.

A word of caution before embarking on this trip through ice cream land with match and saucepan. To avoid that greatest of all fire traps when preparing these torched treats, it is wise to flame most of the spirits in the pan before pouring them over the ice cream in the dish. This not only saves a lot of cracked china, but it also prevents the ice cream from turning into a great bowl of mush.

FLAMING SNOWBALL

1 PINT VANILLA ICE CREAM

3 1/2-OUNCE CAN SHREDDED

COCONUT

1/4 CUP DARK JAMAICA OR

LIGHT PUERTO RICAN RUM

Divide ice cream into 2 equal sections and roll into balls. Toast shredded coconut in oven until it begins to brown. When cool, roll ice cream balls in coconut so they are coated evenly and place in freezing compartment of refrigerator. Serve ice cream balls in individual dishes. Warm rum, ignite, and ladle blazing over ice cream. Serves 2.

Here is an old favorite with a new Southern accent.

PLANTATION SUNDAE

1 PINT VANILLA ICE CREAM	1/4 CUP DARK JAMAICA RUM
1/3 CUP LIGHT MOLASSES	1/4 CUP CHOPPED PECANS
1 TEASPOON LEMON JUICE	(OPTIONAL)

Place ice cream in individual serving dishes. Warm molasses in saucepan. Add lemon juice, rum, and pecans, if desired. When thoroughly heated, ignite and ladle blazing over ice cream. Serves 2.

When you need a real showstopper for dessert, here's something about as hard to ignore as a volcano.

GIN SUNDAE

3 TABLESPOONS GRAPE JAM	1/2 CUP WALNUTS
1 TABLESPOON LIGHT CORN	1/2 CUP DRY GIN
SYRUP	1 QUART VANILLA ICE CREAM

Melt grape jam and corn syrup in flaming pan of chafing dish over direct heat. Add walnuts and pour in gin. When mixture is thoroughly heated, ignite and pour blazing over individual portions of ice cream. A pleasant variation is to serve this recipe with half vanilla ice cream and half chocolate ice cream. Serves 4.

Hot Tips—No. 29

One of the secrets of successful sizzling sundaes is to make sure the ice cream is very, very cold. Long before guests arrive, take the ice cream from the freezer and spoon out individual portions. Place in aluminum foil or some other suitable container and return to the freezer immediately so the ice cream will be rock hard when the time comes for you to light up your dessert. Serving dishes should not be chilled; otherwise they will crack when the flambé sauce is poured over the ice cream. If you're concerned about good china, don't use it. Instead, buy an inexpensive set of clear plastic soup bowls that can be chilled in the freezing compartment of the refrigerator with ice cream in situ, and reserve them for desserts that are put to the match.

This is a seasonal sundae and a singularly good substitute for mince pie.

CHRISTMAS SUNDAE

1 CUP CANNED MINCEMEAT

1/4 CUP ORANGE JUICE

1/4 CUP CURAÇAO OR TRIPLE
SEC

1/4 CUP COGNAC

1 QUART VANILLA ICE CREAM

Pour boiling water into bottom pan of chafing dish until it barely touches bottom of flaming pan. Use low heat to keep water simmering. Place mincemeat and orange juice in flaming pan, cover, and heat thoroughly. Immediately before serving, pour in Curaçao or triple sec and cognac, warm, ignite, and ladle blazing over individual portions of ice cream. Serves 4.

LORDSHIP SUNDAE

1 TABLESPOON BUTTER

1 TABLESPOON PURE MAPLE
SYRUP

2 TABLESPOONS FIRMLY PACKED
BROWN SUGAR

1/2 TEASPOON LEMON JUICE

1/4 CUP RAISINS

1/4 CUP CHOPPED ALMONDS

2 TABLESPOONS DARK JAMAICA
RUM

2 TABLESPOONS 151-PROOF
PUERTO RICAN RUM

1 PINT VANILLA ICE CREAM

Melt butter in flaming pan of chafing dish over direct heat. Add maple syrup, brown sugar, lemon juice, raisins, and almonds. When thoroughly heated, add both rums. Allow time to warm, then ignite and serve blazing over individual portions of ice cream. Serves 2.

You may well wonder whence come the names for some of these ignescent oddments. Desserts denote festivity and, if not identified with their ingredients, should, it would seem, be designated in honor of pleasant places, happy times, or special people. The Lordship Sundae is named after a quiet little town in Connecticut that juts out into Long Island Sound. It was the site of a famous gun club, reputed to be the birthplace of skeet shooting. This delectable dessert was invented as a final cold-weather warmer-upper after the long drive back to New York City and makes an appropriate ending (after a few Gun Club Punches—an après-shooting drink, see Index) to a hearty dinner of roast beef and Yorkshire pudding.

Here is another recipe named after a lovely old club near Chappaqua, New York, containing several hundred acres of virgin woods, lakes, and fine shooting ranges. The Camp Fire Club inspired this dessert, which has been enjoyed on many a winter's eve.

CAMP FIRE JUBILEE

1 TABLESPOON CURRANT JAM	1/4 CUP CHOPPED BLACK
1 TEASPOON GRAPE JAM	WALNUTS
1 TEASPOON FIRMLY PACKED	3/4 CUP RED RASPBERRIES
BROWN SUGAR	3 TABLESPOONS DRY GIN
1/2 TEASPOON LEMON JUICE	3 TABLESPOONS 97-PROOF
GROUND CINNAMON	PUERTO RICAN RUM
PINCH OF GRATED NUTMEG	1 PINT VANILLA ICE CREAM

In flaming pan of chafing dish over direct heat, melt currant and grape jams with brown sugar, lemon juice, several pinches of cinnamon, nutmeg, and walnuts. Immediately before serving, add raspberries, gin, and rum. When warm, ignite and serve blazing over individual portions of ice cream. Serves 2.

A simplified version of this recipe can be made as follows.

RASPBERRIES JUBILEE

2 TABLESPOONS CURRANT JAM

1 TABLESPOON HONEY

$^1/_2$ TEASPOON LEMON JUICE

PINCH OF GROUND CINNAMON

$^3/_4$ CUP RED RASPBERRIES

$^1/_3$ CUP KIRSCH OR FRAMBOISE

1 PINT VANILLA ICE CREAM

In flaming pan of chafing dish over direct heat, melt currant jam with honey, lemon juice, and cinnamon. Immediately before serving, add raspberries and kirsch or framboise. When warm, ignite and serve blazing over individual portions of ice cream. Serves 2.

Some desserts are named after places, some are named after events, and this one is named after a beautiful woman.

BANANAS FLAMBÉ À LA COMTESSE

2 TABLESPOONS BUTTER

$^1/_4$ CUP FIRMLY PACKED BROWN
  SUGAR

2 TEASPOONS LEMON JUICE

$^1/_2$ CUP SHELLED BLACK
  WALNUTS

6 MARASCHINO CHERRIES,
  CHOPPED

2 BANANAS

GROUND GINGER

GROUND CINNAMON

$^1/_4$ CUP DARK JAMAICA RUM

$^1/_4$ CUP 151-PROOF PUERTO
  RICAN RUM

1 QUART VANILLA ICE CREAM

In flaming pan of chafing dish over direct heat, melt butter with brown sugar, lemon juice, walnuts, and cherries. Peel and slice bananas lengthwise, cut in half, and place in pan. Sprinkle bananas with ginger and cinnamon. Sauté lightly, and pour in rum. When warm, ignite and serve blazing over individual portions of ice cream. Serves 4.

Now here is a dish named after a princess, and a Swedish princess at that.

PEACHES PRINCESSA MARGARETHA

4 LARGE RIPE WHITE PEACHES

2 CUPS BOILING WATER

1 CUP GRANULATED SUGAR

VANILLA BEAN (OPTIONAL)

1 TABLESPOON LEMON JUICE

4 TEASPOONS STRAWBERRY JAM

4 TEASPOONS
    BAR-LE-DUC OR RED
    CURRANT JELLY

4 TEASPOONS GREENGAGE PLUM
    PRESERVES

$^1/_2$ CUP COGNAC

$^1/_2$ CUP KIRSCH

1 QUART VANILLA ICE CREAM

$^1/_2$ CUP TOASTED SLIVERED
    ALMONDS

In saucepan, poach whole peaches in boiling water in which sugar has been dissolved. You can add a vanilla bean to water for flavoring if you wish. Remove peaches after several minutes and slip off skins. If they do not come off easily, put peaches back into boiling water and try again. After removing skins, turn off heat. Return peaches to hot water until needed. Add lemon juice. Melt strawberry jam, currant jelly, and greengage plum preserves in flaming pan of chafing dish over direct heat. When thoroughly heated, add warmed, drained peaches that have been sliced in half and have had pits removed. Without stirring, pour in cognac and kirsch. Warm and blaze. Ladle peach and some flaming sauce onto individual servings of ice cream. Sprinkle with toasted almonds. Serves 4.

This recipe was created by Waldemar Ekegårdh, the late proprietor of the famous Opera Källaren restaurant in Stockholm, Sweden. (Reprinted by permission from *Sports Illustrated*, March 14, 1960, © 1960 *Time* Inc.)

Some of the most flavorful flambé desserts are made with a combination of fruits served over ice cream. The following four recipes make a fine flaming finale for a dinner party.

STRAWBERRIES AND BANANAS FLAMBÉ

1 PINT FRESH, RIPE STRAWBERRIES	1/4 CUP CRÈME DE FRAISES LIQUEUR
4 BANANAS	1/2 CUP KIRSCH
GRANULATED SUGAR	1 QUART VANILLA ICE CREAM

Trim stems from strawberries, and peel and slice bananas crosswise into thick pieces. Place in flaming pan of chafing dish over direct heat. Sprinkle with sugar and add liqueur. Simmer gently until fruit is thoroughly heated. Pour in kirsch. When warm, ignite, and serve blazing over individual portions of ice cream. Serves 4.

CHERRIES AND PEACHES FLAMBÉ

2 LARGE RIPE PEACHES

1-POUND CAN PITTED BLACK
    CHERRIES, DRAINED

JUICE OF 2 LEMONS

1 CUP GRANULATED SUGAR

1 1/2 CUPS RED BORDEAUX WINE

1/4 CUP KIRSCH

1/2 CUP COGNAC

1 QUART VANILLA ICE CREAM

Peel and slice peaches. Place peaches and cherries in flaming pan of chafing dish over direct heat. Add lemon juice, sugar, wine, and kirsch. Heat thoroughly, stirring constantly to make sure all sugar is dissolved. Heat cognac and ladle flaming into chafing dish. Serve fruit with a little sauce on individual portions of ice cream. Serves 4 to 6.

PINEAPPLE AND CHERRIES FLAMBÉ

3 TABLESPOONS BUTTER

3 TABLESPOONS BROWN SUGAR

2 TABLESPOONS ORANGE JUICE

1 TEASPOON LEMON JUICE

4 SLICES FRESH OR CANNED
    PINEAPPLE

1/2 CUP MARASCHINO CHERRIES

1/2 CUP KIRSCH

1 QUART VANILLA ICE CREAM

Melt butter in flaming pan of chafing dish over direct heat. Add brown sugar and juices. When sugar is dissolved, add pineapple and cherries and sauté gently until thoroughly heated. Pour in kirsch. When warm, ignite and blaze. Serve slice of pineapple on each plate, place scoop of ice cream on top, and pour cherries and sauce over ice cream. Serves 4.

DANISH SUNDAE

2 RIPE BANANAS

4 SECTIONS COCKTAIL ORANGE
PRESERVED IN SYRUP

2 TABLESPOONS BUTTER

2 TABLESPOONS FIRMLY PACKED
BROWN SUGAR

1 TABLESPOON HONEY

1 TEASPOON LEMON JUICE

2 TABLESPOONS CHOPPED
BLACK WALNUTS

3 TABLESPOONS CHERRY
HEERING

$^1/_3$ CUP DRY GIN OR KIRSCH

1 QUART VANILLA ICE CREAM

Peel and split bananas and cut into small pieces. cut orange sections into small pieces. Place fruit in flaming pan of chafing dish over direct heat. Add butter, brown sugar, honey, lemon juice, and walnuts. Sauté gently until bananas begin to brown. Pour in Cherry Heering and gin. When heated, ignite and blaze. Serve over individual portions of vanilla ice cream. Serves 4 to 6.

When one says that the stately Hotel de Crillon is located in the "very center of Paris" that well-worn phrase takes on new meaning. You can dine in the palatial Les Ambassadeurs—and it *is* palatial because the Crillon was a royal palace in the eighteenth century—and look out upon the Place de la Concorde and the beginning of the Champs Élysées. The Crillon's great kitchen is in keeping with its surroundings: *grand luxe*.

This house spécialité: a festive soufflé with sautéed pears flamed with pear brandy is a perfect ending to a memorable meal.

BISCUIT SOUFFLÉ GUANAJA POÊLÉE DE POIRE WILLIAMS FLAMBÉE

9 OUNCES BITTERSWEET CHOCOLATE

1/2 CUP BUTTER

1 1/2 CUPS EGG WHITES (12–14 EGGS)

1/2 CUP PLUS 2 TEASPOONS GRANULATED SUGAR

4 EGG YOLKS

1 GENEROUS POUND RIPE PEARS

PINCH OF GROUND CINNAMON

JUICE OF 1/2 LEMON

4 TO 6 TABLESPOONS PEAR BRANDY (*POIRE* WILLIAMS)

Melt chocolate in double boiler, add 6 tablespoons of the butter and blend. In a mixing bowl, beat egg whites with 1/2 cup sugar until smooth. Add egg yolks to stiff egg whites. Cool chocolate mixture to about 100° F. and gently fold into mixing bowl with egg whites making sure egg whites do not fall. Pour mixture into 3-inch soufflé molds which have been lined with buttered and sugared paper collars and bake for 10 minutes in a 500° F. oven. While soufflé is baking, skin and halve pears and place them in heated frying pan with remaining butter and brown lightly. Add 2 teaspoons sugar and cinnamon and caramelize. Then add lemon juice and a little water to provide some pan juices. Check pears for doneness. They should be fork tender. Remove soufflés from oven. They should be delicately crunchy. Place on warmed serving plates and remove top crust. Pour brandy over pears in frying pan, and when warmed, ignite and flambé. Carefully spoon pears and pan juices on top of soufflés. Serves 4.

Delicious little quickie sundaes or parfaits can be made as a last-minute dessert by pouring a tablespoon of your favorite liqueur into a parfait glass, plopping in a small scoop of ice cream, and decorating with a cube of sugar, saturated with lemon extract, that has been pressed into a marshmallow. Ignite the lemon extract and you have a miniature flaming sundae. Here are some cordials that work especially well: Cherry Heering, crème de menthe, crème de cacao, Chambord, Frangelico, yellow Chartreuse, Galliano, Grand Marnier, apricot brandy, Cointreau, blackberry liqueur, mandarine, sloe gin, Benedictine, crème de cassis, crème d'ananas, and crème de noyaux.

Here are three offbeat recipes employing grapes, marrons, and, of all things, cloudberries. In case you are unfamiliar with marrons, they are those wonderful chestnuts from France usually found preserved whole or chopped in vanilla-flavored syrup. As for cloudberries, they are a seldom-seen fruit resembling yellow raspberries that grow in the very coldest parts of northern Sweden and Norway. Although practically unknown in this country, they are very good indeed, particularly as a topping for ice cream.

PÊCHES AUX MARRONS FLAMBÉES

6 SMALL PEACHES

BOILING WATER

2 TABLESPOONS LIME JUICE

3 TABLESPOONS LIGHT CORN
  SYRUP

1 1/2 TABLESPOONS HONEY

1 TABLESPOON BUTTER

PINCH OF GROUND GINGER

PINCH OF GROUND CINNAMON

TWO 9 1/2-OUNCE JARS
  MARRONS

1/4 CUP JAMAICA RUM

1/4 CUP 151-PROOF DEMERARA
  RUM

1 QUART VANILLA ICE CREAM

Dip peaches in boiling water to which you have added 1 tablespoon of the lime juice. After a few minutes when skins are loose, remove, peel, and slice. In flaming pan of chafing dish over direct heat, add corn syrup, honey, butter, remainder of lime juice, ginger, cinnamon, and entire contents of both jars of marrons. Simmer for at least 5 minutes. Add peaches and simmer for another 5 minutes until thoroughly heated. Add rums and when warm, ignite, blaze, and serve over individual portions of ice cream. Serves 6.

GRAPES FLAMBÉ

1/2 CUP LIGHT CORN SYRUP

2 TABLESPOONS LEMON JUICE

2 CUPS WHITE SEEDLESS
  GRAPES

1/2 CUP COGNAC OR KIRSCH

1 QUART VANILLA ICE CREAM

Heat corn syrup and lemon juice in flaming pan of chafing dish over direct heat until boiling. Add grapes and baste in mixture until thoroughly inundated in syrup. Add cognac or kirsch and when warm, ignite and blaze. Serve over individual portions of ice cream. Serves 6.

Cloudberry sauce is available in jars at most Scandinavian delicatessens and many gourmet food shops. The $14^1/2$-ounce jar is a convenient size and will last for a considerable length of time after opened when stored in the refrigerator.

FLAMING CLOUDBERRIES

1 CUP CLOUDBERRY SAUCE   1 QUART VANILLA ICE CREAM
$1/2$ CUP GIN OR VODKA

Heat cloudberry sauce in flaming pan of chafing dish over direct heat. When thoroughly warmed, add gin or vodka, blaze, and pour over individual servings of ice cream. Serves 4.

Hot Tips—No. 31

Some fruits, such as peaches, have an unpleasant habit of turning dark after they are peeled. To eliminate the blemishes that result from exposure to the air, keep the fruit immersed in water to which has been added a tablespoon or two of lemon or lime juice. This is called acidulated water and will not affect the taste of the fruit concerned—provided, of course, that you don't use too much lemon or lime juice.

Here is a great dessert for an after-theater supper.

FLAMING HONEY SUNDAE

3 TABLESPOONS BUTTER

1 CUP HONEY

1/4 CUP APPLE JUICE

1/4 CUP WHITE RAISINS

1/3 CUP CHOPPED BLACK
WALNUTS

1/2 CUP JAMAICA RUM

1 QUART VANILLA ICE CREAM

Melt butter and simmer with honey, apple juice, raisins, and walnuts in flaming pan of chafing dish over direct heat. When mixture begins to boil, add rum. When warm, ignite, blaze, and pour over individual portions of ice cream. Serves 4 to 6.

Omelets are good any time, morning, noon, or night, especially when flambéed with rum or cognac.

SOUFFLÉED OMELET FLAMBÉ

8 EGGS, SEPARATED

1/2 CUP GRANULATED SUGAR,
PLUS EXTRA

BUTTER

1/2 CUP DARK JAMAICA OR
BARBADOS RUM, WARMED

Beat yolks, gradually adding sugar, until yolks are light. Beat egg whites until firm, and carefully fold them into yolks. Butter flameproof platter well and make mound of omelet mixture. Mold carefully with spatula until it has been sculptured into desired shape. Bake in hot oven (375° to 400° F.) for about 20 minutes. Remove platter to table, sprinkle with a little granulated sugar, pour on warmed rum, ignite, and blaze. Serves 4.

Here are two marvelous omelet recipes from France. *Omelette Normande* is a great favorite in Normandy.

OMELETTE NORMANDE

2 TO 3 MEDIUM RIPE APPLES	1/2 CUP CALVADOS OR
GROUND CINNAMON	APPLEJACK
1/2 CUP BUTTER	8 EGGS
1/4 CUP GRANULATED SUGAR	1 TABLESPOON WATER
1/4 CUP CREAM OR	SALT
HOMOGENIZED MILK	

Peel, core, and slice apples very thin and sprinkle with cinnamon. Melt half the butter in a pan and sauté apples slowly until brown. Add 3 tablespoons of the sugar and stir in cream or milk and 1 or 2 tablespoons of the Calvados or applejack. Simmer slowly while preparing omelet. Beat eggs briskly with the water in mixing bowl and prepare omelet according to the general instructions given at the beginning of Chapter 2. Add salt to taste. When eggs are nearly cooked, but still moist and runny on top, spread apple mixture over half of omelet, fold over, and turn out on heated platter. Sprinkle with remaining sugar. Warm remainder of Calvados or applejack, and ladle flaming over omelet at table. Serves 4.

OMELETTE AU COGNAC

8 EGGS	1/2 CUP COGNAC
1 TABLESPOON WATER	3 TABLESPOONS BUTTER
SALT	1 TO 2 TABLESPOONS SUGAR

Break eggs in mixing bowl, add water, salt to taste, and beat very briskly with fork for about 30 seconds. While beating eggs, add about half the cognac, a few drops at a time. Melt butter in omelet pan over high heat until butter froths. When foam subsides, but before butter browns, reduce heat, pour in egg mixture, and stir briskly with fork so eggs are well distributed in pan. Slide pan back and forth while eggs cook and lift up edges of omelet with spatula to make sure all liquid is in contact with bottom of pan. When omelet is done, turn out on heated plate, sprinkle with sugar, warm remainder of cognac, ignite, and pour blazing over omelet. Serves 4.

In the whole sparkling spectrum of flambéed desserts, there is probably no recipe that is more popular, or more deserving of popularity, than *crêpes flambées*. There is great opportunity for innovation and originality in making your own special crêpe recipes once you have mastered the technique of making these thin little pancakes. Proper equipment is important, and while crêpes can be made in a skillet, a crêpe pan makes the job somewhat easier and is the proper accoutrement for your chafing-dish burner.

Coat the flaming pan of your chafing dish very lightly with butter and place it over direct heat until it begins to smoke. Remove the pan from the heat and pour approximately 1 heaping tablespoon batter in the middle of the pan. Quickly tilt the pan and swirl the batter in all directions so that it thinly covers the bottom. Return the pan to the heat. When the top of the crêpe is set, lift up the edge with a spatula to see if it has turned a golden brown. When the desired state of brownness is reached, slide the spatula under the crêpe and flip it over. It should cook no more than 30 seconds on second side. Slide the cooked crêpe onto a heated plate and keep it warm by covering it with foil and placing it in a slow oven. With a little practice you will be able to make several dozen crêpes in no time. Here are the important points to remember: Do not overbeat the batter. This makes the crêpes tough. Do not overcook the crêpes, and turn them only once. Keep the crêpe pan hot, and coat it lightly with butter before putting in new batter. Some cooks find it easier to make thin crêpes by covering the entire bottom of the pan with batter. Do not be concerned if the crêpes are not an even golden brown on both sides as long as they have been cooked properly. Use the side that is evenly browned on top, as this is the most attractive way to present your crêpes. Crêpes can be prepared as much as a day in advance of serving, so that you do not have this task to perform at the last minute.

Here is a reliable basic recipe.

CRÊPES SUCRÉES I

4 EGGS

1 CUP SIFTED ALL-PURPOSE
    FLOUR

2 TABLESPOONS GRANULATED
    SUGAR

1 CUP WATER

1 CUP MILK

Beat eggs with wire whisk, add flour and sugar, and continue to beat until mixture is smooth. Gradually add water and milk, and mix until batter is about the consistency of thick cream. If you have a blender, sift dry ingredients and add eggs one at a time, mixing well at low speed until there are no lumps. Then gradually stir in water and milk. Let batter rest for an hour or two before using. Follow cooking directions on pages 245–46. Makes about 24 crêpes, approximately 6 inches in diameter.

Dessert crêpes should be very thin, very light, and delicate. If you would like a thicker crêpe for use with fillings, here is an alternate recipe.

CRÊPES SUCRÉES II

1 CUP SIFTED ALL-PURPOSE
    FLOUR

$1/4$ CUP GRANULATED SUGAR

$1/8$ TEASPOON SALT

3 EGGS

2 TABLESPOONS MELTED
    BUTTER

MILK

Prepare batter as in the preceding recipe, starting with dry ingredients and adding eggs, and then finally melted butter. Add just enough milk to give batter consistency of thick cream. Follow cooking instructions on pages 245–46.

Now we are ready for the most famous crêpe dish of them all: *Crêpes Suzette*. *Crêpes Suzette* are reputed to be named after a very attractive dinner companion of King Edward VII. Henri Charpentier, a master chef who held forth at the Café de Paris in Chicago for many years, claims to have been the originator of this outstanding dish. Whatever the circumstances of its creation, the fact remains that it is one of the most distinguished of all the great family of flammable fare and, if made properly, it will unerringly live up to its reputation.

CRÊPES SUZETTE

4 SUGAR CUBES

2 ORANGES WITH GOOD RIND

$^1/_4$ CUP GRANULATED SUGAR

$^1/_2$ CUP BUTTER

$^1/_2$ CUP TRIPLE SEC OR
    CURAÇAO

1 RECIPE *CRÊPES SUCRÉES I*
    (SEE INDEX)

$^1/_2$ CUP COGNAC

Rub sugar cubes vigorously over rind of an orange until all sides of sugar are saturated with orange oil. Remove zest (orange-colored part of peel) with vegetable peeler and mince finely. Mash sugar lumps in mixing bowl. Mix with zest, a little additional sugar, and half the butter. Slowly add orange juice and beat mixture until light and smooth. Place mixture in flaming pan of chafing dish over direct heat. Add remainder of butter and melt. Add a little triple sec or Curaçao and bring to near boil. Place each crêpe carefully, one at a time, in hot sauce, baste well, fold crêpe into quarters, and move to edge of chafing dish. Repeat this until all crêpes have been basted and folded. Use additional butter if needed. Sprinkle crêpes with sugar. Cover them with cognac and remainder of triple sec, ignite, and blaze. Spoon blazing liquid over crêpes and serve with some of the sauce. Serves 6.

Here is an interesting variation of crêpes resulting from a delicious amalgamation of several fruit flavors.

CRÊPES JEAVONS

1 RECIPE *CRÊPES SUCRÉES I* (SEE INDEX) MADE INTO 12 LARGE CRÊPES

3 TABLESPOONS BUTTER

3 TABLESPOONS FIRMLY PACKED BROWN SUGAR

2 TABLESPOONS ORANGE JUICE

2 TABLESPOONS GRAPEFRUIT JUICE

DASH OF LEMON JUICE

$^1/_4$ CUP TRIPLE SEC

$^1/_4$ CUP PEACH BRANDY

Prepare crêpes in advance, and keep warm. Melt butter in flaming pan of chafing dish over direct heat. Add brown sugar and juices, stirring until sugar is dissolved in mixture. When sauce is very hot, add a little triple sec. Baste crêpes one at a time in sauce and fold into quarters. When all crêpes are folded in pan, pour in remainder of triple sec and peach brandy, stir into sauce, ignite, and blaze. Serve crêpes with sauce. Serves 3 or 4.

In Normandy *Gâteau de Crêpes à la Normande* is very popular and, as you might suspect, is made with Calvados.

GATEAU DE CRÊPES À LA NORMANDE

4 OR 5 LARGE RIPE APPLES

$^1/_2$ CUP GRANULATED SUGAR,
 PLUS EXTRA

GROUND CINNAMON

1 VANILLA BEAN

$^1/_4$ CUP CREAM OR
 HOMOGENIZED MILK

$^1/_2$ CUP CALVADOS OR
 APPLEJACK

4 TABLESPOONS MELTED
 BUTTER

1 RECIPE *CRÊPES SUCRÉES II*
 (SEE INDEX) MADE INTO 18
 OR 20 CRÊPES

2 TABLESPOONS CHOPPED OR
 SHREDDED COCONUT

3 TABLESPOONS CHOPPED
 BLACK WALNUTS

1 GENEROUS CUP WHIPPED
 CREAM (OPTIONAL)

Peel, core, and slice apples very thinly. Place in sauce pan. Add sugar and a few pinches of cinnamon and boil in water to cover, with vanilla bean, until apples are very tender. Pour off excess water. Stir in cream or milk and 2 or 3 tablespoons of the Calvados or applejack. Let apples simmer for a few more minutes. Lightly butter large baking dish and place one crêpe in bottom. Spread thin layer of apple mixture on crêpe. Continue to add crêpes and apples in alternating layers until all crêpes are piled high as in a layer cake. Pour on remainder of melted butter and sprinkle with sugar, shredded coconut, and chopped walnuts. Place in hot oven (about 450° F.) and heat thoroughly. Warm remaining Calvados or applejack, pour over mound of crêpes, ignite, and blaze. Baste with flaming sauce, cut crêpes like a cake, and serve in individual plates with a little sauce and a dollop of whipped cream, if you wish. Serves 6.

Once you have become addicted to these slim pancakes, there is no end to the flavor combinations that are possible. Here are seven variations.

RASPBERRY CRÊPES

1-POUND JAR VERY BEST
SEEDLESS RASPBERRY
PRESERVES
1 RECIPE *CRÊPES SUCRÉES II*
(SEE INDEX) MADE INTO 18
OR 20 CRÊPES

LEMON JUICE
CONFECTIONERS' SUGAR
$1/2$ CUP FRAMBOISE, WARMED

Place small amount of preserves on each crêpe and roll very tightly. Place in flameproof dish, sprinkle with a few drops of lemon juice and confectioners' sugar, and put in very hot oven (475° F.) under broiler for a few minutes until heated thoroughly. Remove to hot platter. Pour on warmed framboise, ignite, and blaze. Serves 6.

CRÊPES AUX BANANES FLAMBÉES

3 RIPE BANANAS

1/4 CUP BUTTER

GROUND GINGER

GROUND CINNAMON

1/2 TEASPOON LEMON JUICE

1 RECIPE *CRÊPES SUCRÉES II*
(SEE INDEX) MADE INTO 18
TO 20 CRÊPES

CONFECTIONERS' SUGAR

1/2 CUP JAMAICA RUM

Prepare crêpes as directed in recipe for *Crêpes Sucrées II*. Set aside and keep warm. Peel and slice bananas lengthwise. Cut into small pieces and place in flaming pan of chafing dish in which you have melted butter, sprinkle with ginger and cinnamon, add lemon juice, and sauté. After bananas have browned, move them to the side of the chafing dish to make room for a crêpe. Place portion of sautéed bananas in crêpe, fold, sprinkle with sugar, and move to side of chafing dish. Add additional butter and lemon juice if necessary. Repeat this process until all crêpes have been filled. When thoroughly warm, pour in rum, ignite, and blaze. Serve warm with a portion of sauce. Serves 6.

CRÊPES AUX FRAISES FLAMBÉES

2 PINTS FRESH STRAWBERRIES

1/2 CUP GRANULATED SUGAR

1/2 CUP WATER

1/2 CUP KIRSCH

1 RECIPE *CRÊPES SUCRÉES II*
(SEE INDEX) MADE INTO 18
TO 20 CRÊPES

Wash strawberries, cut off stems, and slice. Marinate in sugar dissolved in water with approximately half the kirsch. Heat strawberry mixture in skillet or flaming pan of chafing dish over direct heat. Add crêpes one by one and baste in sauce. Fold crêpes into quarters, and when thoroughly heated, add remainder of kirsch, ignite, and blaze. Serves 6.

❧

HAWAIIAN CRÊPES FLAMBÉES

3 TABLESPOONS BUTTER

2 TABLESPOONS FIRMLY PACKED
   BROWN SUGAR

2 TABLESPOONS HONEY

2 CUPS FINELY CHOPPED FRESH
   OR CANNED PINEAPPLE

1 RECIPE *CRÊPES SUCRÉES II*
   (SEE INDEX) MADE INTO 18
   TO 20 CRÊPES

$^1/_2$ CUP JAMAICA RUM

Melt butter in flaming pan of chafing dish over direct heat. Add sugar, honey, and pineapple and simmer until bubbling. Add crêpes one by one. Baste each in sauce, add a little pineapple mixture, roll up, and move to side of flaming pan. Add additional butter and sugar if necessary. When crêpes are well heated, pour in rum, ignite, and blaze. Serves 6.

❧

Here is an old favorite from Alsace.

CRÊPES STRASBOURGEOISES

¹/₄ CUP CONFECTIONERS'
    SUGAR, PLUS EXTRA
¹/₂ CUP BUTTER
¹/₂ CUP KIRSCH

1 RECIPE *CRÊPES SUCRÉES II*
    (SEE INDEX) MADE INTO 18
    TO 20 CRÊPES

Cream confectioners' sugar into butter and add 1 tablespoon of the kirsch. Spread crêpes with butter mixture, roll up, and place in heatproof baking dish. Sprinkle with a little additional sugar and glaze quickly under broiler in hot oven (475° to 500° F). Remove from oven and place on flameproof platter. Warm remaining kirsch, pour over crêpes, ignite, and blaze. Serves 6.

CRÊPES NEGRESCO

3 TABLESPOONS BUTTER
¹/₂ CUP CONFECTIONERS'
    SUGAR
JUICE OF 1 LARGE ORANGE
1 RECIPE *CRÊPES SUCRÉES II*
    (SEE INDEX) MADE INTO 18
    TO 20 CRÊPES

1 CUP APRICOT PRESERVES
¹/₂ CUP GRAND MARNIER

Melt butter in flaming pan of chafing dish over direct heat. Add half the confectioners' sugar and orange juice. Bring to boil. Add crêpes one by one and baste until thoroughly saturated with mixture. Add scant tablespoon of the apricot preserves to each crêpe, roll up, and place on side of chafing dish. Cover crêpes with remainder of confectioners' sugar. Pour in Grand Marnier, ignite, and blaze. Serves 6.

GATEAU DE CRÊPES AUX PÊCHES

2 LARGE RIPE PEACHES

¹/₂ CUP CONFECTIONERS'
SUGAR

¹/₂ TEASPOON GROUND
CINNAMON

¹/₂ TEASPOON GROUND CLOVES

1 RECIPE *CRÊPES SUCRÉES II*
(SEE INDEX) MADE INTO 18
TO 20 CRÊPES

¹/₂ CUP 100-PROOF BOURBON,
WARMED

WHIPPED CREAM (OPTIONAL)

Poach peaches in hot water to cover, remove skins, and slice thinly. Cover with confectioners' sugar and sprinkle with cinnamon and cloves. Stack crêpes in heatproof baking dish, alternating each crêpe with thin layer of sliced peaches. Heat in medium oven (350° F.) for a few minutes until warmed through. Remove from oven, sprinkle with additional confectioners' sugar, pour on warmed bourbon, ignite, and blaze. Top with whipped cream if you wish. Serves 6.

Spectacular specialties in flame make a great ending to a scintillating supper or an evening of haute cuisine. We assume that you will have some confirmed firebrands as guests, so don't be afraid to fire up a storm that will provide a real climax to your festivities. These recipes have stood the critical inspection of the most fastidious fire-eaters in food-dom.

In 1898 César Ritz opened a hotel in the Place Vendôme in the heart of Paris. The Hotel Ritz Paris set a new standard for ultra-luxury hostelries that exerts its influence to this very day. Even the name "Ritz" has become synonymous with a majestic lifestyle once enjoyed only by royalty and those who possessed great wealth and position. César Ritz had the great good judgment to choose as his *chef des cuisines* Auguste Escoffier, who in a very short time made the Ritz kitchen the culinary center of Paris—a gastronomic Olympus by which all other purveyors of *cuisine classique* were judged. Indeed the Hotel Ritz Paris today is not only a superb place to dine, but it offers a graduate-level cooking school, the *Ritz-Escoffier Ecole de Gastronomie Française*, for those who wish to raise their culinary skills to a superprofessional level. Herewith is one of the Ritz's famous flambé desserts.

NORMAN APPLE TART
(*Tarte Normand*)

1 CUP ALL-PURPOSE FLOUR, SIFTED	1 EGG
1/4 CUP BUTTER, CHILLED	1/2 CUP GRANULATED SUGAR
3 TABLESPOONS SHORTENING	SEVERAL DROPS OF VANILLA EXTRACT
SALT	1 POUND APPLES
6 TABLESPOONS MILK	CONFECTIONERS' SUGAR
6 TABLESPOONS CRÈME FRAICHE OR HEAVY CREAM	1/4 CUP CALVADOS

Mix flour, chilled butter, and shortening and several pinches of salt in a mixing bowl. Add cold water a little at a time until dough is smooth and handles easily. Roll out dough on a lightly floured pastry board. Line an 8-inch tart ring with dough. Chill while you prepare custard mixture and apples. Beat milk, crème fraiche or heavy cream, egg, sugar, and vanilla in mixing bowl. Peel apples, seed, and cut into wedges $1/2$-inch thick. Arrange slices on dough, sprinkle with confectioners' sugar, and strain custard mixture over apples. Bake for 35 minutes in a preheated, hot (450° F.) oven. Remove tart from oven. Heat Calvados in a small saucepan, ignite, and pour over tart. After flames have died out, place tart on serving platter and lift off ring. May be eaten warm or cold. Serves 6.

PINEAPPLE MAUNA LOA

1 LARGE RIPE PINEAPPLE

1 CUP BROKEN ALMOND
   MACAROONS

$1/2$ CUP CHOPPED PECANS OR
   MACADAMIA NUTS

$1/2$ CUP CHOPPED DRIED
   APRICOTS

$2/3$ CUP PEACH PRESERVES

$1/2$ CUP DARK JAMAICA RUM

Select a very attractive large pineapple, as it will become the container for this dessert dish when served. After washing to remove dirt, very carefully make lengthwise cut so that about two-thirds of pineapple is intact. Cut skin away from one-third of pineapple you have removed. Dice fruit and set aside, then with small knife carefully remove all fruit in larger portion. Discard core, dice fruit, and leave pineapple shell and crown of leaves intact. Mix diced pineapple with macaroons, pecans or macadamia nuts, dried apricots, and peach preserves, and place this filling in pineapple shell. Cover pineapple with aluminum foil and place in moderate oven (350° F.) for about 30 minutes. Then remove foil from pineapple shell but keep wrapped around crown, and bake for another 20 to 30 minutes. Place pineapple on heated flameproof platter. Warm rum, ignite, and ladle blazing into fruit. Serves approximately 6.

If you like macaroons and bananas, here is a Caribbean dish you will enjoy.

BANANAS MARTINIQUE

6 BANANAS (RED PREFERRED)

LIME JUICE

2 TABLESPOONS BUTTER

1 CUP SWEET RED WINE

1 CUP FIRMLY PACKED BROWN
SUGAR

$^1/_2$ TEASPOON GROUND
CINNAMON

$^1/_2$ TEASPOON GRATED NUTMEG

$^1/_4$ TEASPOON GROUND CLOVES

2 TEASPOONS GRATED ORANGE
PEEL

$1^1/_2$ CUPS CRUMBLED
MACAROONS

1 CUP FINELY CHOPPED
ALMONDS

$^1/_2$ CUP DARK MARTINIQUE,
JAMAICA, OR DEMERARA
RUM, WARMED

Peel bananas, split lengthwise, then cut in half. Sprinkle with lime juice and sauté in butter until brown. In saucepan, make syrup using any sweet red wine that is *unfortified* (a wine to which brandy has *not* been added), add brown sugar, cinnamon, nutmeg, cloves, and orange peel. Place bananas in buttered casserole. Cover with syrup and then top with an even layer of macaroons and almonds. Brown in medium oven (350° F.) When color is a light golden brown, remove casserole and ladle warmed rum, blazing, over top. Serves 3 or 4.

Here is an old American favorite, updated with a flaming dress.

APPLE CHARLOTTE IN FLAMES

3 POUNDS CHOICE RED EATING
   APPLES

2 CUPS GRANULATED SUGAR

2 TABLESPOONS SHERRY

$^1/_4$ CUP BUTTER

2 CUPS DRIED BREAD CRUMBS

$^1/_2$ CUP COGNAC, WARMED

Pare apples, remove seeds, and slice thinly. Place apples in bowl with a little less than $^1/_2$ cup of the sugar. Add sherry, cover, and let stand for several hours. Butter shallow baking dish or casserole and place layer of sliced apples on bottom, followed by layer of bread crumbs. sprinkle with a little sugar and dot with butter. Repeat procedure until all apples are used. Place dish in shallow pan of hot water and bake in medium (350° F.) oven for $1^1/_2$ hours. Remove and blaze with warmed cognac. Serves 8 hungry Apple Charlotte fans. Can be topped with whipped cream if you wish.

And speaking of old favorites, here is an American apple dish of German origin that makes an easily prepared flambéed dessert.

PRINCE EUGENE'S
APPLE PANCAKE FLAMBÉ

$1/2$ CUP MILK

$1/2$ CUP SIFTED ALL-PURPOSE
FLOUR

3 EGGS

1 TEASPOON GRANULATED
SUGAR

PINCH OF SALT

1 LARGE APPLE

2 TABLESPOONS BUTTER

1 TABLESPOON HONEY

GROUND CINNAMON

LEMON JUICE

$1/3$ CUP CALVADOS, APPLEJACK,
OR BOURBON

Prepare batter by mixing milk, flour, eggs, sugar, and salt in mixing bowl. Pare apple, remove seeds, slice, and sauté with butter and honey in large iron skillet. Butter should thoroughly coat bottom and sides of pan. Pour in batter and place pan in hot (425° F.) oven. When pancake has risen and is nearly done (approximately 10 to 12 minutes), powder with additional sugar and cinnamon. Dot with additional butter, return to oven, and bake until brown. Immediately before serving, sprinkle a little lemon juice on pancake. Warm Calvados, applejack, or bourbon, ignite, and ladle flaming into skillet.

For a change of pace, why not have a go at one of these pyrological puddings?

DUCHESS PUDDING

2 CUPS HEAVY CREAM

1/2 CUP DARK JAMAICA OR
    LIGHT PUERTO RICAN RUM

PINCH OF SALT

1/4 CUP GRANULATED SUGAR

CINNAMON STICK

5 TABLESPOONS SIFTED ALL-
    PURPOSE FLOUR

3 EGG YOLKS, PLUS 1 EGG,
    BEATEN

CRACKER CRUMBS

FINELY GROUND ALMONDS

1/2 CUP BUTTER

Scald cream in saucepan. Place in double boiler, add 2 teaspoons of the rum, salt, sugar, and cinnamon stick, and simmer slowly while blending in flour. If batter is lumpy, add just enough water to make it smooth and creamy. Add lightly whipped egg yolks and blend until mixture is thick and smooth. Pour into cake pan and allow to cool, then slice into small servings and coat with cracker crumbs, beaten egg, and finely ground almonds in that order. Melt butter in flaming pan of chafing dish over direct heat and brown cream squares over high heat. Warm remaining rum and pour over squares, ignite, and blaze. Serves 6 to 8.

ARABIAN NIGHTS PUDDING

4 EGGS

1 CUP CHOPPED PITTED DATES

3/4 CUP CHOPPED PECANS

1 1/4 CUPS GRANULATED SUGAR

1/4 CUP ALL-PURPOSE FLOUR

2 TEASPOONS BAKING POWDER

2 TEASPOONS VANILLA
EXTRACT

WHOLE NUTS

CANDIED PINEAPPLE

CANDIED CHERRIES

1/2 CUP TRIPLE SEC

Beat eggs in mixing bowl. Add dates, pecans, sugar, flour, baking powder, and vanilla and mix thoroughly. Line ring mold with lightly greased aluminum foil so cake will not stick. Pour batter into mold and bake in a 350° F oven for 45 minutes. Cool, place on flameproof serving dish, and decorate with nuts, pineapple, and cherries. Heat triple sec, ignite, and ladle flaming over pudding. Serves 6 to 8.

Hot Tips—No. 32

A zesty, all-purpose flaming sauce for plum puddings and fruitcakes will add a little extra glamour to the holidays. Carefully remove the outer peel from an orange and cut it into small, julienne strips. Place orange slices in a saucepan with 1 tablespoon butter and sauté lightly. Add 2 tablespoons honey, 1/2 cup cognac, and 1/4 cup Curaçao or triple sec. Blend well. When heated, ignite and ladle blazing over a cake or pudding.

Meredith Frederick, the pastry chef at New York's famous Post House restaurant, finds challenge and satisfaction in creating monumental desserts. This recipe—in three parts—may seem daunting at first glance, but it is definitely worth the effort.

FLAMING BANANA BREAD PUDDING

Banana Bread Recipe

2 CUPS CAKE FLOUR	1 TEASPOON VANILLA EXTRACT
1 TEASPOON BAKING POWDER	2 EGGS
1 TEASPOON BAKING SODA	3 RIPE BANANAS, MASHED
$^1/_2$ TEASPOON SALT	1 CUP COARSELY CHOPPED
$^3/_4$ CUP BUTTER, SOFTENED	WALNUTS
$1^1/_2$ CUPS GRANULATED SUGAR	$^1/_2$ CUP BUTTERMILK

Preheat oven to 350° F. In bowl, combine flour, baking powder, baking soda, and salt and set aside. In a separate mixing bowl, beat butter until creamy. Add sugar, vanilla, eggs, bananas, and walnuts. In three portions, blend in flour mixture and buttermilk. Turn into a greased and floured loaf pan. Bake for 45 minutes to 1 hour until firm to the touch. Cool and set aside.

Pudding Recipe

2 CUPS MILK	1 LOAF BANANA BREAD
2 CUPS HEAVY CREAM	(ABOVE), CUT UP INTO
6 EGGS	CUBES
$^3/_4$ CUP GRANULATED SUGAR	

Preheat oven to 350° F. In saucepan, bring milk and cream to a boil. In mixing bowl, beat eggs with sugar until lightened, then slowly blend in hot milk and cream. Place bread cubes in greased rectangular pan and pour pudding mixture on top. Set pan with pudding into a larger rectangular pan; fill outside pan with water until three-quarters full. Bake in oven for 40 minutes, or until custard is fully set. Chill custard in refrigerator.

SAUCE RECIPE

2 CUPS HEAVY CREAM	$^1/_3$ CUP GRANULATED SUGAR
VANILLA BEAN, SPLIT IN HALF	$^1/_4$ CUP COGNAC
5 EGG YOLKS	

In saucepan, bring cream, with $^1/_2$ vanilla bean, to boil. In mixing bowl, beat egg yolks with sugar. Slowly blend in hot cream. Put mixture in another saucepan and cook very slowly over low heat until thickened, or until sauce coats the back of a spoon. Strain sauce through a fine sieve and cool in refrigerator.

To serve, cut bread pudding into 2-inch squares and put on skewers. Bring pudding to table on platter. In small saucepan, warm cognac, ignite, and pour flaming onto pudding. Pour sauce over pudding and extinguish flames. Serves 8 to 10.

Babas au rhum is a great classic French recipe that you can prepare at home easily with a little practice. *Babas* are designed to absorb or imbibe syrups as well as liqueurs; consequently they are always a juicy, tender, thoroughly mouth-watering dessert.

BABAS AU RHUM

$^1/_4$ OUNCE DRY YEAST

$^1/_2$ CUP WARM WATER

$1^1/_2$ CUPS FLOUR

2 EGGS

$^1/_2$ CUP WARM MILK

6 TABLESPOONS BUTTER

1 TABLESPOON GRANULATED
SUGAR

$^1/_2$ TEASPOON SALT

3 TABLESPOONS RAISINS

Dissolve yeast in warm water in mixing bowl. Add flour, eggs, and warm milk. Mix dough well, adding additional milk if necessary to make it very soft—about consistency of very thick cream. Sprinkle with flour, cover with towel, and put in warm place for about 1 hour, or until double in size. In mixing bowl, knead butter until very soft and creamy, then blend in sugar and salt. After dough has risen, push it down, add butter mixture, raisins, and mix well. Butter muffin pans. Fill each cup half full with dough and put pans in a warm place. After 20 to 30 minutes, or when dough has risen to top of pan, place in preheated hot (425° F.) oven and bake for 10 to 15 minutes until golden brown. Remove *babas* from pan and serve warm with Duquesne Sauce (see next recipe). Makes about 16 *babas*.

DUQUESNE SAUCE

6 TABLESPOONS LIGHT CORN
SYRUP

4 TABLESPOONS PURE MAPLE
SYRUP

3 TABLESPOONS BUTTER

2 TEASPOONS LEMON JUICE

$^1/_4$ TEASPOON GROUND
CINNAMON

$^1/_4$ CUP JAMAICA RUM

$^1/_4$ CUP COGNAC

Mix all ingredients except rum and cognac in saucepan or flaming pan of chafing dish over direct heat and warm gently. Do not heat too much or sauce will taste scorched. Place *babas* in pan and baste well with hot sauce. Pour in rum and cognac, and continue to baste *babas* until they have absorbed some of the mixture. Ignite, blaze, and baste *babas* with flaming sauce. Serve immediately with sauce.

One of the most distinguished desserts was created by Auguste Escoffier for Nellie Melba, the famous singer and celebrity of another day. Attesting to the power and prestige of a great chef and a great culinary creation is the fact that many, many people know about the dessert but relatively few know about the personage for whom it was created. *Pêche* (or Peach) *Melba* is easy to make, and although the original version was not flamed, we must remember that Madame Melba was an opera singer and not a pyrophile—being no doubt duly concerned about the effect of smoke and fire on a delicate, sensitive, and highly trained throat.

PÊCHE MELBA

2 CUPS WATER

1 CUP PLUS 3 TABLESPOONS
   GRANULATED SUGAR

VANILLA BEAN

2 LARGE RIPE PEACHES

$^2/_3$ CUP FROZEN RASPBERRIES

$^1/_3$ CUP RED CURRANT JELLY

1 TEASPOON ARROWROOT

DASH OF LEMON JUICE

1 QUART VANILLA ICE CREAM

$^1/_4$ CUP KIRSCH, WARMED

Combine water and 1 cup sugar with small piece of vanilla bean in saucepan. Boil until all sugar is dissolved. Peel and halve peaches, remove pits, and poach fruit in syrup until tender. Remove peaches, drain, and chill. In second saucepan, thoroughly mix raspberries, currant jelly, and 3 tablespoons sugar and bring to a boil. Make a smooth paste with arrowroot and a little cold water. Add to raspberry sauce and cook, stirring constantly, until it is smooth and clear. Add lemon juice and purée sauce by pushing through a fine sieve. Place 1 scoop of ice cream in flameproof bowl or goblet for each serving, and top with peach half. Pour raspberry sauce over peaches, and ladle a little warmed kirsch, blazing, over each portion. Serves 4.

Hot Tips—No. 33

It has probably occurred to you by now that the servings given for the recipes in this book are purposely on the generous side. This is based on the simple proposition that, when entertaining, it is better to have a little too much rather than a little too little. Nothing is so sad to behold as a skimpy portion. It is understandable for food manufacturers to try to make their products appear to be good values by indicating that they serve a goodly number of people. The fact that these are ascetics on strict diets is a matter of importance to you, because if you're not having a group of ascetics for dinner, in many cases you will be hard put to come out with the advertised number of adult-size portions. A good rule of thumb to follow when buying food for a special occasion is simply to reduce the number of servings listed on the label by about half.

Peaches and vanilla ice cream have such an affinity for each other, we had to include this recipe named for another famous lady who distinguished herself in other fields of endeavor.

PEACHES POMPADOUR

2 LARGE RIPE PEACHES

3/4 CUP GRATED ALMONDS

1/2 CUP GRANULATED SUGAR

2 DASHES OF LEMON JUICE

1 TABLESPOON ORANGE
  MARMALADE

1 EGG WHITE, BEATEN HARD

1 QUART VANILLA ICE CREAM

1/2 CUP BOURBON OR LIGHT
  PUERTO RICAN RUM

Place peaches in boiling water for several minutes to loosen skins. Peel, slice in half, remove pits, and place in casserole or flameproof baking dish. In mixing bowl, place almonds, sugar, lemon juice, and orange marmalade with egg white. If mixture is too dry, add a little water. Spread mixture on top of each peach half and place in hot (450° F.) oven till light brown and crusty (approximately 2 to 3 minutes). Remove and place peach halves and a little syrup over individual portions of ice cream. Warm bourbon or light Puerto Rican rum, ignite, and pour blazing over peaches and ice cream. Serves 4.

When I was very young, my mother brought me to New York for a birthday dinner at The Rainbow Room perched sixty-five floors above Rockefeller Center. She called it "The most beautiful restaurant in the world." It was. It still is. The spectacular view of the city through two-story-high windows, the live music, the revolving dance floor, and a menu filled with legendary dishes from the age of Art Deco make this a very special place. The Rainbow Room's signature dessert, Baked Alaska, is a great favorite (122,000 were sold in a single year) and reflects the joy of dining here. Ruth Reichl, *The New York Times* restaurant reviewer, describes the experience: "The band segued into 'I'll Take Manhattan' just as the waiter arrived with Baked Alaska. Holding out the silver platter he showed off the pretty ice cream cake covered with meringue. Then he heated a small pot of brandy and poured the burning alcohol over the top. The blue flames flickered across the frozen swirls of sugar, a joyous reminder of how much fun life can be."

RAINBOW BAKED ALASKA

Ice Cream Cake Recipe

1 POUND SPONGE CAKE	1 PINT VANILLA ICE CREAM
1 PINT CHOCOLATE ICE CREAM	6 EGG WHITES
1 PINT RASPBERRY SORBET	$^1/_3$ CUP GRANULATED SUGAR

On a large plate arrange 4 slices of sponge cake approximately 6 to 8 inches in diameter and $^1/_4$-inch thick. Mound chocolate ice cream into an inverted bowl mold (plastic container). Cover with slice of sponge cake. Mound raspberry sorbet on top of sponge cake layer. Cover raspberry sorbet with layer of sponge cake. Mound vanilla ice cream on top of sponge cake layer. Freeze ice cream cake mold overnight (12 hours). Remove frozen ice cream cake from mold by turning upside down onto plate. (Chocolate ice cream will be top layer). Make meringue by whipping egg whites with sugar until stiff. Put meringue in pastry bag with $^1/_2$-inch tip and pipe in swirls onto ice cream cake, making certain to cover completely. Freeze for 2 hours.

Fruit Sauce

³/₄ CUP WATER	¹/₄ CUP BLUEBERRIES
²/₃ CUP GRANULATED SUGAR	¹/₂ CUP STRAWBERRIES
SMALL VANILLA BEAN	
¹/₄ CUP RASPBERRIES	¹/₃ CUP BRANDY

Combine water, sugar, and vanilla bean in saucepan and bring mixture to a boil. Remove from stove, set aside to cool for 30 minutes, then stir in fruit.

To serve, bake ice cream cake in preheated hot (500° F.) oven for 1 minute, until lightly browned. Heat brandy in small pot and, at table, ignite and pour blazing over Baked Alaska. Serve immediately with fruit sauce on the side. Makes about 8 servings.

This recipe was created by Pastry Chef Alain Oster.

Flaming desserts in general and the desserts in this chapter in particular should be regarded not just as fiery furbelows but rather as elegant and exhilarating finales to gracious evenings of drinking and dining. A good dessert can't make up for a drab dinner, but it can do much both psychologically and gastronomically to put just the right bright touch where it might be needed most. Fire lovers seem to be in complete agreement on at least one thing: When the final curtain is rung down on the dinner table, it is far more festive, and frequently more flavorful, if it is a curtain of flames.

EIGHT

Twenty-six Sure-fire Ways to Fix Coffee

$\overset{\bullet}{A}$ good cup of coffee is the crowning glory of a great dinner. Its overwhelming popularity as the American national beverage cannot be questioned. We simply have to look around us to observe the obvious fact that outside of water, coffee is probably the most available drink.

Everyone has a preferred way of making coffee. Many favor the percolator, which recirculates water through the coffee grounds. Others wouldn't part with their automatic electric drip coffeemaker. They like the drip method because the hot water seeps through the grounds rather than continuously boiling through them. Another popular method is the vacuum process, which allows all the water to come into contact with the grounds for an optimum infusion time period and then the brew and the spent grounds are expeditiously separated. For coffee drinkers who prefer a strong, dark coffee, the answer is the espresso method whereby hot water and steam is "expressed" through the grounds.

Whatever method you prefer—percolator, drip, vacuum, or espresso—there are plenty of reliable coffeemakers from which to choose. Finding the best coffee beans for your taste, however, is a far more fascinating—and challenging—pursuit. You may want to begin your search with some of the basic varieties favored by professional blenders, such as Arabica beans grown in Colombia, Nicaragua, El Salvador, and Honduras. Arabica is the most widely planted coffee type which grows at the higher altitudes in South and Central America and East Africa. To attain a balanced blend, Arabicas are mixed with Robusta varieties grown in low-lying areas of India and Uganda where Arabica cannot survive.

Start by sampling good, mild varieties such as Bourbon Santos from Brazil, Sumatra from Indonesia, India's Malabar, and Kenya coffee. Then move up to more pungent, assertive beans like Hawaiian Kona, Mexico's Coatepec, Maracaibo from Venezuela, Jamaican Blue Mountain, and Yauco Selecto from the mountains of Puerto Rico. Rich, full-bodied coffees like Medellín and Maragogipe are grown in Colombia. Also rich and distinctive are Cobán from Guatemala; Mocha from Yemen; and Harar from Ethiopia.

Since coffee-growing areas girdle the earth's tropical zones, just finding new coffee types to sample can become a serious hobby. All you need to get started is a dependable coffeemaker, an inexpensive coffee grinder; sample bags of roasted coffee beans; and a compulsive, inquisitive lust for coffee.

Here is some very sage advice on how you can be sure of making a good cup of coffee every time gleaned from those who work in the coffee trade.

1. *Get the proper grind for your coffeemaker. This is important to everyone (except instant-coffee lovers). It's not really a matter of just making do, because good coffee is a delicate commodity, and unless the water has an opportunity to remove the flavor locked up in those little pulverized coffee beans, you're really not getting what you deserve from your coffeepot. If the grind is too coarse, a lot of the flavor and the aroma that should go into your cup instead go out with the grounds.*

2. *There is no substitute for freshness. Once ground coffee is exposed to the air, it deteriorates after a week or ten days, much more than most people realize. It's not too noticeable if you're drinking the coffee every day, but go away on a two-week vacation, come back, and then try some coffee that's been around for a while and taste the difference. Refrigeration helps, but it is better to buy only what you need for a week or so.*

3. *Coffee should be precisely measured. The approved standard measure for all types of coffeemakers is 2 level tablespoons for each ³/₄ cup (6 ounces) of water.*

4. *Your equipment should be sparkling clean. Some utensils, such as beer mugs, salad bowls, and even omelet pans, improve with age and with minimal cleaning, but this does not hold true with coffeemakers. The tarlike residue that remains in your coffeemaker after you have brewed coffee will not in any way contribute to the next batch you make except to infuse it with a bitter, stale flavor.*

5. *Whenever possible, try to use your coffeemaker to its full capacity and never, under any circumstances, under 75 percent of its rated capacity. It is impossible to expect a percolator that was designed*

to make 10 cups of coffee do as well when making half that amount.

6. *Brewing time is important, and for this reason, all good automatic coffeemakers are designed to make coffee within recommended time limits. Coffee that's brewed too quickly is weak, flat, and tasteless, and coffee that is overbrewed has a tendency to be pungent and bitter. Under no circumstances boil coffee.*

7. *When coffee is ready, it should be served immediately. It is not recommended to allow coffee to stand for more than an hour after brewing. Coffee cannot be reheated successfully after long periods of time. It may be stronger but it won't be better.*

The increase in travel by Americans to Europe and points east has done much to popularize exotic methods of coffee making and unusual recipes for coffee drinking. And the renaissance of the coffeehouse has done much to broaden our awareness of the versatility of coffee. Hence, *caffè espresso,* once a curiosity, is now quite commonplace in every large city and in many small towns. An espresso maker is simply a device that "expresses" live steam through the coffee grounds, yielding a thick, rich, very dark coffee that is usually drunk in demitasse cups. A part of the reason for the darkness of *caffè espresso* is the method of roasting the beans. They appear to be almost burned, but work quite well in an espresso machine or in a drip pot of Italian origin, called a *macchinetta.* Coffee produced by the *macchinetta* is similar to that which is served in France as *café filtre.*

Another type of coffee that has become famous in history and literature is Turkish coffee. Its method of preparation is as fascinating as the drink itself, although some feel that the resulting product is a little too sweet for American tastes. Turkish coffee is prepared by using a long-handled brass or copper container, called an *Ibrik.* Even if you don't care to have Turkish coffee as a staple in your diet, the Turkish coffeemaker itself is very handy for other things, such as heating spirits to be used in flambéed dishes.

One of the most delicious after-dinner coffee recipes is an American creation known as *café brûlot*. It is not difficult to make, and contrary to the opinion of some, there is no one single, immutable recipe for this fine drink. It is concocted by combining spices, such as cloves and cinnamon, with sugar and citrus fruit peel, such as lemon and orange, adding warm cognac, and flambéing for a few moments in a specially shaped flameproof container known as a *brûlot* bowl, then quickly pouring in hot, strong, black coffee to extinguish the flames and thus prevent too much combustion or burning off of the cognac. It is then poured with a ladle into demitasse cups. Attractive *café brûlot* bowls and ladles are available in most stores where chafing dishes and similar gourmet cooking equipment are sold. It is not absolutely necessary, however, to have a *brûlot* bowl, since this recipe can be made successfully in a saucepan or a chafing dish.

Café brûlot is believed to have originated in New Orleans, where it remains popular to this day. It is traditional for special occasions such as New Year's and Christmas, employing, as a rule, *café filtre* or New Orleans drip coffee, which is made very strong and, in accordance with the taste of the local population, contains chicory. The word *brûlot* is quite appropriate, for it means both "seasoned" and "incendiary" in French, which aptly describes this fire lovers' favorite. Here is a traditional recipe for *café brûlot*, followed by some popular variations. Once you get the knack of making this delightful drink, you will undoubtedly want to try inventions of your own.

CAFÉ BRÛLOT

2 CINNAMON STICKS

8 TO 10 WHOLE CLOVES

5 OR 6 SUGAR CUBES,
DEPENDING ON SWEETNESS
DESIRED

OUTER PEEL (ZEST) OF $^1/_2$
ORANGE

OUTER PEEL (ZEST) OF $^1/_2$
LEMON

4 OUNCES COGNAC, WARMED

1 PINT HOT, STRONG BLACK
COFFEE

Place all ingredients, except cognac and coffee, in *brûlot* bowl or chafing dish. Soften sugar cubes with a few drops of water and mash into orange and lemon peel. Add warmed cognac and thoroughly mix ingredients. Ignite and blaze for a few moments, then pour in coffee. Makes 4 demitasse servings.

COMFORT-ABLE CAFÉ BRÛLOT

4 SUGAR CUBES

2 CINNAMON STICKS

6 WHOLE CLOVES

SMALL PIECE LEMON PEEL

$^1/_2$ SPICED PEACH, THINLY
SLICED (FOUND IN MANY
SPECIALTY FOOD STORES)

4 OUNCES SOUTHERN
COMFORT, WARMED

1 PINT HOT, STRONG BLACK
COFFEE

Place all ingredients except coffee and liqueur in *brûlot* bowl or chafing dish. You can substitute a little syrup from peaches in place of sugar cubes if you wish. Mix well. Pour in warmed Southern Comfort, ignite, blaze for a few moments, and then pour in coffee. Makes 4 demitasse servings.

CAFÉ BRÛLOT AU CHOCOLAT

1 TABLESPOON HONEY OR
  SIMPLE SYRUP (SEE INDEX)

1 CINNAMON STICK

6 WHOLE CLOVES

OUTER PEEL (ZEST) OF $^1/_2$
  ORANGE

3 OUNCES 100-PROOF VODKA,
  WARMED

2 OUNCES KAHLÚA OR CRÈME
  DE CACAO, WARMED

1 PINT HOT, STRONG BLACK
  COFFEE

Place honey or Simple Syrup, cinnamon, cloves, and orange zest in *brûlot* bowl or chafing dish. Pour in warmed vodka and Kahlúa or crème de cacao. Mix well, ignite, and blaze. After a few moments, pour in coffee. Makes 4 demitasse servings.

CAFÉ BRÛLOT B AND B

4 TO 6 SUGAR CUBES

OUTER PEEL (ZEST) OF $^1/_2$
  LEMON

OUTER PEEL (ZEST) OF $^1/_2$
  ORANGE

2 CINNAMON STICKS

6 TO 8 WHOLE CLOVES

4 OUNCES B AND B LIQUEUR,
  WARMED

1 PINT HOT, STRONG BLACK
  COFFEE

Place all ingredients, except liqueur and coffee, in *brûlot* bowl or chafing dish. Soften sugar cubes with a few drops of water and mash into lemon and orange peel. Add warmed B and B liqueur. Ignite and blaze for a few moments. Pour in coffee. Makes 4 demitasse servings.

SCOTTISH CAFÉ BRÛLOT

2 CINNAMON STICKS

6 TO 8 WHOLE CLOVES

5 SUGAR CUBES (OR HONEY TO TASTE)

OUTER PEEL (ZEST) OF $1/2$ LEMON

OUTER PEEL (ZEST) OF $1/2$ ORANGE

2 OUNCES DRAMBUIE LIQUEUR

3 OUNCES SCOTCH

1 PINT HOT, STRONG BLACK COFFEE

Mix cinnamon sticks, cloves, sugar, and fruit zest in *brûlot* bowl or chafing dish, substituting honey for sugar cubes if you wish. Mix Drambuie and Scotch and warm. Pour in warmed Drambuie-Scotch mixture. Ignite, blaze for a few moments, and then pour in coffee. Makes 4 demitasse servings.

CAFÉ BRÛLOT GRAND MARNIER

2 SUGAR CUBES

2 CINNAMON STICKS

6 TO 8 WHOLE CLOVES

OUTER PEEL (ZEST) OF $^1/_2$
ORANGE

OUTER PEEL (ZEST) OF $^1/_2$
LEMON

SMALL PIECE VANILLA BEAN

3 OUNCES GRAND MARNIER,
WARMED

2 OUNCES COGNAC, WARMED

1 PINT HOT, STRONG BLACK
COFFEE

Place all ingredients, except liquor and coffee, in *brûlot* bowl or chafing dish. Moisten sugar cubes with a few drops of water and mash into lemon and orange peel. Add warmed Grand Marnier and cognac. Mix well. For an additional flourish, place another sugar cube in bowl of ladle with small amount of cognac. Ignite and pour blazing into bowl. Allow to burn for a few moments and pour in coffee. Makes 4 demitasse servings.

CAFÉ BRÛLOT FRAMBOISE

2 TABLESPOONS HONEY OR
SIMPLE SYRUP (SEE INDEX)

2 CINNAMON STICKS

6 WHOLE CLOVES

OUTER PEEL (ZEST) OF $^1/_2$
LEMON

OUTER PEEL (ZEST) OF $^1/_2$
ORANGE

4 OUNCES FRAMBOISE, WARMED

1 PINT HOT, STRONG BLACK
COFFEE

Place all ingredients, except framboise and coffee, in *brûlot* bowl or chafing dish. Pour in warmed framboise, ignite, blaze for a few moments, and then pour in coffee. Makes 4 demitasse servings.

All *cafés flambés* are simply variations of four basic ingredients: coffee, spices, fruits, and sweetening agents and spirits. They are known by various names in addition to *café brûlot*, such as *café diable*, *café diablo*, *café diabolique*, *café royale*, and a host of special names following the usual culinary practice of dedicating recipes to people, places, or events. Here are a few of the more famous blazable brews that have well established pyric popularity.

CAFÉ ROYALE NO. 1

4 SUGAR CUBES

1 PINT HOT, STRONG BLACK
    COFFEE

4 OUNCES 100-PROOF BOURBON

Place sugar cube in each of 4 demitasse cups and fill almost full with coffee. Using teaspoon, carefully float 1 ounce of bourbon on top of coffee in each cup. When coffee has warmed bourbon, ignite and blaze for a few moments. Then stir bourbon into coffee with spoon to extinguish flames. Serves 4.

CAFÉ ROYALE NO. 2

4 SUGAR CUBES

1 PINT HOT, STRONG BLACK
    COFFEE

4 OUNCES COGNAC

Place sugar cube in each of 4 demitasse cups and fill almost full with coffee. Using teaspoon, carefully pour 1 ounce of cognac on top of coffee in each cup. When coffee has warmed cognac, ignite and blaze for a few moments. Then stir cognac into coffee with spoon to extinguish flames. Serves 4.

CAFÉ KIRSCH

4 SUGAR CUBES

1 PINT HOT, STRONG BLACK
  COFFEE

4 OUNCES KIRSCH

Place sugar cube in each of 4 demitasse cups and fill nearly full with coffee. Pour kirsch in small saucepan (a long-handled Turkish coffeemaker will do very nicely). Warm kirsch, ignite, and pour blazing into each cup. Serves 4.

CAFÉ DIABLE

2 CINNAMON STICKS

6 TO 8 WHOLE CLOVES

4 OR 5 WHOLE COFFEE BEANS

2 OUNCES COGNAC

2 OUNCES ORANGE CURAÇAO
  OR TRIPLE SEC

1 PINT HOT, STRONG BLACK
  COFFEE

Place all ingredients, except coffee, into *brûlot* bowl or chafing dish. Warm under low heat and mix well. Ignite and blaze for a few moments. Then pour in coffee. Makes 4 demitasse servings.

FLAMING IRISH COFFEE

BOILING WATER

2 OUNCES IRISH WHISKEY,
WARMED

1 CUP HOT, STRONG BLACK
COFFEE

1 TO 2 TEASPOONS FIRMLY
PACKED BROWN SUGAR, OR
SWEETEN TO TASTE

DOLLOP OF WHIPPED CREAM

Scald 8-ounce Irish coffee glass or mug with boiling water. Pour out water and add warmed whiskey. Ignite and blaze for a very few moments. Pour in coffee and add brown sugar. Mix well until sugar is dissolved. Top with whipped cream. Serves 1.

COFFEE GROG

1 TEASPOON BUTTER

1 TABLESPOON FIRMLY PACKED
BROWN SUGAR

PINCH OF GRATED NUTMEG

12 WHOLE CLOVES

4 CINNAMON STICKS

4 SMALL SLICES LEMON PEEL

4 SMALL SLICES ORANGE PEEL

1/2 PINT DARK JAMAICA RUM

1 PINT HOT, STRONG BLACK
COFFEE

WHIPPED CREAM

Cream butter and brown sugar with nutmeg. Into each of 4 large flame-proof mugs, place approximately 1 teaspoon of butter–brown sugar mixture, 3 cloves, 1 cinnamon stick, 1 slice of lemon peel, 1 slice of orange peel, and 2 ounces of the rum. Stir well, ignite, and blaze. After a few moments, pour in coffee to extinguish flames. Stir again and top with whipped cream. Serves 4.

One of the real secrets of good coffee is the water in which it is brewed. For this reason, water should never be drawn from the hot tap because scale and other mineral deposits in the pipes can affect the flavor of the brewed coffee. More important is whether the water you use is hard or soft. Soft water makes the best coffee. If you live in an area where the water is hard, you will be well advised when planning a party for coffee lovers to buy a bottle of spring water and use it to brew your coffee. You'll be surprised how good the coffee tastes.

Most of the coffees presented thus far are popular and well known, or at least recognizable, since they are basic recipes or variations thereof that are in the realm of experience of most coffee lovers. Here is a rare baker's dozen, a connoisseur's collection of café concoctions most of which are unknown (and some just invented), guaranteed to make thermally tantalizing conversation pieces and good drinks as well.

CAFÉ BARBADOS

BOILING WATER	1 CUP HOT, STRONG BLACK
1 TEASPOON COCONUT SYRUP	COFFEE
2 GROUND CARDAMOM SEEDS	1 TEASPOON 151-PROOF
PINCH OF GROUND CINNAMON	DEMERARA RUM
1 OUNCE BARBADOS RUM	DOLLOP OF WHIPPED CREAM

Scald flameproof mug with boiling water. Mix coconut syrup, cardamom seeds, cinnamon, and Barbados rum in mug. Pour in coffee. Carefully

float Demerara rum on top. Ignite and blaze. Stir to extinguish flames.
Add whipped cream. Serves 1.

CAFÉ COPACABANA

1 TABLESPOON COCONUT SYRUP	PEEL OF $1/2$ ORANGE
1 TABLESPOON FALERNUM	1 OUNCE CRÈME DE CACAO
2 CINNAMON STICKS	1 PINT HOT, STRONG BLACK
2 WHOLE CLOVES	COFFEE
6 ALLSPICE BERRIES	4 OUNCES 86-PROOF DEMERARA
$1/2$ TEASPOON GROUND GINGER	RUM

Mix all ingredients, except rum, in flaming pan of chafing dish over direct heat. Warm rum in ladle, ignite, and pour blazing into chafing dish.
Makes 4 servings.

CAFÉ ORANGERIE

GRATED OUTER PEEL (ZEST) OF	1 PINT HOT, STRONG BLACK
1 ORANGE	COFFEE
1 TABLESPOON COCONUT SYRUP	4 OUNCES BARBADOS OR
1 TABLESPOON ORGEAT SYRUP	HAITIAN RUM
GROUND CINNAMON	WHIPPED CREAM

Blend peel, coconut and orgeat syrups, and generous sprinkling of cinnamon in flaming pan of chafing dish over direct heat. Pour in coffee and mix well. Warm rum in ladle, ignite, and pour blazing into chafing dish. Serve in mugs and top with generous portions of whipped cream. Serves 4.

CAFÉ DE LA PAIX

1 TABLESPOON ORANGE
  MARMALADE
4 SMALL CINNAMON STICKS
4 SMALL PIECES ORANGE PEEL

1 PINT *CAFFÈ ESPRESSO* OR
  CAFÉ FILTRE
2 OUNCES DARK JAMAICA RUM
2 OUNCES COGNAC

Place orange sections, cinnamon sticks, and peel in flaming pan of chafing dish over direct heat and pour in *caffè espresso* or *café filtre*. Mix well and bring to boil. Warm rum and cognac in ladle, ignite, and pour blazing into chafing dish. Makes 4 demitasse servings.

CAFÉ COINTREAU

OUTER PEEL (ZEST) OF $^1/_2$
  LEMON, GRATED
1 PINT HOT, STRONG BLACK
  COFFEE

4 OUNCES COINTREAU

Place a little grated lemon peel in each of 4 coffee cups. Fill nearly full with coffee. Warm Cointreau in ladle, ignite, and pour blazing into each cup. Serves 4.

CAFÉ NAPOLEON

2 TABLESPOONS HONEY

OUTER PEEL (ZEST) OF $^{1}/_{2}$
   ORANGE

1 TEASPOON LEMON JUICE

2 CINNAMON STICKS

8 WHOLE CLOVES

1 PINT HOT, STRONG BLACK
   COFFEE

2 OUNCES B AND B LIQUEUR

1 OUNCE KÜMMEL

1 OUNCE PUERTO RICAN RUM

1 OUNCE COGNAC

WHIPPED CREAM

FRESHLY GRATED NUTMEG

Place all ingredients except spirits, whipped cream, and nutmeg into flaming pan of chafing dish over direct heat. Bring to a simmer but do not boil. Add B and B, kümmel, and rum and mix well. Warm cognac in ladle, ignite, and pour blazing into chafing dish. Serve in large cups or mugs, and top with whipped cream sprinkled with freshly grated nutmeg. Serves 4.

Hot Tips—No. 35

Some recipes for flaming coffee specify that the flaming of a small amount of liqueur be done over the coffee in a teaspoon. There is nothing wrong with this method, except that it lacks the elegance, flair, and excitement of blazing spirits in a chafing dish. The most dramatic effect is achieved when you warm the spirits in a small container, such as a ladle or a Turkish coffeemaker, ignite the spirits, and pour them in a cascade of flames into the individual cups. The alternate method is to float spirits carefully on top of the coffee, ignite, and blaze.

Here is a truly elegant drink named in honor of the very special person for whom it was created.

CAFÉ DIANA

1 TEASPOON LEMON JUICE

4 MINCED MARASCHINO
    CHERRIES

2 TEASPOONS MARASCHINO
    CHERRY JUICE

4 SMALL PIECES CINNAMON
    STICK

GROUND GINGER

1 TEASPOON ORANGE
    MARMALADE

4 WHOLE CLOVES

GROUND CINNAMON

GRATED NUTMEG

1 PINT HOT, STRONG BLACK
    COFFEE

4 OUNCES PEACH BRANDY

Place all ingredients except coffee and peach brandy into flaming pan of chafing dish over direct heat. Add brandy and when thoroughly warmed, ignite, blaze for a moment or two, then pour in coffee. Makes 4 servings.

CAFÉ JACQUES

HOT, STRONG BLACK COFFEE

4 OUNCES COGNAC

KIRSCH

Pour coffee into 4 cups until almost full. Heat cognac in ladle, ignite, and pour blazing into each cup. When flames are extinguished, add dash of kirsch to each. Serves 4.

CAFÉ MANDARINE

HOT, STRONG BLACK COFFEE

2 OUNCES 100-PROOF VODKA

2 OUNCES MANDARINE
NAPOLÉON LIQUEUR

Pour coffee into 4 cups until nearly full. Warm mixture of vodka and liqueur in ladle or small pan, ignite, and pour blazing into each cup. If you prefer additional sweetness or a stronger tangerine flavor, simply add a little more liqueur to each cup without flaming. Serves 4.

CAFÉ CACAO

1 PINT HOT, STRONG BLACK
COFFEE

4 SMALL PIECES LEMON PEEL

2 OUNCES 100-PROOF VODKA
2 OUNCES CRÈME DE CACAO

Fill 4 cups almost full with hot coffee and add lemon peel to each. Warm vodka–crème de cacao mixture in ladle or small pan, ignite, and pour blazing into each cup. Serves 4.

CAFÉ NORMAND

4 SMALL PIECES CINNAMON
    STICK
4 SUGAR LUMPS
1 PINT HOT, STRONG BLACK
    COFFEE

4 OUNCES CALVADOS OR
    APPLEJACK

Place cinnamon stick and sugar lump in each of 4 cups and fill almost full with coffee. Warm Calvados or applejack in ladle, ignite, and pour blazing into each cup. Serves 4.

CAFÉ DE MENTHE

1 PINT HOT, STRONG BLACK
    COFFEE
2 OUNCES 100-PROOF VODKA

2 OUNCES CRÈME DE MENTHE
CRÈME DE CACAO
WHIPPED CREAM

Fill 4 coffee cups almost full with coffee. Warm vodka and crème de menthe in ladle, ignite, and pour blazing into each cup. Add dash of crème de cacao, and a little whipped cream. Serves 4.

CAFÉ ANESONE

1 PINT HOT *CAFFÈ ESPRESSO*   4 OUNCES ANESONE LIQUEUR

Fill 4 demitasse cups nearly full with coffee. Warm liqueur in ladle, ignite, and pour blazing into each cup. Makes 4 demitasse servings.

The humble coffee bean, source of so much flavor, fragrance, and satisfaction, whether served plain or glorified in flames, has always been and will continue to be the most auspicious way to end a lovely evening of good food, good companionship, and good cheer.

If by now you have wearied of twenty-six ways of flaming coffee, here is just one way of blazing hot chocolate.

ALHAMBRA ROYALE

1 PINT HOT CHOCOLATE   4 OUNCES COGNAC
4 SMALL PIECES LEMON PEEL   WHIPPED CREAM

Fill 4 cups nearly full with hot chocolate, and add piece of lemon peel to each. Warm cognac in ladle, ignite, and pour blazing into each cup. Stir well and top with whipped cream. Serves 4.

This creamy cold-weather bracer doesn't even need to be flamed. It was invented for Prince Bertil of Sweden, where the winters are long.

CHOKLAD PRINCE BERTIL

4 TEASPOONS COCOA

4 TEASPOONS SUGAR

4 SCANT CUPS MILK

4 OUNCES TRIPLE SEC

WHIPPED CREAM

Mix cocoa and sugar with a little cold milk to make it thick and creamy, and stir till smooth. Bring remaining milk to a boil and pour into cocoa, stirring well. Pour in triple sec, mix, and serve in individual cups. Top with whipped cream. Serves 4.

NINE

A Glossary of Flambé Fuels

The following is a more or less comprehensive list of flaming fuels, considered from the point of view as to what burns best in the spirit world in relation to *cuisine flambée*. We are concerned basically with two characteristics, flavor and flammability, and the direct application of these attributes to cooking.

First, and of major importance, is the flavor. If it does not stand up when compounded or combined with other spirits, sweetening agents, spices, herbs, fruits, or other food ingredients, it is of little value in flambé cookery. Many fine liqueurs have flavors so delicate and fleeting that while alone they are perfectly acceptable, in mixed drinks or with food they are utterly valueless. Other spirits, with flavors hearty enough to hold their own in combination with other ingredients, for some reason or another do not satisfactorily survive cooking. If a particular spirit loses character when flamed, or has an objectionable residual flavor, then irrespective of its other benefits, it has no place in flaming food.

As to flammability, there are many liqueurs available that have good flavor properties but whose alcoholic content is so low that they will not burn satisfactorily. Some of these flavors are so desirable, however, that it is advantageous to add high-proof neutral spirits, such as grain alcohol, vodka, or even a high-proof gin, so that the underproof liqueur is brought up to a higher level of ignitability. If a liqueur is less than 60 proof (30 percent alcohol), you probably should plan to bump it up with a stronger-proof spirit. Sometimes, as the saying goes, "The game is not worth the candle," for the addition of vodka or grain alcohol to a low-proof liqueur causes too much dilution. While there isn't any doubt that any cordial can be coaxed into a state of combustion by this process, there is some question as to the ultimate benefit.

You will find that the majority of flambéing is done with the old staple, high-proof spirits, such as brandy, whisky, rum, gin, and vodka. Other distilled spirits, such as the various fruit brandies, which in France are called *alcools blancs,* also hold up very well in the flambéing process. Liqueurs or cordials—not to be confused with true brandies—are infusions of fruits, herbs, spices, or other flavoring agents with spirits that may or may not subsequently be redistilled or aged. They are subject to wide variations in taste and alcoholic content depending on type and brand.

So herewith is a guide to what is best, with particular emphasis on taste and burnability, for the convenience of those who wish to continue to experiment and innovate in the exciting, heady world of flaming food and drink.

ABSINTHE—Possibly one of the most interesting of all liqueurs, with a bitter, pronounced licorice flavor, which has many uses as a flavoring agent and an ingredient in numerous mixed drinks. The original formula, which contained wormwood, is reputed to have made blithering idiots out of those who drank it regularly. Consequently, it is available in the United States and most Western countries sans wormwood. Pernod Fils owns the original absinthe formula, which it now manufactures in a number of countries. One of a large family of similarly flavored liqueurs, Pernod is excellent for flambéing.

AGUARDIENTE—This generally refers to a strong, cheap, unaged rum or brandy popular in Spain and South America. Not recommended.

AMER PICON—A bitter cordial, very popular in France as an apéritif. It has a surprisingly broad application to many mixed drinks but very limited use as a flavoring in cooking.

ANESONE—A liqueur, like anisette, made from anise, with a pronounced licorice flavor. It is made in Italy with a high-enough alcohol content to make it useful for flambéing and in some mixed drinks.

ANIS—The Spanish version of anisette. Basically a liqueur made from anise, which is extremely popular in countries bordering the Mediterranean and in South America. Varies widely in alcohol content, although some of these liqueurs will run as high as 96 proof. A clear, colorless liquid with a distinctive licorice flavor. See *Anisette*.

ANISETTE—A very popular liqueur, made of anise, which dates back to ancient Greece. Anise is the essential flavor ingredient of anisette and similar drinks, such as ouzo from Greece, Syrian arak, and Pernod. Some versions are sweet, others are dry, and the proof runs from very low to up to 96 proof, which means that the stronger varieties are quite suitable for flambéing, particularly with coffee and certain kinds of desserts. Also used in some mixed drinks.

APPLE BRANDY—Popularly known as applejack in the United States; called "Jersey Lightning" in Prohibition days. In France it is called Calvados. This is a true brandy, distilled from apples or hard cider, and frequently runs as high as 100 proof. It is excellent for flambé cookery as well as mixed drinks. See *Calvados*.

APPLEJACK—The popular name in the United States for apple brandy. The term generally refers to apple brandies made in America and not to imported products. As far as flambéing is concerned, whether domestic or imported, it is an exceptionally robust spirit, with an excellent residual apple flavor. Also good in many mixed drinks.

APRICOT BRANDY—A true brandy, not to be confused with apricot liqueurs or cordials. Of sufficient strength for flambéing, especially good for desserts.

APRICOT LIQUEUR—A generic term for a number of sweet apricot-flavored liqueurs with a brandy base, such as Abricotine and Apry. These liqueurs, although endowed with good flavor, are sometimes too low in alcohol content for effective flambéing without the addition of high-proof spirits.

AQUAVIT (also spelled akvavit)—The great, universally popular Scandinavian drink usually taken very cold and neat. It might best be described as flavored vodka. The flavoring agent usually is caraway seed although other flavorings also are used. Aquavit varies from country to country, the best-known being the Danish product, which is named after the little town of Aalborg. While the pronounced caraway flavor limits its use in mixed drinks, this is an advantage in flambé cookery, in which it has many applications.

ARAK—A pungent, aromatic rum from the island of Java, near Batavia, commonly referred to as Batavian or Batavia arak. This is an excellent product, not unlike brandy, and it is very popular in The Netherlands and Scandinavia, where it is used to make Swedish punsch. It is excellent both for cocktails in which dry rum is called for and for many flambé dishes, because of its relatively high proof.

ARMAGNAC—A fine brandy made in the southeastern corner of France. It is not so well known as cognac and has a drier, more pronounced taste. It can be used in all or nearly all recipes calling for cognac. It has an excellent flavor, preferred by some brandy drinkers, and is good for flambéing.

ARRACK or RACK—A distillate of rice or sugarcane, not to be confused with Batavia arak or punsch. Many versions of this spirit are found throughout the Far East under different names, made from a host of different ingredients, with wide variations in quality and proof. Although it is usually of sufficient proof for flaming, it has little application in food preparation.

ARRACK PUNSCH—Another name for Swedish or caloric punsch, which is made from a base of Batavia arak. See *Swedish punsch*.

B AND B LIQUEUR—A combination of Benedictine and brandy, made by the makers of Benedictine, which results in a drier product. Can be flambéed in any situation calling for the use of Benedictine alone.

BARBADOS RUM—A light-bodied rum with a distinctive, aromatic, and pleasant flavor that can be used interchangeably with Puerto Rican and Cuban rums. Excellent in a number of mixed drinks and frequently used in flambé recipes.

BATAVIA ARAK—See *Arak*.

BENEDICTINE—A distinguished and venerable liqueur, known throughout the world by its famous initials, D.O.M. (Deo Optimo Maximo, which means: "To God, Most Good, Most Great"). It is made at Fécamp, France, by an organization that has nothing to do with the Benedictine religious order. It is very aromatic and extremely distinctive with an unforgettable flavor. It has never really been successfully imitated, although many have tried. Its delicate flavors limit its use to only a very few mixed drinks, and although it can be flambéed, Benedictine must be used with care when combined with other ingredients lest its essential flavors be overwhelmed.

BLACKBERRY BRANDY—A true distilled brandy, not to be confused with blackberry liqueur. Good when drunk straight and also excellent for flambé dessert dishes.

BLACKBERRY LIQUEUR—A blackberry-flavored liqueur, sometimes employing a blackberry brandy as a base with the addition of a little red wine. Its low proof does not make it particularly good for flambéing, unless some high-proof neutral spirits are added.

BOROVICKA—A dry Czechoslovakian brandy, made from juniper berries and of relatively high proof. It resembles gin so far as its flavor is concerned.

BOURBON WHISKY—A straight whisky that, by law, must be distilled from a fermented grain mash that contains no less than 51 percent corn. Any whisky distilled in the United States must be aged for at least two years. Bottled-in-bond whisky must be 100 proof and at least four years old. The name bourbon comes from Bourbon County, Kentucky. It has an endless number of uses in mixed drinks and is becoming more and more popular as a flavoring in cookery. It is easily flambéed and can be used, in some instances, interchangeably with cognac, except that bourbon has a slightly sweeter residual taste.

CALVADOS—A fine apple brandy from Normandy, similar to applejack, but far smoother because of longer aging. Its pleasant and distinctive apple flavor and aroma make it valuable for many mixed drinks and a host of flambé recipes.

CAMPARI—An unusual, aromatic, bitter liqueur made in Italy. It is excellent in a number of mixed drinks but has little application in cooking.

CANADIAN WHISKY—A blended whisky that is light and pleasant, usually made from corn, rye, wheat, and barley malt. A fine-quality product, generally well aged and valuable in a number of mixed drinks and some flambé recipes calling for whisky.

CERTOSA—A variety of liqueurs of different flavors and colors with a vague taste of Chartreuse, made by an order of monks near Florence. Its primary use is as an after-dinner liqueur. It has very little application in mixed drinks or cookery.

CHARTREUSE—Another old, famous, and widely imitated proprietary liqueur, made by the monks of the Carthusian Order, near Grenoble, France. Two types of Chartreuse are generally available: the yellow, which is 86 proof, and the green, which is 110 proof. The secret formula, which has never been successfully duplicated, employs a brandy base and a variety of herbs and spices. As with Benedictine, the pronounced but delicate flavors of both green and yellow Chartreuse limit their use in mixed drinks and in flambé cookery.

CHERRY BRANDY—See *kirschwasser*.

CHERRY LIQUEUR—A rich, sweetish fruity cordial made of fresh cherries, employing a brandy base. Perhaps the best-known cherry liqueur is the outstanding Danish product Cherry Heering. Can be flambéed quite successfully for desserts, with the addition of a little vodka or gin.

COFFEE LIQUEURS—There are a host of products on the market, many of them excellent. Among the better-known names are Tia Maria, Kahlúa, crème de café, and crème de moka, which has an interesting overtone of bitter almonds. Tia Maria has a rum base. While all of these liqueurs are tasty, their low proof does not make them suitable for flaming unless neutral spirits are added to bolster up the alcohol content.

COGNAC—The royal family of brandies, coming from a strictly delimited area, known as the Cognac District, which lies in the south of France, near Bordeaux. Of the eight areas in the district, the most highly regarded are known as the Petite and Grande Champagne sections, from which comes the best of all cognacs, called "Fine Champagnes"—not to be confused with the area in northern France from whence comes the well-known bubbly wine. Cognac has many, many uses in cooking, in mixed drinks, and as a *digestif* and restorative. It perhaps is the most commonly used of all spirits for flambéing.

COINTREAU—A proprietary name for triple sec, which is very popular as an after-dinner liqueur, a necessary ingredient in many mixed drinks and in all manner of *cuisine flambée*. Alcohol content: 80 proof.

CORDIAL MEDOC—A proprietary liqueur made of brandy, orange Curaçao, and crème de cacao in Bordeaux, France. Essentially an after-dinner liqueur, but with interesting flavor possibilities for certain flambé dessert recipes.

CRÈME D'ANANAS—A pineapple-flavored liqueur with an alcohol content of about 60 proof. Limited use with some desserts.

CRÈME DE BANANES—A banana-flavored liqueur with limited value as a flavoring agent, since the banana essence does not seem to come through when mixed with other ingredients.

CRÈME DE CACAO—A heavy, sweet liqueur made from cocoa beans and vanilla. It is an excellent flavoring for desserts, but its low proof makes it difficult to flame without the addition of neutral spirits. Also called for in a few mixed drinks.

CRÈME DE CAFÉ—Looks like crème de cacao but tastes like coffee. Can be used when coffee liqueurs are called for. Not for burning.

CRÈME DE CASSIS—A sweet liqueur made from black currants. Has broad use as a flavoring ingredient, particularly for desserts, but the proof is so low that it cannot, for practical purposes, be flambéed successfully.

CRÈME DE CELERI—A cordial that derives its flavor from celery. More of a curiosity than anything else, with no known application in mixed drinks or cooking.

CRÈME DE FRAISES—A strawberry-flavored liqueur, generally low in proof, with a delicate flavor. Has a few applications as a flavoring agent for desserts and some mixed drinks.

CRÈME DE FRAMBOISES—A sweet raspberry-flavored liqueur with a relatively low alcohol content. Good as a flavoring syrup for some desserts and as an after-dinner cordial.

CRÈME DE MENTHE—One of the most popular of all liqueurs. Sweet and refreshing with a relatively low alcohol content. Obtainable in both white and dark green versions. Called for in a variety of mixed drinks. Makes a very refreshing after-dinner liqueur when poured over shaved ice and a good flavoring medium for many desserts. Not recommended for extensive flambéing.

CRÈME DE NOYAUX—A low-proof liqueur, made from bitter almonds and apricot pits that are crushed and fermented with spices. Can be used for a few desserts as a sweetening agent and also as an after-dinner drink.

CRÈME DE ROSE—A liqueur flavored with vanilla and the oil of rose petals. Alcohol strength: 60 proof. Limited use for flavoring purposes.

CRÈME DE THÉ—A tea-flavored liqueur. A cordial with no application in *cuisine flambée*.

CRÈME DE VANILLE—A sweet cordial, made from vanilla beans. Alcohol content runs around 60 proof. Limited use as a flavoring agent.

CRÈME DE VIOLETTE—Same as Crème Yvette.

CRÈME YVETTE—An extremely sweet liqueur with the flavor of violets. Alcohol content: about 60 proof. Has some use as a flavoring syrup.

CURAÇAO—Named after an island in the Dutch West Indies, the origin of a particularly fine bitter orange peel from which this liqueur is made. The colors range from white to orange, and the alcohol content runs from 60 to 90 proof. The best Curaçao is reputed to come from The Netherlands. It has many applications in flambé cookery as well as mixed drinks.

DAMIANA—A French liqueur with a rather vague flavor that may have some value as an after-dinner liqueur but has little use in either mixed drinks or cooking.

DEMERARA RUM—Similar to dark Jamaica rum, except that it has a very aromatic, pungent, spicy flavor that makes it valuable for mixed drinks. The alcohol content of some Demerara rums is very high, running up to 151 proof and sometimes even higher. Excellent for flambé cookery, particularly desserts.

DRAMBUIE—A proprietary liqueur made in Scotland with a Scotch base, sweetened with heather honey. Made by a secret formula that is reputed to have been brought to Prince Charles Edward in 1745 by a French admirer. An excellent after-dinner liqueur. Used in some mixed drinks and a few dessert recipes. Alcohol content: 80 proof.

FIOR D'ALPE (also known as *fiori alpini* and *flora dell'alpi*)—A sweet, aromatic liqueur, produced in northern Italy and Switzerland, easily recognized by the twig, covered with rock candy crystals, found in every bottle. An after-dinner liqueur with very limited use in drink mixing or cooking.

FRAISE—A true brandy, colorless and aromatic, part of a family of distilled spirits known in France as *alcools blancs*. A good after-dinner drink with some important uses in flambé desserts. Not to be confused with crème de fraises, which is a sweet liqueur.

FRAMBÒISE—A true brandy, distilled from mashed raspberries, with a pronounced raspberry taste and aroma. Like other true brandies, a really good framboise is difficult to obtain and is relatively expensive, but worth the price, since it is superb as an after-dinner liqueur and also has many applications in flambé cookery.

FRANGELICO—A flavorful, aromatic liqueur made in Italy from wild hazelnuts.

GALLIANO—A zesty liqueur from Livorno, Italy, resembling Chartreuse and named after an Italian military hero. Alcohol content is 80 proof. It has application in some mixed drinks and certain flambé recipes.

GIN—Essentially a flavored spirit with a distinctive juniper essence, derived from juniper berries and a variety of botanicals. Gin formulas vary from brand to brand. With one or possibly two exceptions, the best gins, known as London dry, are imported into the United States from England. Gin has wide application in mixed drinks and in flambé cookery.

GOLDWASSER—Also known as *eau-de-vie de Danzig*. Originally made in Danzig from an old proprietary formula, it has a vague but pleasant citrus flavor and is distinguished by the tiny flecks of real gold leaf that swim around in the bottle when it is shaken. Mainly an after-dinner liqueur, with little application in mixed drinks or cooking.

GRAND MARNIER—An extremely fine liqueur, made with oranges and cognac, resulting in a smooth, dry flavor that makes it excellent in many mixed drinks and as an after-dinner liqueur. It has unlimited applications in flambé cookery and can be used wherever an orange liqueur is indicated.

GRAPPA—A colorless brandy, which is strong and similar to marc. Not generally recommended for mixed drinks or flambé dishes.

HERBSAINT—An absinthe substitute made in Louisiana that can be used in mixed drinks and in flambé recipes specifying absinthe. See *Pernod*.

HOLLAND GIN—Sometimes referred to as Jenever gin, this has a pungent, malty flavor that limits its use in mixed drinks and for cooking. In Europe it is served cold in small glasses and taken neat, much like vodka or aquavit.

IRISH MIST—A pleasant-tasting, sweetish proprietary liqueur, made from Irish whiskey and heather honey. It is excellent when taken straight with coffee and has some important uses in mixed drinks and flambé cookery.

IRISH WHISKEY—Similar to Scotch except that it lacks the singularly smoky flavor of Scotch, because of a difference in the malting process. Irish whiskey is smooth, full-bodied, and well aged, and is an excellent spirit whether taken neat, blended in mixed drinks, or used in flambé recipes.

IZARRA—An exotic, highly aromatic liqueur from Spain's Basque country. Limited use as a flavoring in a few dishes.

JAMAICA RUM—Distilled from sugarcane or sugarcane products such as molasses. It is full-bodied, with a distinctive molasses flavor. Invaluable in many mixed drinks and in a number of flambé recipes.

KAHLÚA—A pleasant, coffee-flavored liqueur, made in Mexico. Its low proof and distinctive flavor make it impractical for flambé cookery. It is mainly an after-dinner drink and has some use in desserts.

KIRSCHWASSER—Also known simply as kirsch. Along with cognac and Armagnac, it is probably one of the most famous of fruit brandies. It is a strong, colorless distillate of cherries and cherry pits and is made in Alsace, the Black Forest region of Germany, and Switzerland. Because it has the most vigorous flavor characteristics of all the non-grape fruit brandies, it has extensive applications in flambé cookery.

KÜMMEL—A colorless liqueur of ancient origin that is flavored with cumin or caraway seed. Its relatively high proof makes it flammable, but it has limited value in either flaming dishes or mixed drinks.

LIQUEUR D'ANIS—An anise liqueur from France, mainly used as an after-dinner drink.

LIQUEUR D'OR—See *Goldwasser.*

LIQUEUR JAUNE—Basically an imitation of yellow Chartreuse.

MANDARINE—A light, flavorful liqueur, made in Belgium from the dried peel of tangerines. Limited use in mixed drinks but, with the addition of high-proof vodka or neutral spirits, can be used in some flambé recipes that specify an orange liqueur. Proper name: Mandarine Napoléon Grande Liqueur Impèriale.

MARASCHINO—A liqueur made from wild marasca cherries from Dalmatia as well as other ingredients, resulting in a colorless, sweet liqueur that is used in many mixed drinks and, with the addition of neutral spirits, in some flambé dessert recipes.

MARC—Also known as *eau-de-vie de marc*. A brandy distilled from grape pomace of the wine press, which imparts a dry, strong, woody taste. It lacks the refinement and smoothness of cognac, Armagnac, and the various *alcools blancs*. Limited use in mixed drinks and in flambé cookery.

MARTINIQUE RUMS—Sometimes referred to as French rums. They are heavy-bodied and similar in flavor to Jamaica rums, except drier. Called for in a number of rum drinks and valuable in several flambé recipes.

MEAD—An ancient Anglo-Saxon beverage celebrated in song and story. Made of fermented honey, malt, water, and herbs or spices. Regarded as a historical curiosity with no known applications to modern drink mixing or cuisine.

MIRABELLE—A true brandy or *alcool blanc*, distilled from French yellow plums. Like all colorless fruit brandies, good mirabelle is hard to get and expensive since so much fruit is involved in its manufacture. It is by far the best of all the true plum brandies. Excellent as an after-dinner liqueur and as an ingredient in a number of flambé dishes, especially desserts.

OJEN—A Spanish version of absinthe. One of the many anise-flavored liqueurs popular in countries surrounding the Mediterranean. Little application in cookery but can be used in mixed drinks calling for absinthe.

OKOLEHAO—A distilled spirit from Hawaii called for in a few cocktails but with no known application in flambé cookery.

OLD TOM GIN—A sweetened version of London dry gin, called for in a few mixed drinks and several flambé recipes.

OUZO—An anise-flavored liqueur, very popular in Greece. Can be used as an absinthe substitute in mixed drinks and occasionally in flambé cooking.

PARFAIT AMOUR—See *crème de violette.*

PEACH BRANDY—A true distilled brandy, made of peaches and peach pits. Has use in many mixed drinks and a number of flambé recipes. Where peach brandy is called for, Southern Comfort, which is not technically a brandy, will be found to be very satisfactory.

PEACH LIQUEUR—A sweet cordial, flavored with peaches, not to be confused with peach brandy. Used occasionally in mixed drinks and for desserts.

PEAR BRANDY—A true distilled brandy, known as *eau-de-vie de poire* or *poire Williams,* the latter being derived from a Swiss variety called the Williams pear. A colorless spirit, with a definite pear aroma and taste, it is sometimes available with a large pear in the bottle. A delightful after-dinner drink and also useful in a few flaming desserts.

PERNOD—The proprietary name of the original absinthe formula that is still made by the firm of Pernod Fils except for the absence of a single ingredient—wormwood, which has been banned by law in most countries. Pernod is an excellent absinthe substitute and is indicated in many mixed drinks and flambé recipes. See *absinthe.*

PLUM BRANDY—See *mirabelle.*

PRUNELLE—A sweet liqueur from France, flavored with plums, sometimes made with a plum brandy base. Not to be confused with plum brandy. Used mainly as a flavoring agent and an after-dinner liqueur.

PUERTO RICAN RUM—Distilled from sugarcane juices or molasses. Characterized by light body and dryness. Excellent in numerous mixed drinks and many flambé recipes.

PULQUE—Fermented sap of the maguey plant, which must be drunk fairly fresh, and is highly regarded by the Mexicans. No known value in mixed drinks or in cooking.

QUETSCH—A colorless brandy distilled from purple plums, similar to slivovitz and mirabelle but not nearly as good as the latter. Some use in mixed drinks and a few flambé dishes.

RAKI—Another anise-flavored liqueur, popular in Greece and Turkey. Of little or no use in mixed drinks or cooking.

ROCK & RYE—An old American favorite made with fresh fruits, rock candy, and rye whisky. Once considered a cold preventive. Some use in mixed drinks and occasionally as a flavoring for dessert.

RYE WHISKY—A distilled spirit that by law must contain at least 51 percent rye grain. Used extensively in blended whiskies but also excellent as a straight whisky. It has an unusual, interesting nutty flavor. Can be used in many mixed drinks and also has some applications in flambé cookery.

SCOTCH WHISKY—Usually a blend of malt and grain whiskies. World-famous for its characteristic smoky taste, which it acquires from peat. Must be at least three years old but is usually aged longer. Considered by many as the world's finest whisky. Has many uses in mixed drinks and in numerous flambé dishes.

SLIVOVITZ—A true distilled brandy, made from plums. It has a strong, distinctive flavor and aroma, but it is not up to the quality of mirabelle, which is considered the best of all plum brandies. Has limited use in mixed drinks and flambé dishes.

SLOE GIN—A sweet, pleasant-tasting liqueur, made of sloe berries, which impart a distinctive flavor. Not a true gin or even a berry, but an extract of a wild plum. Excellent in some mixed drinks and as a flavoring for desserts.

SOUTHERN COMFORT—An outstanding American proprietary liqueur, with a distinctive peach flavor, made from a secret formula. It is sometimes described as a peach brandy or a peach bourbon. It is excellent in a number of mixed drinks and has many applications in flambé cookery. Alcohol content: 100 proof. Can be used in recipes specifying peach brandy.

STREGA—A spicy, yellowish liqueur based on a secret formula that has been made by the Alberti family at Benevento, Italy, for over a hundred years. Beneficial in many mixed drinks and a number of flambé recipes, particularly desserts.

SWEDISH PUNSCH—Sometimes called caloric punsch because it is supposed to impart heat. Actually a sweet liqueur with a base of Batavia arak, mixed with other ingredients. No significant application in mixed drinks or cookery.

TEQUILA—A distilled spirit from the maguey plant. The national drink of Mexico. Usually drunk straight with salt and lime. Available in white and gold varieties, the latter presumably aged for several years before being bottled. Highly underrated with great potential for cocktails and flambé cooking.

TRIPLE SEC—A sweet generic orange liqueur, similar to Curaçao and Cointreau. Called for in a number of mixed drinks and valuable in many flambé recipes. Alcohol content: 80 proof.

VAN DER HUM—An aromatic liqueur from South Africa. Made from a number of ingredients, but the flavor of tangerine predominates. Called for in a few mixed drinks and some flambé recipes.

VEILLE CURE—An aromatic herb liqueur, produced near Bordeaux. It is good as an after-dinner drink but has little known use in mixed drinks or cookery.

VODKA—Distilled from fermented mash of grain or potatoes. It is tasteless, colorless, and odorless and therefore can be mixed with anything. Originated in Russia, where it is served cold and taken neat. Can be used to pep up almost any mixed drink and has unlimited applications in flambé cookery, especially in its 100-proof form.

Index